Apache Solr

A Practical Approach to Enterprise Search

Dikshant Shahi

Apress®

Apache Solr: A Practical Approach to Enterprise Search

ISBN-13 (pbk): 978-1-4842-1071-0

ISBN-13 (electronic): 978-1-4842-1070-3

Managing Director: Welmoed Spahr
Acquisitions Editor: Celestin Suresh John
Development Editor: Matthew Moodie
Technical Reviewer: Shweta Gupta
Editorial Board: Steve Anglin, Pramilla Balan, Louise Corrigan, James DeWolf, Jonathan Gennick, Robert Hutchinson, Celestin Suresh John, Michelle Lowman, James Markham, Susan McDermott, Matthew Moodie, Jeffrey Pepper, Douglas Pundick, Ben Renow-Clarke, Gwenan Spearing
Coordinating Editor: Rita Fernando
Copy Editor: Sharon Wilkey
Compositor: SPi Global
Indexer: SPi Global

Distributed to the book trade worldwide by Springer Science+Business Media New York, 233 Spring Street, 6th Floor, New York, NY 10013. Phone 1-800-SPRINGER, fax (201) 348-4505, e-mail orders-ny@springer-sbm.com, or visit www.springer.com. Apress Media, LLC is a California LLC and the sole member (owner) is Springer Science + Business Media Finance Inc. (SSBM Finance Inc.). SSBM Finance Inc. is a Delaware corporation.

For information on translations, please e-mail rights@apress.com, or visit www.apress.com.

Apress and friends of ED books may be purchased in bulk for academic, corporate, or promotional use. eBook versions and licenses are also available for most titles. For more information, reference our Special Bulk Sales–eBook Licensing web page at www.apress.com/bulk-sales.

Any source code or other supplementary materials referenced by the author in this text is available to readers at www.apress.com/. For detailed information about how to locate your book's source code, go to www.apress.com/source-code/.

To my foster mother, Mrs. Pratima Singh, for educating me!

Contents at a Glance

Contents

About the Author

Dikshant Shahi is a software engineer with expertise in developing search engines and enterprise applications using Java technologies. He is currently working as a solution architect at The Digital Group, focusing on developing a suite for advanced text processing and for incorporating semantic capabilities in Apache Solr.

Dikshant developed interest in search engines during his college days, where he submitted his thesis on developing a personality-based search engine. In his first job, he initially worked on developing enterprise applications and then on a project to build a distributed log processing search engine. After evaluating various alternatives, Apache Solr was chosen. It was Solr 1.3 and the year 2008, and his journey with Solr began. Since then, he has developed several search engines catering to industries including e-commerce, healthcare, music, mobile, manufacturing, and legal. He has worked on diverse problems related to full-text and metadata search, textual fingerprinting, log processing, and analytics.

He loves coding and building disruptive systems. He is the developer of TripBuddy, a chatbot that answers your travel questions, which won the Tnooz Travel Hackathon. He has keen interest in the fields of information retrieval, natural language processing, and machine learning. When not at work, you can find him backpacking solo!

About the Technical Reviewer

Shweta Gupta is a Smarter Commerce specialist with IBM. She is a commerce consultant for the WebSphere Commerce product, with a key focus on performance and search, enabling customers to achieve their business goals and objectives from their e-commerce implementations. Shweta is a subject-matter expert on Solr search, an important component of e-commerce that supports best-in the-industry search capabilities.

Shweta lives in Pune, India with her husband and enjoys outdoors and nature. You can reach her at LinkedIn (in.linkedin.com/in/shwetalakhimpur) and Twitter (@shwetalakhimpur).

Acknowledgments

My first vote of thanks goes to my daily dose of caffeine (without which this book would not have been possible), my sister for preparing it, and my wife for teaching me to prepare it myself. Thanks to my parents for their love!

Thank you, Celestin, for providing me the opportunity to write this book; Rita for coordinating the whole process; and Shweta, Matthew, Sharon, and SPi Global for all their help to get this book to completion. My sincere thanks to everyone else from Apress for believing in me.

I am deeply indebted to everyone whom I have worked with in my professional journey and everyone who has motivated me and helped me learn and improve, directly or indirectly.

A special thanks to my colleagues at The Digital Group for providing the support, flexibility, and occasional work break to complete the book on time. I would also like to thank all the open source contributors, especially of Apache Lucene and Solr; without their great work, there would have been no need for this book.

As someone has rightly said, it takes a village to create a book. In creating this book, there is a small village, Sandha, located in the land of Buddha, which I frequented for tranquility and serenity that helped me focus on writing this book.

Thank you!

Introduction

This book is for developers who are building or planning to build an enterprise search engine using Apache Solr. Chapters 1 and 3 can be read by anyone who intends to learn the basics of information retrieval, search engines, and Apache Solr specifically. Chapter 2 kick-starts development with Solr and will prove to be a great resource for Solr newbies and administrators. All other chapters explore the Solr features and approaches for developing a practical and effective search engine.

This book covers use cases and examples from various domains such as e-commerce, legal, medical, and music, which will help you understand the need for certain features and how to approach the solution. While discussing the features, the book generally provides a snapshot of the required configuration, the command (using curl) to execute the feature, and a code snippet as required. The book dives into implementation details and writing plug-ins for integrating custom features.

What this book doesn't cover is performance improvement in Solr and optimizing it for high-speed indexing. This book covers Solr features through release 5.3.1, which is the latest at the time of this writing.

What This Book Covers

Chapter 1, Apache Solr: An Introduction, as the name states, starts with an introduction to Apache Solr and its ecosystem. It then discusses the features, reasons for Solr's popularity, its building blocks, and other information that will give you a holistic view about Solr. It also introduces related technologies and compares it to other alternatives.

Chapter 2, Solr Setup and Administration, begins with Solr fundamentals and covers Solr setup, steps for indexing your first set of documents and searching them. It then describes the Solr administrative features and various management options.

Chapter 3, Information Retrieval, is dedicated to the concepts of information retrieval, content extraction, and text processing.

Chapter 4, Schema Design and Text Analysis, covers the schema design, text analysis, going schemaless, and managed schemas in Solr. It also describes common text-analysis techniques.

Chapter 5, Indexing Data, concentrates on the Solr indexing process by describing the indexing request flow, various indexing tools, supported document formats, and important update request processors. This is also the first chapter that provides the steps to write a Solr plug-in, a custom UpdateRequestProcessor in this case.

Chapter 6, Searching Data, describes the Solr searching process, various query types, important query parsers, supported request parameters, and steps for writing a custom SearchComponent.

Chapter 7, Searching Data: Part 2, continues the previous chapter and covers local parameters, result grouping, statistics, faceting, reranking queries, and joins. It also dives into the details of function queries for deducing a practical relevance ranking and steps for writing your own named function.

Chapter 8, Solr Scoring, explains the Solr scoring process, supported scoring models, the score computation, and steps for customizing similarity.

Chapter 9, Additional Features, explores Solr features including spell-checking, autosuggestion, document similarity, and sponsored search.

Chapter 10, Traditional Scaling and SolrCloud, covers the distributed architectures supported by Solr and steps for setting up SolrCloud, creating a collection, distributed indexing and searching, shard splitting and ZooKeeper.

Chapter 11, Semantic Search, introduces the concept of semantic search and covers the tools and techniques for integrating semantic capabilities in Solr.

What You Need for This Book

Apache Solr requires Java Runtine Environment (JRE) 1.7 or newer. The provided custom Java code is tested on Java Development Kit (JDK) 1.8 and requires Apache Maven.

The last chapter requires downloading resources required by Apache OpenNLP and WordNet.

Who This Book Is For

This book expects you to have basic understanding of the Java programming language, which is essential if you want to execute the custom components.

■ ■ ■

CHAPTER 1

Apache Solr: An Introduction

Search is ubiquitous and has become part of our digital life! You open your browser, and it is highly likely that your home page is your preferred search engine. The search engine of your smartphone is just a swipe away. Open an e-commerce web site, and the search box appears right at the center or top of the page. Basically, every portal that has data to expose needs a search engine. This proves how critical a search engine is for an enterprise or a product that it's building.

Enterprises today have a tremendous amount of information to expose, and this volume will keep growing. It's nearly impossible and tedious to browse through all the data to find relevant information. The only solution to the problem is a search engine.

If you have lots of data and struggle to find desired information when you need it and in a manner that you need, then that data is almost worthless and it's time to call for the development or upgrading of your search engine. Because you are reading this chapter, I assume that you are building or planning to build a search engine, and you understand why you need one for your enterprise. So without much ado, let's proceed.

The goal of this book is to help you develop a search engine by using the open source Apache Solr. First you need to understand that each search engine is different and has its own unique challenges that need to be addressed differently. We will explore common problems and their solutions and provide approaches to resolve specific problems during the flow of this book.

This chapter starts with an introduction to Apache Solr and provides a high-level view of its features. It touches upon several facets of Solr so that you have a comprehensive understanding before starting on your proof of concept or development.

This chapter covers the following topics:

- Important features of Solr

- Important components of Solr

- Use of Solr beyond its search engine capabilities

- Comparison of Solr with other solutions

- Technologies used in Solr's ecosystem

Overview

Solr (pronounced *solar*), is an enterprise-ready, blazingly fast, and highly scalable search platform built using Apache Lucene. Over the years and with such a vibrant community, Solr has matured to a level that it provides all the much needed features out of the box as well as provisions to customize it. It is cloud ready and powered for robustness, fault tolerance, and reliability.

Solr is written in Java and runs as a stand-alone server. Getting started is extremely easy. All you need to do is run a script with a start/stop command. Being purely configuration based, Solr requires only that you register the components with each other. Even without any knowledge of Java, you can build a decent search engine, as long as you don't need customization. Solr also provides a graphical administrator interface for easy monitoring, which can be accessed from the browser by pointing to the port you are running the search engine on.

■ **Note**   Apache Lucene is a popular open source search library written entirely in Java. It is widely used for indexing a large collection of documents and supporting full-text search.

Inside Solr

To choose a framework, you evaluate it on aspects such as internals, features, capabilities, usability, performance, and scalability. This section will answer some of your questions, including what's inside Solr, how to configure it, and how to use it. The features covered in this section might not be what makes Solr so popular, but they're important to know as part of your basic understanding of Solr. The next section covers the features that make Solr popular, and with that you will have comprehensive knowledge of Solr's features. The following points provide a quick overview of Solr's features:

> *Inverted index*: Lucene builds an inverted index of the documents that you add to Solr, and at query time it searches the index for matching documents. You can think of an inverted index as similar to the index at the end of this book.

> *Vector space model*: By default, Lucene uses the vector space model (VSM) along with the Boolean model to determine the relevance of a document with respect to a user query. In a nutshell, the Boolean model approves, and the VSM ranks.

> *Config-based*: `solrconfig.xml` and `schema.xml` are the two primary configuration files of Solr. The `schema.xml` file primarily defines the fields of your schema and the behavior of those fields (how the text will be tokenized while indexing and querying). Almost everything else goes in `solrconfig.xml`. You can also go schemaless and let Solr create fields automatically while indexing the data. The configurations can be edited manually or modified dynamically by calling the respective APIs. As of Solr 5.0, you can even upload JAR files through an API call.

> *Analysis chain*: Your search query and the documents being indexed go through a chain of analyzers and tokenizers (the output of one tokenizer is fed to another in the chain). The output of the last tokenizer is the term that is indexed and matched against.

> *Java*: Solr and Lucene are written in Java. Solr 5.0 requires Java 7+ to run. To customize any feature of Solr, you need to extend the appropriate Java class.

> *SolrJ*: Solr bundles a Java client library that can be used for indexing documents and querying for results. Libraries are also available for other languages such as Perl and Python.

What Makes Apache Solr So Popular

Apache Solr is one of the most widely used search solutions, with millions of downloads, tens of thousands of applications in production, and hundreds of commits every month. The following are some of the factors that make it so popular:

Lucene: Solr uses the Lucene search library at its core and wraps it to add features and expose it as a RESTful service that can be accessed over HTTP. Development of Solr and Lucene merged in March 2010, and both the code bases reside in the same trunk in Apache Subversion (SVN); hence you are sure to get all the latest Lucene features in your latest Solr release.

Highly scalable and fault-tolerant: You can add or remove computing capacity to Solr, just by adding or removing replicas of your instance as needed. SolrCloud even abstracts your application from knowing how the data is distributed and saves you from getting into further nuances such as load balancing and sharding. Data indexed to Solr can be replicated among multiple instances; so even if one instance goes down, the data will still be accessible.

Enterprise ready: Solr is well proven and trusted by many leading organizations for their search requirements and for handling extensive loads. It can be deployed in stand-alone, traditional distributed architecture or in cloud mode based on the need of the organization, big or small.

Full-text search: As Solr is built on top of Lucene, it provides all the matching capabilities needed including token, phrases, fuzzy, wildcard, spell-check, and autocomplete.

RESTful XML/JSON over HTTP: Solr is exposed as a RESTful web service and can be accessed over HTTP. Data can be exchanged in XML, JSON, CSV, and binary format.

Flexible and extensible: Solr has a versatile range of features available out of the box. Still, if it doesn't fit your needs, no worries; Solr is flexible and extensible. You can modify and customize the behavior of components by extending the Java classes and adding the configuration for the created class in the appropriate file.

Easy configuration: If you know your schema, you can predefine it; otherwise, you can choose to go schemaless and let Solr define the fields. Also, you can modify your configuration through API calls.

Comprehensive admin interface: This is another feature that makes Solr fairly easy to use. Solr provides a feature-powered and user-friendly interface, accessible over HTTP right in your browser. It provides almost all the required insights, enabling you to view configuration files; inspect the text analysis; add/delete shards; manage logs in real time; search, add, delete, and update documents; trigger the data-import process; view threads and system properties; and a lot more.

Vibrant community: Solr, a project by the Apache Software Foundation (ASF), has a vibrant and growing community of more than 100 developers and committers. With every release, many features are added and improvements are made. The project has matured to such a level that it has an incredibly versatile set of features available out of the box.

Major Building Blocks

The classes of Solr and Lucene are organized and layered. Each has been designed to perform a specific job. All you need to do is configure them appropriately in the config files, so that they register with each other as needed. Solr also allows you to write custom components and plug them in. Broadly speaking, the following are some of the major building blocks and important components of Solr:

Request Handler: All the requests that you make to Solr are processed by one of the classes implementing `SolrRequestHandler`. You configure the handler to map to a specific URI endpoint, and the requests made to this endpoint start getting served by it.

Search Component: A search component defines the logic to implement the features provided by the search handler. These components should be registered in a `SearchHandler`, a request handler which serves the user query. For example, features such as query, spell-checking, faceting, and hit-highlighting are implemented as components and are registered to SearchHandler. Multiple components can be registered to a search handler.

Query Parser: This translates the user query into instructions that Lucene understands. They are generally registered in the `SearchComponent`, a component that defines the logic for performing a search.

Similarity: This class determines how Lucene weights terms and scores a document. If you want to change the scoring behavior, this is the class to extend.

Response Writer: This decides how the response to the user query should be formatted. For each response type such as XML, JSON, or Velocity, there exists a separate response writer.

Analyzer/tokenizer: The smallest unit of data that Lucene understands is a token. The implementations of `Analyzer`, `tokenizer` or `TokenFilter` decide how to break the text into tokens.

Update Request Processor: While indexing your document, you can invoke a set of `UpdateRequestProcessors` as part of your chain to perform custom actions upon your data.

History

In 2004, Solr was created as an in-house project by Yonik Seeley at CNET. In early 2006, CNET donated this project to the Apache Software Foundation. After a period of incubation, Solr was released. In time, features such as distributed search, hit-highlighting, enhanced searching and indexing capabilities, faceting, spell-checking, cloud capabilities, and innumerable others have been added—making its community of users, contributors, and committers one of the most vibrant today. The following indicates how Solr matured:

Solr 1.x: This was an enterprise-ready version of the product. Solr 1.3 was released in January 2007. Solr 1.4 was released in November 2009 with enhancements to indexing, searching, replication, and rich document indexing and better database integration.

Solr 3.x: In March 2011, development of Solr and Lucene projects merged, so there was no 2.x version of Solr. The next release of Solr was directly labeled 3.1 to match the Lucene version. Solr 3.x was focused on feature additions such as spatial search, and integrations such as UIMA for processing pipelines, Velocity for the UI, and so on.

Solr 4.x: Solr 4.0 was primarily about distributed search and about SolrCloud making Solr even more reliable, fault-tolerant, and scalable.

Solr 5.x: Solr 5.0 was released in February 2015 with a focus on ease of use and hardening. Recent releases have focused on security, analytics and extending the APIs. Refer to the next section for details.

What's New in Solr 5.*x*

Solr 4.x introduced SolrCloud, a new approach and design toward distributed search and scalability. Release 5.x presents Solr as a stand-alone server with the following major changes:

Stand-alone server: If you are an existing user of Apache Solr, it's time to see it from a new perspective. It's no longer distributed as a WAR (web archive) file that you should deploy in your favorite servlet container, but as a stand-alone server that you should use to solve your business problems and not bother about deployment details. This has been done to better utilize the container's networking stack features.

Ease of use: Solr 5.0 is easier to get started and use. Starting, stopping, and exposing Solr as a service is as simple as running a command. It also provides better self-discovery, is more organized, and is even more configurable. The administration UI has been refactored by using AngularJS for a better user experience.

Distributed IDF: Inverse document frequency, one of the most important factors in Solr scoring, can now be computed globally.

New APIs: New APIs have been introduced, and existing APIs have been extended. The JSON Request API allows search requests to have a JSON body.

Security: Solr 5.2.0 has introduced a pluggable authentication module and provides a Kerberos-based plug-in. An authorization framework is also provided.

Analytics: The facets module has been extended to support analytics and aggregations.

Clusterstate splitting: Splitting of the `clusterstate` to per collection makes SolrCloud more scalable. The cluster will know only what it needs to know, and not everything.

Beyond Search

Solr has evolved beyond its search engine capabilities and can be secondarily used as a datastore. If you are using Solr for indexing and searching requirements and also need a datastore, it would be worth evaluating Solr as an alternative NoSQL solution. NoSQL solutions such as MongoDB support full-text search so that they can cater to your simple search requirements. Similarly, Solr can be leveraged as a datastore, though that's not its primary use case. Updates in Lucene are implemented as deletions and additions and might not be the best candidate for systems that need frequent updates. Also, when selecting a NoSQL database, evaluation is done on many parameters. Unfortunately, discussion on that is beyond the scope of this book.

Also, Solr can be used as an analytical tool for simple requirements such as counting, slicing, and grouping. A data analysis system must be able to handle a huge volume of data, and Solr is a proven and blazingly fast technology for that. Hence, you can use Solr to perform some analytics on the indexed data. Solr 4.9 allows you to plug in a custom analytics algorithm through the AnalyticsQuery API. Solr 5.0 supports OLAP operations out of the box through the search analytics component. Solr 5.2 supports HyperLogLog, the probabilistic approach for counting distinct values.

Solr vs. Other Options

This section compares Solr to relational databases and Elasticsearch. I chose to compare Solr to relational databases so that developers new to search and NoSQL can understand and relate to Solr from the perspective of databases. In contrast, Elasticsearch is another popular open source search engine, and its comparison can help you understand where Solr stands in relation to it and whether you should evaluate Elasticsearch as well for your use.

Relational Databases

Traditional SQL databases are designed to query tables to find matching results and do not have the capability to rank those results. When you develop your search engine, you want your results to be ranked on a certain basis, with reasoning behind why a particular document ranks at a particular position or above another document. For example, a document might rank at the top of the result set based on logic such as the maximum number of tokens that match in the document, the rarity of the tokens in the corpus, the document being the most recent, or a combination of other parameters. The following are some of the major differences between Solr and traditional databases:

> *Relevance ranking*: Solr ranking is based on a combination of the Boolean model and vector space model. Documents are approved by the Boolean model, and those approved documents are ranked using the VSM. In contrast, traditional databases only find documents that should form part of the result set; they have only the approval process and no provision for ranking the documents.

> *Normalized vs. denormalized*: The data in relational databases is supposed to be normalized, and a relationship is established between the tables. But data in Solr is denormalized and flattened. Solr does support joins, but the behavior and implementation is different and less powerful than table joins. If the data is stored in a table and is to be imported to Solr, it should be denormalized by your indexer program or by the dataimport contrib module of Solr.

> *Schema vs. schemaless*: Relational databases need a schema to be defined at the time of creating the table. If you want to add a new column, the table needs to be altered. But Solr is flexible. If you know your schema, you can define it in the configuration file or you can go schemaless.

> *Scale up vs. scale out*: One area where Solr excels and gets the edge in enterprise systems is that it scales out easily. It's difficult for relational databases to scale out; they generally scale up, which is costly. In traditional Solr architecture, data can be distributed and sharded. SolrCloud makes scaling out even easier and it can run on a cluster of commodity machines.

> *Text analysis and navigation*: Solr provides flexible text analysis and navigational features, which makes perfect sense for developing a search engine. These features are totally missing in traditional databases.

What's important to understand here is that preferably, Solr should be used as a secondary datastore that imports data from a primary datastore such as a traditional database. Whenever you make a change to the indexing process or upgrade a Solr version (or something similar), you might need to build your index from scratch. Having a primary datastore simplifies the reindexing process.

Elasticsearch

Elasticsearch is a popular and widely used open source search engine. Both Solr and Elasticsearch are built on top of Lucene, have vibrant communities, and are commercially backed. The difference is in the way each builds a wrapper and implements features on top of Lucene. The following are some of their key differences:

Lucene: Solr aces Elasticsearch in terms of Lucene. Because development of Solr and Lucene are merged, Solr always has the same version as Lucene. With Solr, you always get the latest version of Lucene, whereas Elasticsearch might be a few releases behind. At the time of writing this chapter, Solr 5.3.1 runs Lucene 5.3.1, whereas Elasticsearch 1.6.0 runs Lucene 4.10.4.

Open source: Both Solr and Elasticsearch are open source. However, Solr is a project from the Apache Software Foundation and so is open source in the true sense; even you can be a committer. Elasticsearch is backed by its founding company, Elastic, and only their employees can commit.

History: Solr was open sourced in 2006 and at that time was the only popular open source search engine. Elasticsearch was released in 2010 and despite being younger, it has become quite popular and widely used.

Distributed and scalable: Solr's initial focus was core search problems and features related to querying, faceting, and so forth. It supported distributed search in the form of a traditional master-slave architecture. Elasticsearch was released with a truly distributed and scalable architecture, which was the key differentiator. Later Solr 4.0 caught up in supporting distributed and scalable architecture with SolrCloud.

Cluster management: Solr uses Apache ZooKeeper, an extremely popular and mature solution for maintaining configuration. In turn, Elasticsearch has a built-in framework called Zen Discovery, which is more vulnerable to the split-brain problem. In a split-brain scenario, one cluster appoints two masters, which leads to data loss.

REST endpoints: Both expose REST endpoints. Elasticsearch is purely JSON in and JSON out, whereas Solr supports multiple formats including XML, JSON, CSV, and binary.

Push queries: Percolation is a feature in Elasticsearch that informs the application when new documents match your specified condition. Solr doesn't support push queries.

Analytics, monitoring, and metrics: Solr is more focused on text search and supporting features. But when it comes to analytics and monitoring, Elasticsearch excels. It offers innumerable options for monitoring, whereas the support in Solr is limited. The ELS stack (Elasticsearch, Logstash, and Kibana combined together), allows you to get actionable insights in real time. The stack is widely used for requirements related to log management.

Text analysis: In Solr, analyzers should be predefined or configured by using managed APIs. In Elasticsearch, analyzers can be set even while querying.

Ease of use: Elasticsearch has always been easy to get started and run, but the recent Solr 5.0 is not far behind. If you are running Solr in schemaless mode, indexing and searching is just a two-step process: download and start. But Solr generally expects you to configure two XML files, schema.xml and solrconfig.xml. The files are well documented but require some understanding, which can offer better manageability in the long run.

Related Technologies

Through the course of this book and while developing solutions for your requirements, you will come across some related projects. I cover these projects in as much detail as needed throughout the book. If you want to dive further into them, refer to their respective manuals. These projects are as follows:

Apache ZooKeeper: This controls the heartbeat of SolrCloud. It is a central service for maintaining cluster configurations, store statuses, and synchronization information in a fault-tolerant and highly available manner. For SolrCloud to function, at least one ZooKeeper instance should be up and running.

Apache OpenNLP: This is a Java library for natural language processing of text. It supports tasks to understand and interpret text written in human languages. In this book, you will learn to apply these techniques to build a powerful search engine.

Apache UIMA: If your data is unstructured, the Solr UIMA contrib module can be used to give structure to the data. UIMA allows us to define a custom pipeline for analyzing a large volume of unstructured text and annotating the extracted metadata, which can be added to Solr fields.

Carrot clustering: You can cluster your similar or semantically related search results together by using Carrot2, and you can do so with just a few changes in your XML configuration.

Apache Tika: This toolkit provides a framework for parsing and extracting contents and metadata from files in many different formats such as Word, PPT and PDF. Solr provides a Solr Cell framework which uses this toolkit for indexing contents and metadata from such files.

Summary

This chapter presented a quick introduction to Apache Solr, with an overview of what's inside Solr, what makes Solr so popular, and why you should use it in your projects. I also briefly presented the new additions to Solr. With its current maturity, Solr is not limited as a search engine and is being widely used as a NoSQL datastore and as an analytical engine.

The next chapter covers how to set up Solr and how things work inside. Chapter 3, which is about the concepts of information retrieval and the internals of how the search engine works, is independent of other chapters and can be read out of sequence.

Resources

The official Apache Solr web site is `http://lucene.apache.org/solr/`. The latest version of Solr can be downloaded from this location. Along with each release binary, Solr provides official documentation specific to the release, details of changes, and Javadocs.

The Solr cwiki (`https://cwiki.apache.org/confluence/display/solr/Apache+Solr+Reference+Guide`) and wiki (`https://wiki.apache.org/solr/`) are two primary sources for Solr information available online. The cwiki is a Confluence site maintained by the ASF community, and all the commits are performed by Solr committers. The information available is officially approved and verified. If you have a suggestion on any cwiki page, feel free to add it as a comment. Committers will respond or make appropriate changes based on the suggestion.

The Solr wiki is an easily editable collection of web pages maintained by the community and hosted over the MoinMoin web engine. Anyone with permission can edit the pages. If you want edit permission, write to the Solr mailing list or IRC channel.

To ask questions, discuss issues, or contribute to the community, refer to the Solr resources page at `http://lucene.apache.org/solr/resources.html` for more information.

CHAPTER 2

■ ■ ■

Solr Setup and Administration

Indexing and searching are the two primary operations performed in Solr. *Indexing* is the process of adding content to a Solr index to make it searchable. But before you can index, you first need to set up Solr. The primary focus of release 5.0 was improving ease of use, which has made Solr setup process extremely easy. The steps are so simple that if you run Solr in schemaless mode, enabling Solr to dynamically guess the field type and define fields, the whole setup process can be performed in few minutes.

This chapter begins by presenting Solr fundamentals, including its terminology and directory structure. You'll then set up Solr and briefly index and search sample documents. For the benefit of first-time users or those migrating from 4.x releases, this chapter takes a simple demonstration approach. You'll see more-advanced examples as you proceed through the chapters and gain some background about those Solr features and components.

In addition, you will learn about Solr's primary user options and administrative features. Throughout these explanations, you'll see how Solr used to work in earlier releases. For ease of understanding and convenience, this chapter assumes an environment with a single Solr instance (or server). Chapter 10 focuses on a distributed approach and SolrCloud, which enables support for replication, scalability, and fault tolerance.

This chapter covers the following topics:

- Solr as a stand-alone server

- Important terminology and directory/file structure

- Utility scripts

- Web admin interface

- Core management

- Instance management

- Common exceptions

Stand-Alone Server

Solr runs as a stand-alone server that comes prebundled with everything you need to get your instance up and running. Prior to release 5.0, Solr was distributed as a WAR file. To deploy it, you either used the prebundled Jetty instance or copied dist/solr-<version>.war to Tomcat or another servlet container. But now Solr abstracts the deployment process and needs you to see it as a stand-alone server without worrying about the where and how of deployment. If you have used a previous version, you need to erase that knowledge from your memory and start using the scripts provided for administration. For those of you who are curious about how it's deployed now, Solr internally uses the Jetty servlet container—but that's an implementation detail, and you should think of it as a stand-alone server. The flexibility to deploy Solr in other containers has been withdrawn to better utilize the container's networking stack features.

Figure 2-1 uses an example of Tomcat to depict how Solr differs as a server and in its deployment in releases 4.x and 5.x.

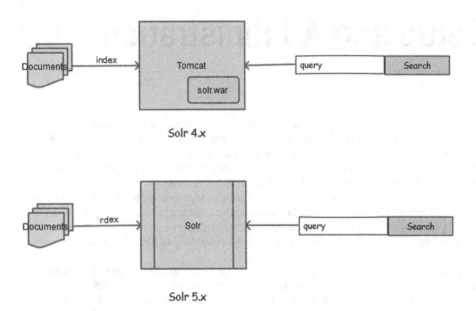

Figure 2-1. *Solr versions 4.x and 5.x*

You can sniff solr.war in the server/webapps directory in releases older than Solr 5.3.0.

■ **Note** The term *stand-alone server* here refers to the new perspective you see Solr from and doesn't refer to an environment with a single Solr instance. In SolrCloud mode, each stand-alone server referred to here is an instance (or node).

Prerequisites

Apache Solr is written in Java, and the only prerequisite for installing Solr 5.3.1 is Java 7 or greater. Using update version u55 or later is recommended. Using a prior version is strongly discouraged. If your machine is running Java 8, that's even better, as it can improve performance. Before proceeding, please check your Java version as shown here:

```
$ java -version
java version "1.8.0_31"
Java(TM) SE Runtime Environment (build 1.8.0_31-b13)
Java HotSpot(TM) 64-Bit Server VM (build 25.31-b07, mixed mode)
```

For Solr versions older than 4.8.*x*, you can use Java 6. If the preceding command doesn't find a Java installation on your machine, you can download a copy from www.oracle.com/technetwork/java/javase/downloads/index.html. For installation steps, refer to www.java.com/en/download/help/download_options.xml.

Download

You can download the latest binary of Solr from http://lucene.apache.org/solr/downloads.html. The download page contains a reference to Apache mirror sites. Click the suggested option or any of the backup sites and download the latest binary (zip or tar).

After completing the download, extract the directory from the compressed binary by using an appropriate tool or as shown here:

```
$ tar -xvf solr-5.3.1.tgz (*nix)
$ unzip solr-5.3.1.zip (Windows)
```

Terminology

To avoid ambiguity and understand Solr better, it's important to know a few terms as well as the files used in the context of Solr. Before we proceed any further, this section presents the common terms, followed by SolrCloud-specific terms, and then some of the important files.

General Terminology

The following is a list of general terms that are used across all types of Solr setups:

> *Solr instance*: This generic term is used in the context of an application server—for example, a Tomcat instance or Jetty instance. Here it refers to a Solr server running inside a Java Virtual Machine (JVM). Zero or more cores can be configured to run inside a Solr instance. Each Solr instance requires a reference to a separate Solr home directory.

> *Solr core*: Each of your indexes and the files required by that index makes a core. So if your application requires multiple indexes, you can have multiple cores running inside a Solr instance (instead of multiple Solr instances, each containing one core). Physically, each core maps to a subdirectory in the Solr home directory.

> *Solr home*: This is the directory that Solr refers to for almost everything. It contains all the information regarding the cores and their indexes, configurations, and dependencies. This book uses the term $SOLR_HOME to refer to this directory.

Solr shard: This term is used in distributed environments, in which you partition the data between multiple Solr instances. Each chunk of data on a particular instance is called a *shard*. The shard contains a subset of the whole index. For example, say you have 30 million documents and plan to distribute these in three shards, each containing 10 million documents. You'll need three Solr instances, each having one core with the same name and schema. While serving queries, any shard can receive the request and distribute it to the other two shards for processing, get all the results and respond back to the client with the merged result.

SolrCloud Terminology

In Solr, you can have two types of distributed architecture: traditional and SolrCloud. The traditional approach to distributed search, available since release 1.3, uses master-slave architecture. In this approach, the index is created on the master server, which is replicated to one or more slave servers dedicated to searching. This approach has several limitations, which you will learn about in Chapter 10.

To address these limitations, SolrCloud was released in version 4.0. This revolutionary approach sets up a cluster of Solr servers to provide fault tolerance and high availability and to offer features such as distributed indexing, centralized configuration, automatic load balancing, and failover.

SolrCloud introduced new terms that are a bit different from those of a traditional architecture. If you are using SolrCloud, it's important to remember these terms. For simplicity, this book uses the terms related to traditional architecture unless we are doing something specific to SolrCloud. The following list defines the key terms associated with SolrCloud:

Node: A single instance of Solr is called a node in SolrCloud.

Cluster: All the nodes in your environment together.

Collection: A complete logical index in a cluster. All the shards in a collection use the same set of configuration files.

Shard: A logical portion, or slice, of a collection. Each shard consists of one or more replicas of the index for redundancy.

Replica: The physical copy of a shard, which runs in a node as a Solr core.

Leader: Among all the replicas of a shard, one is elected as a leader. SolrCloud forwards all requests to the leader of the shard, which distributes it to the replicas.

ZooKeeper: ZooKeeper is an Apache project widely used by distributed systems for centralized configuration and coordination. SolrCloud uses it for managing the cluster and electing a leader.

Important Configuration Files

You can develop a full-fledged search engine and take it to production, without writing even a single line of Java code. Solr makes this possible by allowing you to configure all the features and schema just by making XML changes. You can put a feature in place by registering the components and chaining them appropriately in XML-based configuration files. The following are some of the primary configuration files:

> solr.xml: On starting a Solr instance, solr.xml is the first file that Solr looks for in the $SOLR_HOME directory. This file primarily contains SolrCloud-related information. Its configuration is applicable to the Solr instance, while other files are specific to a core. Solr used to refer to this file for identifying the cores to be loaded. In release 4.4, automatic core discovery was introduced, and the provision to make entries in solr.xml was deprecated and is no longer supported as of version 5.0.

> solrconfig.xml: This file contains core-specific configurations and definitions related to request handling, response formatting, indexing, configuring other components, managing memory, caching, and making commits.

> schema.xml: Contains the whole schema—the definition of fields, its type (also called a fieldType) and scoring strategy, if any. The fieldType defines the text analysis to be performed on the field to control the matching behavior while indexing and searching.

> core.properties: Solr refers to this file for core discovery. This is a Java properties file that contains configuration specific to the core, such as the name of the core and the path of the data directory. You can also define your custom properties as key-value pairs in this file and refer to it in Solr configuration files for value substitution. It can sit in any subdirectory and at any depth, and that directory is treated as a core directory. The only limitation is that the same directory hierarchy cannot have multiple core.properties (you cannot create a core inside another core).

Directory Structure

To set up and use Solr, you need to understand two sets of directory structures. One is the Solr distribution (the directory extracted from a downloaded tar or zip) and another is the Solr home directory, which contains the indices and configurations of all the cores.

Solr Installation

The directory structure of the Solr 5.x distribution is different from the previous releases. This change has been made to make Solr more organized and easier to use. Figure 2-2 shows this new directory structure. An ellipsis (...) signifies that the directory contains other files or directories.

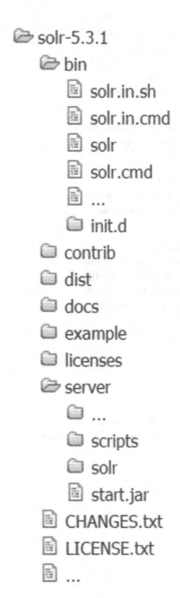

Figure 2-2. *Solr installation directory structure*

The following is a description of all the directories and important files in the Solr distribution directory:

bin: This contains the utility scripts for starting, stopping and administrating Solr. Introduced in version 4.8, this directory contains scripts for both Windows and *nix machines. The following list describes these scripts:

- solr/solr.cmd: The script you use for starting, stopping, and other administrative purposes. Upcoming sections cover this in more detail.

- solr.in.sh/solr.in.cmd: Environment file for settings specific to the instance.

- oom_solr.sh: Using this script, you can force-kill the Solr instance running on a specific port. There is no corresponding utility for Windows.

- solr.<port>.port: When you start the Solr instance by using the script, this file is created. It is for internal use and is automatically deleted on stopping the instance.

- post: Script for indexing documents to Solr.

- install_solr_service.sh: If you want to install Solr as a service, this script lets you do that in an interactive manner.

- init.d: A directory you can refer to, if you want to run Solr by using the init process in a Unix environment.

contrib: Apart from core libraries, Solr contains other libraries that are part of Solr but are contributions from other projects and are used as needed. This directory contains the following subdirectories, each of which makes a module:

- analysis-extras: This contains additional analyzers for internationalization and multilingual support.

- clustering: The previous chapter mentioned Carrot2. This directory contains plug-ins for implementing clustering when using Carrot2 in Solr.

- dataimporthandler: If Solr is your secondary store and a SQL database is your primary store, you need not worry about writing your own client program to fetch data from the database and index it. DataImportHandler is a contributed plug-in that allows you to import data from various sources with few XML changes. It is not limited to databases and can be used to import data from XML and HTTP data sources.

- dataimporthandler-extras: This contains additional plug-ins that you may need while importing data by using DataImportHandler.

- extraction: To extract data from rich documents such as Microsoft Word documents or Adobe PDFs, you can use the Apache Solr Content Extraction Library (Solr Cell). This plug-in uses Apache Tika for extraction, which we mentioned in Chapter 1.

- langid: If all your text is not in English, you may need this module in your project. The Apache Solr Language Identifier plug-in allows you to identify the language of the text and handle it appropriately.

- map-reduce: This experimental module enables you to build an index by using map-reduce jobs.

- morphlines-cell: This is an experimental module for content extraction.

- morphlines-core: This is another experimental plug-in, which depends on the Kite Morphlines framework to perform Extract, Transform, and Load (ETL) of huge data volumes quickly and easily when loading into Solr.

- uima: Not everything in this world is perfect, and that may be true of your data. If your data is not structured, you can use an Unstructured Information Management Architecture (UIMA) project while indexing the data.

- velocity: If you want to design a UI for your search engine, you can do it right inside Solr, by using the Apache Velocity templating engine.

docs: This contains documentation specific to the Solr version you have downloaded.

licenses: This contains the licensing information for all the libraries provided with Solr.

server: This directory by default is the central place for everything related to a Solr instance. It contains the server, your Solr home directory, and the logs. It also contains the Jetty configuration files, which can be modified to change the behavior of the server; however, you should refrain from doing this because Solr wants you to ignore implementation details. For any customization, you should tune the properties available in the bin scripts. For a production environment, it's advisable to configure the Solr home and log location to be different from the server directory. The following are the subdirectories in the server directory:

- contexts: Solr uses Jetty internally, and this directory contains the deployment descriptor required by Jetty for Solr.

- etc: This directory contains Jetty configuration files.

- lib: This contains the Jetty and other libraries required by the Solr instance.

- logs: By default, the Solr logs are created in this directory.

- modules: It is used by Jetty for containing module definitions.

- resources: This contains the configuration files such as log4j.properties.

- scripts: This contains utility scripts for SolrCloud.

- solr: This is the default Solr home directory, which you learned about in the "General Terminology" section. We discuss it in more detail in the next section.

- solr-webapps: Jetty extracts Solr in this directory.

- start.jar: The executable JAR that is used to start Jetty. Solr 5.3.0 has internally been upgraded to run on Jetty 9. Solr no longer supports running it directly using the "java -jar start.jar" and bin/solr scripts are the only way.

■ **Note** Throughout this book, the term $SOLR_DIST refers to the Solr distribution directory discussed in this section.

Solr Home

The Solr home directory contains Solr configuration files and the indices and is home to everything related to a Solr instance. A Solr instance can have multiple cores, and they are all defined in this directory. A Solr server requires a reference to the home directory, and if it's not provided, will take the default path configured. For a successful core start, Solr requires the configurations and libraries to be available in an appropriate fashion. It is also a good practice to create a lib directory inside $SOLR_HOME or a core directory containing the dependent libraries.

Figure 2-3 shows a sample Solr home directory, containing three cores located at core1, core2/sub-dir1, and core3, respectively, which are detected by the corresponding core.properties file. You can also see a lib directory present in $SOLR_HOME, sharing dependencies among all the defined cores.

Figure 2-3. Solr home directory structure

The following is a description of all the subdirectories and important files in the Solr home directory:

solr.xml: This has been covered in the "Terminology" section.

zoo.cfg: This contains the configuration for ZooKeeper. Chapter 10 covers ZooKeeper. If you are not using SolrCloud, you can ignore this file.

configsets: If you want to share configuration among multiple cores on your instance, you can use configsets introduced in Solr 4.8. The upcoming "Core Management" section covers this in more detail.

lib: Keep all the common libraries in this directory, to share among all the cores.

Core (core1, core2/sub-dir1, core3): In this example, we have three indexes, so we have three cores. This directory is the root to all the core-related files.

- core.properties: Solr refers to this file for autodiscovery of the core. It can be present at any level in the directory tree, and the directory containing the file will be the core root. In Figure 2-3, the directory for core2 is core2/sub-dir1. Hence conf, data, and everything specific to the core should exist in sub-dir1. This file is a Java properties file, in which you can configure the core-specific properties.

- conf: This directory contains all configuration files specific to the core, including solrconfig.xml and schema.xml.

- data: This directory is for your indexes. The index sub-directory contains the Solr index, which is created upon indexing documents. The tlog sub-directory contains your transactional logs, which are critical for ensuring consistency of document writes.

- lib: This directory contains all the dependencies specific to the core.

Hands-On Exercise

You must be eager to quickly get your Solr instance up and begin searching for results. This section takes a simple approach to starting Solr, indexing documents, and searching for results. This overview of the complete process will be helpful in your experiments until we discuss more-detailed examples in upcoming chapters. In the next section, you will explore starting and administrating Solr in more detail.

Start Solr

You can start Solr by using the script provided (since release 4.10) in the distribution bundle.

```
$ cd bin
$ ./solr start
Started Solr server on port 8983 (pid=2108). Happy searching!
```

Now, that your Solr instance has started, you can point your browser to http://localhost:8983/solr. Figure 2-4 shows the Solr admin interface.

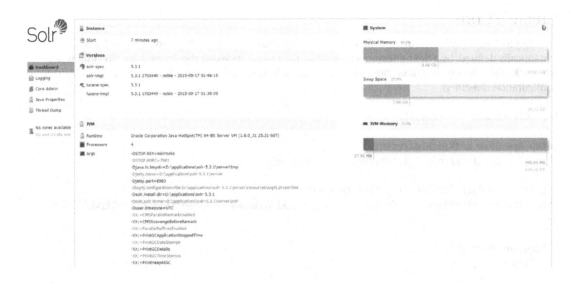

Figure 2-4. *Dashboard, the home page of the Solr admin interface*

If your dashboard displays as in Figure 2-4, Solr has started successfully. In case of error, either this page will not display or an error message will be highlighted at the top of dashboard, as shown in Figure 2-5. If the error is in a specific core, as in Figure 2-5, other cores will work as expected.

Figure 2-5. *Core initialization exception*

At the bottom of the tabs on left-hand side of Figure 2-4, you see "No cores available." This is because we haven't configured any cores yet. As you know, to create an index you need to define a core, and cores are physically located in the SOLR_HOME directory. So first you should know where your SOLR_HOME is or make the server refer to your preferred directory as SOLR_HOME. In the next section, you will create a core in the default SOLR_HOME directory, which is server/solr in the distribution directory.

If you want to run Solr on a specific port, you can do so as follows:

```
$ ./solr start -p 8980
```

-p <portnumber> specifies the port on which you want Solr to run. The preceding command runs Solr on port 8980. This parameter is optional. By default, Solr runs on port 8983.

Also by default, the script runs Solr in background mode, and output is sent to solr-<PORT>-console. log. If you are running Solr for a short duration and want the output to be printed on the console, you can run it with the -f option:

```
$ ./solr start -f -p 8983 -V
```

-V is an optional verbose mode, which can be used even while running Solr in background mode.

Create a Core

The simplest way to create a core in Solr 5.*x* is to go schemaless. In schemaless mode, the fields are dynamically defined, by a field-guess mechanism, at the time of indexing the documents. The following is a quick example of schemaless core creation, which Solr by default creates when you don't provide the configuration directory:

```
$ ./solr create -c hellosolr

Setup new core instance directory:
/home/applications/solr-5.3.1/server/solr/hellosolr

Creating new core 'hellosolr' using command:
http://localhost:8983/solr/admin/cores?action=CREATE&name=hellosolr&instanceDir=hellosolr

{
  "responseHeader":{
    "status":0,
    "QTime":2461},
  "core":"hellosolr"}
```

-c <corename> is the name of the core you want to create.

Refresh your Solr admin page, and you will see that the "No cores available" message is replaced with a drop-down menu listing the core you created.

Index Some Data

Select the hellosolr core and go to the Documents tab. This tab allows you to index documents, right from the interface. Figure 2-6 shows a snapshot of the screen. To index documents, you need to select a Document Type and provide data in that format. Let's index the sample data that comes with Solr and is available in example/exampledocs. Because our core is schemaless, we can index any XML or JSON file in that directory without worrying about the field definition. Use the following steps to index documents in the money.xml file provided by Solr:

1. From the Document Type drop-down list, select File Upload.

2. Browse the money.xml file.

3. Click the Submit Document button to index the documents in that file.

Alternatively, from the Document Type drop-down list, you can select the XML option and paste the documents for indexing. On successful upload or submittal, you will see the response status "success." This status indicates that the documents are indexed but will be ready to serve search requests only after changes are committed. The admin interface triggers this commit by default, so you can start searching for results.

■ **Note** The files in example/exampledocs contain documents in Solr-specified format, and random documents should not be uploaded. To index your own data, create a document adhering to the conventions followed in the sample files.

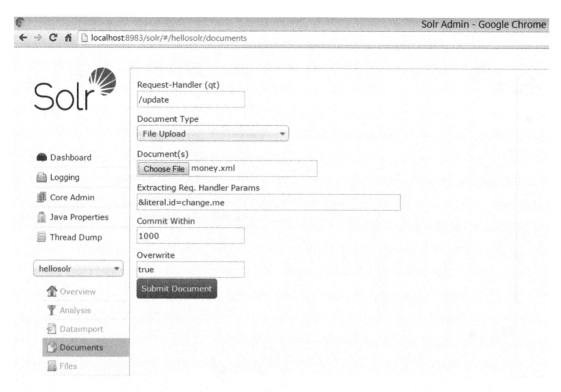

Figure 2-6. *Uploading the file for indexing*

Search for Results

Access the Query tab and then click the Execute Query button. This shows the document you indexed. By default, Solr fetches the top 10 documents from the index. In the Query pane, the q text box contains your query, which you need to specify in the format *fieldname:query*. Here, *:* means all the values in all the fields. If you want results for a specific query, such as all the documents containing the phrase "Bank of America" in the manu field, you can type **manu:"Bank of America"** in the q text box. The wt parameter specifies the response format. Figure 2-7 shows the results in JSON format , with json selected as the wt value.

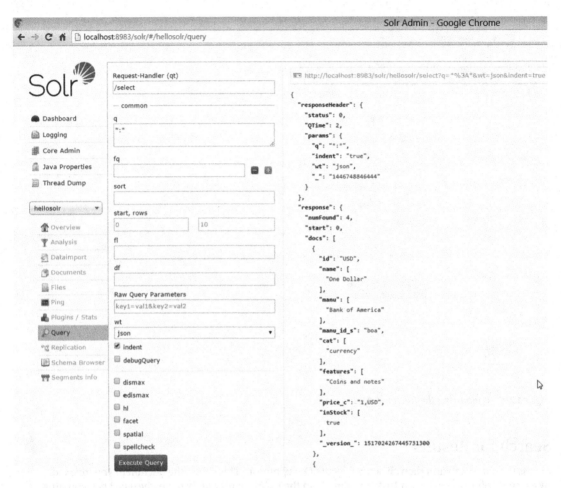

Figure 2-7. *Search results*

Now that you understand the simple process of indexing and searching, you can skip any sections you don't need and jump to those that are relevant to you. However, I suggest you follow the sequence. In the next sections, you will get into the details of setup and administrative tasks.

Solr Script

Solr scripts were introduced in release 4.10 and starting from Solr 5.3.0, the script is the only provision to start Solr. The support for start.jar, the traditional way of running Solr with Jetty, has been withdrawn to support HTTP and HTTPS Jetty modules. So for starting and stopping Solr, the following scripts should be used:

```
bin/solr - *nix
bin/solr.cmd - Windows
```

■ **Note**　To avoid presenting duplicate code, this book uses the name bin/solr to refer to both scripts. The purpose of both scripts is same. Each is specific to its environment.

In this section, you will see in detail how to use the bin/solr script for starting, stopping, and managing Solr. The examples provided here assumes that you are running the script from bin directory on a Windows machine.

Starting Solr

Starting Solr is easy! You already did it in the "Hands-On Exercise" section. In this section, you'll learn a bit more detail about it.

Solr can be started in two modes: stand-alone and SolrCloud. We are ignoring the traditional distributed architecture because it's starting mechanism is the same as for stand-alone mode. By default, Solr runs in stand-alone mode, and this chapter covers that for simplicity. The following command starts Solr with default settings on default port 8983.

```
$ solr start
```

You can provide additional parameters to Solr to override the default settings as shown in the below example.

```
$ solr start -p 8983 -h localhost -m 4g
```

　　-p specifies the server port
　　-h specifies the host name
　　-m specifies the heap size for the JVM. This argument specifies the same value for -Xms and -Xmx
　　If you are running earlier release of Solr, you can start it using the start.jar in server directory as specified below:

```
$ java -jar start.jar
```

The easiest way to learn about the commands supported by the script and the options it provides is by utilizing the help command of the bin/solr script. You will learn to use help menu in the next section.

Using Solr Help

The bin/solr script is verbose and well documented. The best way to proceed further is to use the -help option. This provides all the available commands as well as some examples:

```
$ solr -help
Usage: solr COMMAND OPTIONS
       where COMMAND is one of: start, stop, restart, healthcheck, create, create_core,
       create_collection, delete
```

Here is a stand-alone server example (which starts Solr in the background on port 8984):

```
$ solr start -p 8984
```

The following is a SolrCloud example (which starts Solr in cloud mode using localhost:2181 to connect to ZooKeeper, with a 1GB maximum heap size and remote Java debug options enabled):

```
$ solr start -c -m 1g -z localhost:2181 -a "-Xdebug -Xrunjdwp:transport=dt_socket,
server=y,suspend=n,address=1044"
```

```
Pass -help after any COMMAND to see command-specific usage information,
  such as:    solr start -help or solr stop -help
```

Now, if you know the command that you want to use, you can get further information about its usage, by typing **-help** after the command name:

```
$ solr stop -help
Usage: solr stop [-k key] [-p port]

 -k key      Stop key; default is solrrocks

 -p port     Specify the port the Solr HTTP listener is bound to

 -all        Find and stop all running Solr servers on this host
```

Stopping Solr

You can stop Solr by running the script as follows:

```
$ solr stop -p 8983
```

This stops a Solr instance running on port 8983. Providing either the -p or -all parameter is mandatory. If you specify -all, the command stops all the running nodes. Also, the preceding command stops Solr only if it has been started with the bin/solr script.

When you start Solr with the `bin/solr` script, it creates a `solr-<port>.port` file in the `bin` directory, to identify the running Solr instances and the `stop` command deletes this file.

Restarting Solr

You can restart a running Solr instance with the `restart` command. All the parameters of the start option work with restart; the only difference is that the `-p <port>` option is mandatory. The following is an example command to restart a Solr instance running on port 8983:

```
$ solr restart -p 8983
```

Determining Solr Status

Using the `status` command, you can verify all the running instances of Solr in the box. This command provides the port number on which the instance is running, the path of the Solr home directory, the amount of heap memory allocated, and its consumption status:

```
$ solr status

Found Solr process 8076 running on port 8983
{
  "solr_home":"D:\\applications\\solr-5.3.1\\server\\solr\\",
  "version":"5.3.1 1703449 - noble - 2015-09-17 01:48:15",
  "startTime":"2015-11-05T18:07:32.916Z",
  "uptime":"0 days, 0 hours, 57 minutes, 44 seconds",
  "memory":"80.7 MB (%16.4) of 490.7 MB"}
}
```

Configuring Solr Start

Before starting Solr, you might want to customize properties such as server host/port, heap space allocation, and Solr home. The following are the two common approaches for this customization:

- Setting the properties in the `solr.in` environment file
- Passing the values as arguments to the `solr` script

The environment file is the recommended place to set the properties and is also persistent. The environment is retained between multiple restarts. If you start Solr by passing parameters, it will either override or append to the value(s) of properties defined in the environment file.

You can either read through the comments in the environment file or run this command to find all the Solr startup options:

```
$ solr start -help
```

Admin Web Interface

While running Solr to get a feel for it, you used the Solr admin interface for indexing and searching. The Solr admin UI is an extremely powerful tool that provides Solr administrators and developers deep insight about their cores, instances, and the whole cluster and environment. It provides the user a rich interface for viewing configuration files, running queries, analyzing documents, and much more. The following are the primary reasons for using the Solr admin interface:

JVM properties and thread dump: The Java Properties tab provides the properties of the JVM running Solr such as classpath and memory settings. The Thread Dump tab allows you to inspect server thread information such as thread status, execution time and stacktrace.

Core management: The Core Admin tab in the console allows you to add, unload, reload, rename, optimize, and swap the cores.

Log management: The Logging tab displays log messages with a color scheme. Each color represents a different logging level. The messages are collapsed for convenience, and can be clicked to expand to a detailed view. The tab also allows you to change the logging level of packages and classes on the fly.

Core overview: Select the core, and the "Overview" page loads by default, providing important statistics including the count of documents in the index, total size of the index, last indexed time, replication information, and core directory-related information.

Search: Select a core and then click the Query tab to query, facet, spell-check, or call any custom search handler. This page is used frequently for running, debugging, and evaluating ad hoc queries.

Index: Select a core and click Documents to index XML, JSON, or CSV documents by submitting the form, or you can upload a file from your local drive. If data import is configured in `solrconfig.xml`, you can import data from a database. For this task, the DataImport tab provides an exclusive page.

Analyze: Programmers frequently use the admin interface to analyze the behavior of a field or fieldType. You can click the Analysis tab, enter the text you will index or query in the respective fields, and then click the Analyze Values button. The system provides step-by-step text analysis, performed while indexing and querying, and highlights the text right at the step at which both tokens matched.

Replication: If you are running Solr in a traditional master-slave environment, you can enable, disable, or force replication for the core through the Replication tab.

Browse files: The Files tab lists all the files and directories in the `<core>/conf` directory.

View component statistics: The Plugins/Stats tab lets you view important statistics.

Use the Schema Browser: This screen lets you select a field or fieldType and browse its schema information and the indexed tokens. This screen is extremely useful for exploring the indexed terms. For example, if you want to generate a list of stop words for a field, you can use the indexed terms and the count provided by the browser, to evaluate the candidate stop words.

Visualize the Segments Info: The underlying indexes can be composed of a set of sub-indexes or segments. The "Segments Info" page visualizes these segments and provides metadata about it such as indexed document count and deleted document count.

In Solr 5.1, the UI has been refactored using AngularJS.

Core Management

In Solr, the core contains a single index, its configuration files such as `solrconfig.xml` and `schema.xml`, and other associated files. Each core can have a different index structure and can be used for a different search requirement. A Solr instance, which can have multiple cores, provides a unified administration of all the cores. Solr allows you to create a core on the fly, rename it, unload it, and a lot more. In this section, you will learn how to perform all these tasks without restarting the Solr server.

Config Sets

Solr 4.8 introduced a provision to create Config Sets, a set of sharable configuration files, that can be used for creating new cores. These can be useful in a distributed environment. The Solr 5.*x* distribution also bundles some preconfigured configsets, which you can reference for creating your core instead of writing it all from scratch. These named configsets can be found in the `server/solr/configsets` directory. The following is the list of configsets prebundled in Solr 5.3.1:

> `basic_configs`: This contains the minimal configuration needed for running Solr.

> `data_driven_schema_configs`: If you want to go schemaless, you can use this config. It's configured to support a managed schema with field guessing.

> `sample_techproducts_configs`: This is a full-fledged configuration with most of the optional features enabled. You can use this configset as a starting point for your core configuration.

Create Configset

The default home for the configset directory is SOLR_HOME. You can create a configset as follows:

1. Create a configset directory in SOLR_HOME:

```
$ cd $SOLR_HOME
$ mkdir configsets
```

2. The `configsets` directory is your configset base directory. In this directory, you can create as many subdirectories as you need. The name of each subdirectory indicates the name of that configset:

```
$ cd configsets
$ mkdir configset1 configset2 configset3
```

3. Your named configset subdirectory should contain a `conf` subdirectory with `solrconfig.xml`, `schema.xml`, and other configuration files.

4. If you want to change the name of your configset base directory, you can do it in `solr.xml`:

```
<solr>
  <configSetBaseDir>sharedConfigSets</configSetBaseDir>
</solr>
```

Figure 2-8 shows a configset directory structure.

Figure 2-8. *Config Sets directory structure*

___

■ **Note**   In an upcoming version, Solr will introduce a REST API to manage configsets. This API will allow you to upload the configsets to a template location and use them for core creation.

___

Create Core

Suppose you have a new search requirement that calls for a new schema definition with a different structure. In the previous section, you created a core by using the default schema. In this section, you will learn how to create a core by using an existing configset. In Chapter 4, you will learn how to create a schema and define fields.

If your Solr instance already contains a core, and you want to use the same configuration for the new core, you can create a configset by using that configuration. If the new schema is different, I suggest you use a configset prebundled with Solr. The named configset `sample_techproducts_config` is a good starting point for any schema design, as it defines most of the Solr features.

The following are the ways to create your new core in Solr. After creating a core, validate it either by getting the status or using the Solr admin UI.

bin/solr Script

The bin/solr script can create a new core in any Solr instance running on the machine. The command for creating the core is as follows:

```
solr create -c <corename> -d <confdir> -p <port>
```

corename is a mandatory parameter. Solr automatically creates the specified core directory in SOLR_HOME along with the core.properties file required for core discovery.

confdir is one of the named configsets or the path of the conf directory you want to use. Solr copies the configuration files from this directory to the core directory. If -d is not specified, Solr will use the data_driven_schema_configs configset.

port identifies the local Solr instance in which the core is to be created. If port is not specified, the core will be created in the first running instance that the script finds.

The following is an example command that creates a core named hellosolr, in a Solr instance running on port 8983, using the sample_techproducts_configs configset.

```
$ ./solr create -c hellosolr -d sample_techproducts_configs -p 8983
```

Alternatively, you can use the create_core command with the same options:

```
solr create_core -c <core-name> -d <conf-dir> -p <path>
```

The create option checks whether Solr is running in stand-alone mode or SolrCloud mode on the specified port, and based on that, it invokes either create_core or create_collection. The create_collection option is for SolrCloud mode. You will see an example of collection creation in Chapter 10.

When creating a core by using the script, you should not create the corresponding directory manually, because the script will take care of it.

Core Admin REST API

Another way of creating a core is by calling the Core Admin API. Because it's a REST API, you can call it from your program, using curl or even a browser. If you want to create a core by using the API, you can do so as follows:

```
http://host:port/solr/admin/cores?action=CREATE&name=corename&instanceDir=path/to/
instance&config=solrconfig.xml&schema=schema.xml&dataDir=data
```

corename and instanceDir are mandatory parameters. If you don't provide other parameters, Solr will provide the default value.

You can create a core by using an existing configset as follows:

```
http://host:port/solr/admin/cores?action=CREATE&name=corename&instanceDir=path/to/instance&
configSet=configset1
```

The following is an example that creates a hellosolr core by using the Core Admin API:

```
$ curl http://localhost:8983/solr/admin/cores?action=CREATE&name=hellosolr&instanceDir=
hellosolr&configSet=sample_techproducts_configs
```

Admin Interface

The Solr admin UI provides a screen for creating a core—and for all the operations supported by Core Admin. Although this chapter covers all the administrative options provided by the Core Admin API, it covers only the UI for creating a core.

Open the admin interface in your browser. Open the Core Admin tab and click the Add Core button. Fill in the displayed form with appropriate values and click Add Core. Figure 2-9 shows a snapshot of the screen for creating a core.

Figure 2-9. *Solr admin screen for core creation*

Manually

You can even create a core manually, but that requires a Solr restart. The following are the steps you need to follow for manual core creation:

1. Create a core directory in SOLR_HOME.

2. Create a core.properties file in that directory and define a property name=<corename> inside the file. corename is the name of your core.

3. Copy the conf directory in the newly created core directory.

4. Restart the Solr instance.

Similarly, you can perform other core administration operations manually.

I present this approach to help you better understand core management. You can take this approach while experimenting and during development. But doing this in production will take your Solr instance down and is not recommended.

Core Status

You can get the status of cores that are registered by using the Core Admin API. The following call gives you the status of all the cores. You can make this call even if you haven't registered any cores yet:

```
http://localhost:port/solr/admin/cores?action=STATUS
```

If you are interested in the status of a specific core, you need to pass an additional core parameter with <corename>.

```
http://localhost:port/solr/admin/cores?action=STATUS&core=<corename>
```

The bin/solr script doesn't offer you the provision to get the core status. You can get the status of only your Solr instance by using this script.

Unload Core

If you don't need a core anymore, you can unload it by using the Core Admin API. The endpoint for unloading is shown here, along with the required parameters:

```
http://localhost:port/solr/admin/cores?action=UNLOAD&core=<corename>
```

The core is unloaded only after all the existing requests are served. All new requests to the core will throw a 404 error. Unloading also provides the option to delete the index, data, and core directory by passing the parameters deleteIndex=true, deleteDataDir=true, and deleteInstanceDir=true, respectively.

The deleteInstanceDir operation also deletes its subdirectories. In that case, you don't need to invoke a delete on the data directory or index directory.

The Solr script doesn't offer any provisions for unloading a core.

Delete Core

If you don't need a core anymore, you can delete it in the following ways.

You can use the bin/solr script:

```
solr delete -c <corename> -p <port>
```

Alternatively, you can use the Core Admin REST API:

```
http://localhost:port/solr/admin/cores?action=UNLOAD&core=<corename>&deleteInstanceDir=true
```

Refer to the preceding "Unload Core" section for details of the API.

Core Rename

If you want to change the name of a live core, you can do so by using the Core Admin API as follows:

```
http://host:port/solr/admin/cores?action=RENAME&core=old&other=new
```

This renames the core from the old name to a new name.

Core Swap

If you want to swap the names of two cores, you can use the Core Admin Swap API. You may need this, for example, to swap between the live and standby core:

```
http://host:port/solr/admin/cores?action=SWAP&core=core1&other=core2
```

Core Split

Solr allows you to split an index into two or more indices. You may want to do this when the size of your index grows huge. This is generally done in SolrCloud for shard splitting. Here is the endpoint and supported parameters for splitting the core:

```
http://host:port/solr/admin/cores?action=SPLIT&core=sourcecore&targetCore=core1&targetCore=core2
```

The core parameter indicates the source core that you want to split. For writing to the target core, you need to provide either the targetCore or path parameter. If path is provided, an equal subset of the index will be written to that path. If targetCore is provided, that core must be available. The chunk of index will be merged to the target core. Both path and targetCore parameters are multivalued. The preceding example splits the index in the source core between cores core1 and core2.

Index Backup

Failures do happen, so making a backup always makes you feel safe. You can make a backup in Solr by calling ReplicationHandler, a component for replicating data from the master instance to slave instances. The API for backup is provided here:

```
http://host:port/solr/core/replication?command=backup&name=backup-name&location=backup-location
```

By default, Solr takes a snapshot of the index, with a current timestamp, in the data directory. If a location parameter is provided, the snapshot is taken in an absolute directory or relative to Solr's instance directory as provided. The snapshot directory is suffixed with the provided name or the current timestamp. If your Solr version is older than 5.0, ensure that before calling this API, ReplicationHandler is configured in solrconfig.xml.

You can also configure Solr to take an automatic backup of the index during a commit or optimize and can specify the number of backups to maintain:

```
<requestHandler name="/replication" >
 <lst name="master">
  <str name="replicateAfter">startup</str>
  <str name="replicateAfter">optimize</str>
  <str name="backupAfter">commit</str>
  <str name="maxNumberOfBackups">2</str>
 </lst>
</requestHandler>
```

Solr allows you to track the status of your backup operation by using the details command:

```
http://host:port/solr/core/replication?command=details
```

Index Restore

Solr 5.2 introduced an API for restoring the backed-up index. This API restores the named backup into the current core, and searches will start showing the snapshot data on restore completion. The API for restoring the backup is as follows:

```
http://host:port/solr/core/replication?command=restore&name=<backup-name>
```

Solr doesn't allow you to perform another backup or restore operation while one is in progress. Solr allows you to track the status of a restore operation by using the restorestatus command:

```
http://host:port/solr/core/replication?command=restorestatus
```

In releases earlier than Solr 5.2, you need to restore the index manually. The manual process requires you to stop Solr, rename/delete the index directory, rename the snapshot directory as the index, and then start Solr.

Instance Management

In this section, you will learn to manage and customize features and properties that apply to a Solr instance.

Setting Solr Home

You already know what SOLR_HOME is, but until now we have been referring to the default Solr home. The default home directory since Solr 5.0 is server/solr and for earlier releases it is example/solr. It's good to have the SOLR_HOME path different from your server path, so that upgrades are less painful. If you want your Solr server to point to a different location for your SOLR_HOME, you can do so using one of the following methods:

- Start the Solr script with the -s or -solr.home option:

  ```
  $ ./solr start -s /home/solr
  ```

- Set the SOLR_HOME property in the solr.in environment file:

  ```
  SOLR_HOME=/home/solr (*nix)
  set SOLR_HOME=D:\playground\solr (Windows)
  ```

You can verify the path of SOLR_HOME in the Solr admin UI by looking for -Dsolr.solr.home in the JVM args section. Alternatively, you can run the solr script for getting the status:

```
$ ./solr status
```

When running Solr by using the script, you cannot set the home path by using -Dsolr.solr.home= /path/to/home, because if Solr doesn't find the home path as mentioned previously, it will refer to the default SOLR_HOME.

Memory Management

Heap memory is the space Solr needs to run and do all its processing. Because Solr is written in Java, you can pass the JVM parameters -Xms and -Xmx, which set the initial and maximum size of memory, respectively. By default, Solr 5.3.1 sets the fixed heap size to 512MB, which is reasonable enough for your initial experiments. When you plan to take Solr to production, you should set the value optimally. It's advisable to set -Xms to the same value as -Xmx to avoid a series of heap expansions. The best way to identify the optimal size is through experimentation, because if you set the maximum heap size too low, the system might throw OutOfMemoryError, and if you set it too high, garbage collection will take longer:

```
SEVERE: java.lang.OutOfMemoryError: Java heap space
```

If you receive the preceding error, it's time to increase the heap size. Here is how to set the heap memory:

- Set the SOLR_JAVA_MEM property in the solr.in environment file:

  SOLR_JAVA_MEM="-Xms1024m -Xmx1024m"

- Start Solr with the −m option. With this option, you can set −Xms and −Xmx to be only the same size:

  solr start −m 1g

■ **Caution** Ensure that you set the maximum heap to only a proportion of the total memory and leave appropriate memory for your operating system.

Even after setting the heap memory, if you are still getting OutOfMemoryError, you can take a heap dump to identify the reason for failure. You need to add HeapDumpOnOutOfMemoryError and HeapDumpPath parameters to the GC_TUNE property in solr.in script, as shown here:

```
set GC_TUNE=-XX: +HeapDumpOnOutOfMemoryError ^
-XX:HeapDumpPath=/var/log/dump/
```

This takes a dump of your heap whenever Solr throws OutOfMemoryError. If you get this error next, go to the file created at the specified path and evaluate it.

Log Management

Logging is crucial for debugging and analysis. Your log setting in production will vary from your log setting in development or testing. In this section, you will see how to change the log settings.

Solr uses Log4j for logging and so relies on the log4j.properties file. For Log4j configurations, refer to http://logging.apache.org/log4j/1.2/manual.html.

Log Location

By default, Solr provides a preconfigured log4j.properties file in the distribution server/resources directory and it writes the log messages to the server/logs/solr.log file. If your properties file exists in a different location, you can set it in the solr.in environment file.

```
LOG4J_PROPS=<dir-path>/log4j.properties
SOLR_LOGS_DIR=<log-dir>

LOG4J_PROPS=${solr.solr.home}/path/log4j.properties - relative to $SOLR_HOME
```

Log Level

The default logging level is set to INFO. You might want to change the level based on your needs and environment. You can make permanent changes to the logging level, or temporary ones for debugging if you don't want the changes to persist.

If you want permanent settings that persist between Solr restarts, you can use these steps::

1. Set the level in `log4j.properties`:

    ```
    log4j.rootLogger=INFO, file, CONSOLE
    ```

2. Set the threshold in `solr.xml`. Details are in the upcoming "Log Implementation" section.

    ```
    <int name="threshold">INFO</int>
    ```

If you want to make temporary changes in the logging level, you can use the Solr admin UI. From the Logging/Level tab, you can change the level of the root itself or any package or subpackage. Remember, because these changes are transient, they will be lost upon core reload or Solr restart.

Log Implementation

`solr.xml` also allows you to manage your log. You can disable logging altogether or use a totally different logging implementation, by making changes to `solr.xml`. You can set the size to specify the number of events Solr should buffer before flushing events to the log file. You also can change the logging level. The following is a sample configuration:

```
<solr>
  <logging>
    <str name="enabled">true</str>
    <str name="class">com.ClassName</str>
    <watcher>
      <int name="size">50</int>
      <int name="threshold">INFO</int>
    </watcher>
  </logging>
...
</solr>
```

Common Exceptions

This section presents some of the common exceptions that occur while running Solr and performing administrative tasks.

OutOfMemoryError—Java Heap Space

When memory allocated to JVM is not enough, Solr will throw `OutOfMemoryError`. You need to either allocate more heap space to Solr or optimize your settings. Refer to the previous "Memory Management" section for details.

OutOfMemoryError—PermGen Space

If you feel that heap space and PermGen are same, you are mistaken. You could have enough heap space available for your JVM but run out of PermGen (the permanent generation heap). PermGen space is used by the class loader to store all the metadata such as name, attributes, and methods of the class. The space allocated to them is reclaimed only when their class loader is ready for garbage collection. You get this error only when too many classes are loaded or a memory leak occurs. The first solution is to increase the size of the PermGen heap by passing it as a Java option:

```
-XX:MaxPermSize=256m
```

If you still get this exception after increasing the PermGen size, you need to check for possible leaks in your custom component or look for configuration issues.

TooManyOpenFiles

If you are getting this error, there is no problem with your Solr instance, but your machine has limited the number of open files. You can solve this as follows:

1. If you are using a *nix machine, increase the `ulimit`, as shown next. For a Windows machine, you can use Process Explorer. Refer to `https://technet.microsoft.com/en-us/sysinternals/bb896653.aspx` for more details.

    ```
    ulimit -n 1000000 - *nix
    ```

2. Set `useCompoundFile` to `true` in `solrconfig.xml`. Enabling this will use fewer descriptions while indexing but will lead to performance degradation:

    ```
    <useCompoundFile>true</useCompoundFile> - solrconfig.xml
    ```

3. Use a lower `mergeFactor` in `solrconfig.xml`, which will merge fewer segments and hence fewer open files:

    ```
    <mergeFactor>10</mergeFactor>
    ```

UnSupportedClassVersionException

If the JVM finds that its version number is not supported when loading Solr classes, it throws this exception. If you receive this error, you likely are running Solr on an older version of JVM.

Summary

This chapter started with an overview of concepts and terms used in the world of Solr. You learned to get the first instance of Solr up and running, and then to create a core, index documents, and search for results. You then had a short walk-through of the Solr admin interface. With these, I feel that newbies will have a basic understanding of Solr and will start to feel at home. Then you explored administrative tasks such as instance and core management and learned common exceptions that you might encounter while using Solr. You can use the administrative section as a manual that you can refer to while creating cores or before getting your instance live.

The next chapter is about information retrieval, which is crucial for solving complex problems and excelling at your job. This chapter has little relation to other chapters and can be referred to out of sequence. If you are in a hurry to learn more about indexing and searching documents, you can skip the next chapter and read it when you like.

CHAPTER 3

■ ■ ■

Information Retrieval

The primary focus of this book is to show you how to develop a search engine by using Solr. However, a search engine is no longer a silo and requires integration with several other tools and technologies to meet complex information needs. Other chapters present the features of Solr, its components, their usage, and related examples and use cases, but before you get any further into implementation and anything more serious, let's get an overview of information retrieval.

It's important to understand information retrieval (IR) to herald a holistic view of the bigger picture in search engine development, which is generally ignored. In this chapter, you will learn about the broader concepts, components, and phases involved in the development of an information retrieval system. This knowledge will be beneficial in classifying the retrieval problem into small manageable units and taming it through iterative development. This chapter also covers the tools and technologies that can be utilized to bring intelligence to the search engine and take it to the next level. Although this chapter indicates how these aspects can be hooked into Solr, the concepts can generally be applied to any search engine.

This chapter can benefit not only developers and search engineers, but also project managers and anyone involved in the life cycle of a search engine.

This chapter covers the following topics:

- Introduction to information retrieval

- Data categorization and extraction

- Text processing

- Inverted indexes

- Information retrieval models

- Information retrieval processes

- Result evaluation

Introduction to Information Retrieval

Information retrieval is a set of activities that represent, store and ultimately obtain information based on a particular need. Machine-based information retrieval was introduced in the 1950s, and its need was limited to the research community. Later it was implemented in commercial products and vertical search engines.

Information retrieval is a broad concept, and a search engine is one of its primary applications. Other common areas of its application are in recommendation systems, document classification and clustering, filtering, and question-answering systems. The information to be retrieved can be available in any source, format, and volume and can be applied to almost any domain such as healthcare, clinical research, music, e-commerce, and web search. The use of the system can be limited to a set of people such as lawyers or doctors, or can be used by the whole world.

Information retrieval systems are becoming the dominant form of information access. With the advent of web search engines, a large-scale information retrieval system has been implemented, and this is just the beginning. In the current era of Android and iOS smartphones and their even smarter applications, information needs have increased drastically, and with the Internet of Things, the need for information will be bigger and even more critical. With this, you can imagine the variety and volume of data that the machines need to process in order to support searches relevant to this need.

Search Engines

Search engines are one of the most widely used implementations of information retrieval systems. A web search engine such as Google is one of the most obvious examples. Each search engine has its own challenges, but some of those challenges are related more to information retrieval than search engines. Ranking the relevant documents appropriately and evaluating the effectiveness of a ranking algorithm can be considered IR concerns, whereas performance and scalability are search engine concerns.

Search engines can be broadly divided into several categories, each of which has similar information needs, to some extent. The following is the list of broader categories:

> *Web search*: This crawls through the World Wide Web, extracts the contents from HTML tags, and indexes the information to make it searchable. Some engines also crawl for images and other associated files, and before indexing process the text for other interesting information and links. DuckDuckGo is a typical example of a web search engine developed using Solr.

> *Vertical search*: Vertical search addresses a specific domain, an area of information or industry such as healthcare or finance. The information is generally available in a primary database or data source such as a Word document or PDF file. These types of searches are generally developed to cater to a specialized need.

> *Desktop search*: This is designed to index the files in a user's PC and make it searchable. Some search engines also index the file content along with the metadata to make it searchable. Spotlight in Mac OS X is a typical example.

> *Others*: Information retrieval is no longer limited to text and is being widely used for searching image, audio fingerprints, and in speech recognition.

The goal of any information retrieval system is to turn data into actionable information that satisfies the users' needs. In case of search engines, information pertains to relevant documents that are retrieved for search requests. Figure 3-1 depicts the components in a search system that converts data into information.

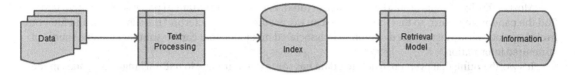

Figure 3-1. *A search system*

In the next sections, you will learn about the important information retrieval components and the process that is generally followed in any search engine development.

Data and Its Categorization

Data is created in different forms to cater to different needs—some for human consumption, such as blogs and posts, and some for machine consumption, such as data in tables or metadata. This data also is available in various formats, such as Word or PDF, and maintained in different data sources.

Based on the nature of the data and its format, the system needs to perform different content-extraction tasks, which can be a simple database query or a complex process such as extracting data from an image.

Before you learn more about content extraction, you first need to understand the data categories. The data to be indexed can be divided into three categories: structured, unstructured and semistructured. Each category is described next.

Structured

Structured data is a piece of information that adheres to a predefined structure. The information is organized into manageable units for efficient storage, processing, and retrieval. The structured data is easier to organize, store, and query when compared to unstructured data. If a relational database or table is a primary source of information, the data is generally structured. A simple example of structured data is a web form or an Excel sheet. The values are logically separated, each of which can be indexed to a different field.

Structured data is easier to ingest as it doesn't require highly sophisticated text parsing and application of retrieval techniques and relevancy rules are more manageable and effective. Also, it is more interoperable and convenient for other machines to consume. Everything around you generates data: your camera, phone, GPS device, and wearables. The more structured their data is, the easier the consumption.

Unstructured

Unstructured data, in turn, cannot be formally defined into manageable units and contains blocks of free-form text that cannot be differentiated by the machine. These blocks are difficult to programmatically interpret, or to identify the associated context and concepts, and can contain ambiguity and junk. They can contain a variety of information (such as person, location, date, number, disease, and symptoms) based on the domain. Examples of unstructured data include text files, PDFs, Word documents, books, journals, and e-mail.

Most of the documents around us are unstructured, and so it's important to process and analyze it to find the patterns in its text, so that the machine can extract the entities, interpret the semantics, and filter out irrelevant data. If the unstructured content has associated metadata, that can be another valuable source of structured information.

It's worth noting that even unstructured data has some structure due to natural language syntax, in the form of chapters, paragraphs, and sentences. Advanced processing pipeline can be applied to this text to extract a plethora of interesting information and build some structure out of it. Have a look at Wikipedia: that's an unstructured form of data that also has some associated structure.

Unstructured text can be structured by using machine-processing techniques such as artificial intelligence. You can use open source tools (for example, Apache UIMA) to build a pipeline that annotates the useful information in the stream of text. Solr provides firsthand support for the UIMA pipeline through processors and filters. Apache Stanbol is another project that allows you to perform semantic content management. If that doesn't work for you, the structure can be handcrafted or crowdsourced by using a platform such as Amazon Mechanical Turk (www.mturk.com/mturk/welcome).

Semistructured

Semistructured data is the third form, which fits between structured and unstructured. This data has some structure that provides convenience in interoperability but cannot be constrained by a schema. There is no specification for the amount of structure; the amount depends on the need. Files in XML format are a classic example of semistructured data. You may have to perform some processing similar to that for unstructured text to extract more meaningful information out of it, but the process is comparatively easier.

Content Extraction

Context extraction is the first process in information flow. In this process, you extract the content from the data source and convert it into indexable documents. In Solr, the process can be performed inside it or in the client application that indexes the documents. You will see more details of document indexing options provided by Solr in Chapter 5.

Let's assume that a search engine is being developed for researchers and scholars. In that case, the majority of content would generally be unstructured and available in PDF, DOC, and PPT format. The extraction of such unstructured data would need fairly complex processing. To index these documents, you first need to detect the content type and then extract the text for indexing. Parsers are available for extracting text from content in different file formats. Table 3-1 provides a list of common file formats and open source tools available for text processing.

Table 3-1. File Formats and Open Source Tools

File Formats	Open Source Tools
PDF	Apache POI Apache PDFBox
Microsoft Word/Excel/PowerPoint	Apache POI Apache OpenOffice
HTML	jsoup HTMLCleaner
XML	Apache Xerces Java Architecture for XML Binding (JAXB) Dom4j Many other SAX and DOM parsers are available Solr DataImportHandler
OCR	Tesseract
Geospatial	Geospatial Data Abstraction Library (GDAL)
E-mail	JavaMail API
Web crawling	Apache Nutch

The extraction process varies based on the data source. If the data is available in a database, it will generally be in normalized form and hence should be flattened before indexing. Solr provides tools for defining the denormalization process, or if you are using an external indexing process, you can do it in that application. You will learn about indexing data from databases in Chapter 5 by using the DataImportHandler Solr module.

An open source project called Apache Tika provides a framework for processing files in many formats. It supports autodetection of content type and allows extracting the content as well as associated metadata. Tika doesn't do all the work of detection and extraction by itself; instead, it wraps around libraries such as Apache POI and Apache PDFBox through its interface to provide a convenient approach for extraction. Tika supports parsing of content in a wide variety of file formats such as package formats (.tar, .jar, .zip), text document (.doc, .xml, .ppt, .pdf, .html), image (.jpeg, .png, .bmp), audio (.mp3, .wav), and more.

The Tika parser eases your task by hiding the complexities of the file formats and from invoking separate parsing libraries. It provides a simple and powerful mechanism for client applications to extract content and metadata. It provides a single API for all extraction tasks and saves you from having to learn and implement a different API for different extraction needs.

Solr provides a framework called Solr Content Extraction Library (Cell), which uses Apache Tika to expose `ExtractingRequestHandler`, a handler for extracting content from files in different formats and indexing it to respective Solr fields. Chapter 5 provides more details on content extraction using Solr Cell.

Text Processing

Raw documents received from the database or text extracted from binary documents, as discussed in the previous section, require processing before being indexed. The processing tasks can be for cleansing, normalization, enrichment, or aggregation of text. The processes are generally chained together to achieve the desired output, and the pipeline depends on your processing needs, which varies depending on the nature and quality of data and the desired output.

In Solr, text processing can be performed at two steps, by the *analysis* process and *update request processors*. The purpose of these steps is to address various text-processing needs. The analysis process caters to individual field-level tokenization and analysis, whereas the update request processor is for other text-processing needs and is scoped to the entire document. Update request processors are also called *preprocessors* or *document processors*.

The text processing varies among different systems and is also different while indexing and searching. For example, the user query might not need cleansing or minimal cleansing. The various text-processing categories are discussed next.

Cleansing and Normalization

Not all data is important, and some important data needs normalization and transformation before being indexed. Common *cleansing and normalization* tasks include removal of punctuation marks, removal of stop words, lowercasing, conversion to the nearest ASCII character, and stemming. These are some of the most fundamental tasks that should be performed in any search engine and are crucial for matching.

Enrichment

Text enrichment is the phase of analyzing and mining of content to find patterns for enrichment, annotation, entity extraction, and applying a variety of intelligence to make the content more usable, understandable, and relevant. The enrichments applied to the text depend on your retrieval needs and the depth of expansion you worry about. Also, it's suggested to experiment with enrichments after your system performs reasonably in terms of cleansing and normalization and retrieves relevant keyword-based matches. The following are some of the enrichments that can be applied on the text:

> *Entity extraction*: If the content being indexed is unstructured, or any of the fields is full-text, you may want to extract entities such as person, organization, and location and annotate the content. Suppose you are indexing text from a clinical trial; you might extract entities such as disease, symptoms, and anatomy from the text, so that the index is more structured. Then, if the user query is detected to be for a particular disease or anatomy, the documents can be appropriately ranked.

> *Part-of-speech tagging*: Words in any language can be classified as a predefined part of speech (such as a noun or a verb) based on the syntax of the language. These parts of speech can be used to form phrases and identify the important concepts in the text that can be boosted to rank the documents appropriately.

> *Thesauri*: A thesaurus (plural: thesauri) is a controlled vocabulary that typically contains a list of words and its related words. The related words are semantic metadata such as synonyms, antonyms, broader and narrower concepts, meronyms, and so forth, and the list of metadata supported can vary between thesauri. WordNet, a generic thesaurus, also contains glosses (definitions) of terms. These thesauri are maintained by communities that periodically update the vocabulary. The vocabularies can be generic (as in WordNet) or specific (such as Medical Subject Headings, or MeSH, which contains deeper lists of terms and is widely used in the field of medical science). The thesaurus you choose depends on your needs, and you may even choose to use multiple thesauri. You can try a live demo of WordNet at `http://wordnetweb.princeton.edu/perl/webwn`.

> *Ontologies*: An ontology is a formal representation of concepts and its relationships, such as broader and narrower concepts, in a particular domain. It's important to note that some thesauri also contain relationships, but they are informal and can be based on usage in the lexicon of a language. Also, thesauri can be universal, whereas ontologies narrow to a domain.

This is just the tip of the iceberg and an active area of research. The processing you do can be anything that is needed for the efficient retrieval and ranking of documents. For example, you may want to do sentiment analysis if the text contains reviews, or text summarization if you are indexing news, journals, or court proceedings.

The processing of text is not necessarily applied only at index time. It can also be applied on the user query, especially for scenarios such as query expansion, concept identification, and intent mining. Question answering is a typical example, whereby the user query goes through a pipeline such as query-type classification.

Table 3-2 lists of common preprocessing types and the freely available tools and resources.

Table 3-2. *Tools and Resources for Processing of Text*

Preprocess	Tools / Resources
Natural language processing	Apache OpenNLP Stanford CoreNLP
Clustering	Carrot 2 Apache Mahout Mallet Weka
Classification	Apache Mahout Mallet Weka
Controlled vocabulary	WordNet Library of Congress Subject Headings (LCSH) Medical Subject Headings (MeSH)
Text-processing framework	Apache UIMA GATE Apache Stanbol Apache cTAKES (Clinical Research)
Knowledge base	DBpedia YAGO

Metadata Generation

Metadata is data about data, which can be a useful source of information for accessing a document and determining its relevancy. Structured metadata allows easier interoperability, exchange, and processing of data by the machine.

Many systems provide metadata for the content automatically, without you worrying about generating it. Web pages have metadata associated in the form of meta-tags, which contain keywords and description of the page content and are used by search engines for topic identification. If you have any interest in photography, you may know that your camera generates metadata in EXIF (Exchangeable Image File) format for each image you click, which includes the camera and lens details, exposure information, and copyright. Recent cameras and mobile phones also store the location information in EXIF format by using the built-in GPS receiver. In Figure 3-2, you can see the metadata of a JPEG image. Imagine that by using this metadata, you can tune the relevancy of a document based on spatial, camera, or other information provided.

Metadata schema standards have been defined by communities such as Dublin Core, which contains terms to describe web and physical resources.

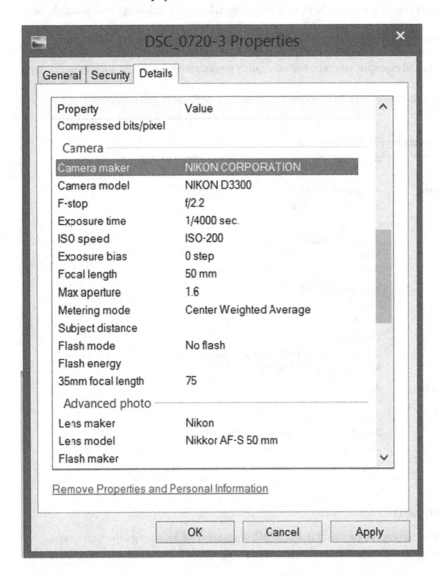

Figure 3-2. Metadata of a JPEG file

If the metadata is not automatically available, you may want to handcraft it or get it from content providers. Also, there are semiautomatic ways of generating it. We won't cover these, as they are beyond the scope of this book.

If the metadata is integrated in the file containing the content, it can be consumed in Solr by using Apache Tika. You will see the steps for this in Chapter 5.

Inverted Index

The data extracted from your data source should be indexed for fast and accurate retrieval. If you have been wondering why the process of adding documents to Solr is generally called *indexing*, then the inverted index is the answer. Solr internally uses Lucene, and when you add documents, it creates an inverted index to make the information searchable.

An *inverted index* is the primary data structure in a typical search engine, which maintains a dictionary of all the unique terms and mapping to all the documents in which they appear. Each term is a key, and its value is a postings list, which is the list of documents the term appears in.

A Lucene data structure is called an inverted index because traversal is backward (or inverted): from terms to documents, instead of from documents to terms as in the case of a forward index. An inverted index is similar to the index at the end of this book, which contains a list of words and corresponding pages in which the words occur. The words are synonymous to terms, and pages are synonymous to documents in Lucene's context. In contrast, a forward index is similar to the table of contents in the beginning of this book.

The approach of an inverted index is term-centric instead of document-centric as in the case of a forward index. For each term in a query, a document-oriented data structure would have to sequentially scan through the terms of all the documents, whereas an inverted index looks up the term in the index and finds the matching documents from the postings list. This approach offers a fast full-text search and much better performance.

Figure 3-3 provides a simplified view of inverted index representation. You can see that when a document is indexed, the terms are added as keys, and its document mapping in a postings list. When a user fires a query, the inverted index provides information about all the matching documents.

The postings list also contains additional information such as frequency of terms in the document, index time boosts, and payloads, which provides convenience and faster searching.

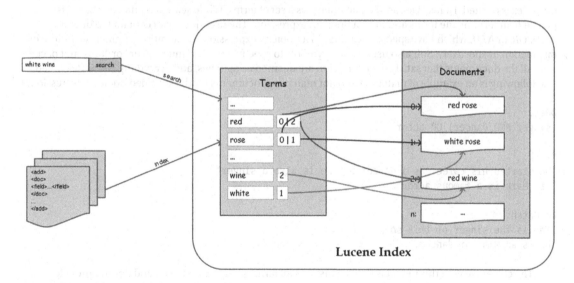

Figure 3-3. *Lucene inverted index*

■ **Note** User query and indexing goes through lots of complex processing, which has been abstracted in Figure 3-3 for simplicity.

Retrieval Models

To search relevant documents, you need a retrieval model. A *retrieval model* is a framework for defining the retrieval process by using mathematical concepts. It provides a blueprint for determining documents relevant to a user need, along with reasoning of why a document ranks above another. The model you choose depends a lot on your information retrieval need. Each model uses a different approach for determining the similarity between query and documents. The model can even be as simple as a Boolean model that returns either 0 or 1 as the value. Also, the implementation by the system can be a variation or an extension of the model that addresses the practical use cases. In Chapter 8, you will see how Lucene modifies the vector space model, which is discussed later in this section.

This section covers the information retrieval models generally used by search engines.

Boolean Model

The *Boolean model* of information retrieval is a simple model based on set theory and Boolean algebra. As the name signifies, it classifies documents as either true or false (either the documents match or don't match).

Let's understand this in Solr's parlance. While indexing, the terms are extracted from documents, and the index is created. Hence, we can see documents as a set of terms. While searching, the user query is parsed to determine the terms and form a Boolean expression. The user query can contain the operators *AND, OR,* or *NOT,* which have special meanings in a Boolean expression—to identify conjunction, union, or disjunction, respectively. Solr also uses + and - symbols to specify terms as "must occur" or "must not occur."

All the documents that satisfy the expression are deemed as matches, and everything else is discarded. The following is an example of matching and not matching documents for the specified Boolean expression:

```
Query:
(singer AND dancer) OR actor

Match:
"He started his career as a dancer but he is also a singer"
"Mr. Mark is a famous actor"

No Match:
"Who is the singer of this song?"
"He is an amateur dancer."
```

The challenge with this model is that it considers all terms as equally relevant and doesn't provide any provision to rank the documents. Hence, you need a more sophisticated model that would rank the document on the basis of relevancy. Another challenge is in conversion of a Boolean query into a Boolean expression.

Vector Space Model

The Boolean model takes you halfway. For a user query, it determines the documents that match, but you may also like to know how relevant the matched documents are. The Boolean model can be acceptable in a system that can consume hundreds to thousands of results. But what if the end user is a human? While searching in Google, you expect the best matches to appear on the first page. When the documents are ranked, you know that the first few results are the most relevant, and you hardly bother about the one that comes after traversing a number of result pages.

The *vector space model* (VSM) is a retrieval model that can be used to rank the indexed document with respect to a user query. The query response contains the documents, along with scores assigned to it, which signifies the degree of similarity with the user query. The document with the highest score is supposed to be the best match.

The vector space model represents each document and query by a vector of term weights in a high-dimensional space and computes a score on the basis of an angle between the query and documents. Figure 3-4 depicts an *N*-dimensional space in which documents are represented as solid lines and a query is represented as strong solid line. VSM uses the following list of steps for relevance ranking:

1. While indexing, represent each document as a weighted vector of term frequency and inverse document frequency

2. While searching, represent the query as a weighted TF-IDF vector

3. Compute the cosine similarity score between the query vector and each document vector

4. Rank documents with respect to the query

5. Return the matching top *N* rows in the response

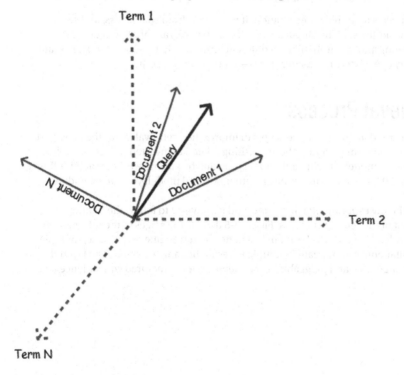

Figure 3-4. Vector space model

The default Lucene scoring algorithm uses a combination of the Boolean model and vector space model for finding relevant documents. The documents that are approved by the Boolean model are ranked by the vector space model. Hence, Lucene computes the similarity only for documents that satisfy the Boolean query. Also, it uses a modified form of cosine similarity for computing the relevance ranking. Chapter 8 covers Lucene scoring in detail.

This model works great for free-text queries. The limitation of this model is that it ignores the relationship between the terms and assumes them to be independent. It considers the text as a bag of words.

Probabilistic Model

The *probabilistic model* ranks the documents by estimating the probability of relevance of documents with respect to the query. The process of estimation is crucial, and this is where the implementations vary from one another. This model is based on the notion that for a query, each document can be classified as relevant or nonrelevant: $P(R|D)$ or $P(NR|D)$.

Language Model

The *language model* is a branch of probabilistic model that ranks the documents on their probability to generate the query terms. It usually uses maximum likelihood estimation to estimate the probability. The process of estimation is broadly done in three steps:

1. Estimate the language model for each document in the corpus and sample them

2. Calculate the probability of observing the query terms in the sample

3. Rank the documents in the order of probability

Because each document makes a sample for estimation, it may suffer from sparseness, and so smoothing should be applied to address it. The language models can be unigram or N-gram. Unigram models, which are more common, split the probability of different terms and ignore the context. N-gram models estimate the probability of each term, considering $N - 1$ terms of prior context.

Information Retrieval Process

In the previous sections, you learned about the key concepts in information retrieval. Now, the good part of the story is that Solr abstracts you from worrying about anything related to inverted indexes as well as implementation details of retrieval models. The default model provided by Lucene works great for full-text search and most retrieval needs. If you want to integrate any other retrieval model, you can extend the existing Java classes.

Information retrieval is a highly experimental discipline, and it's advised to follow the iterative development and improvement of the retrieval process. Figure 3-5 depicts the stages of the information retrieval process that ultimately leads to the development of a better search engine. In practice, multiple stages can be performed simultaneously or repeated multiple times in the same iteration. The layered architecture of Solr and the configurable and pluggable components offer the required convenience and flexibility.

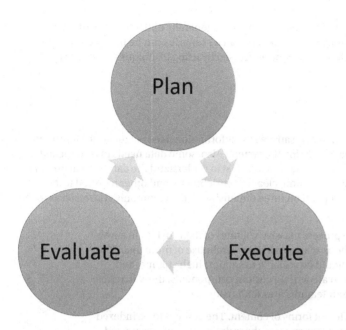

Figure 3-5. *Stages in information retrieval process*

Plan

Planning is an extremely crucial task, especially in the field of information retrieval, which is a time-consuming process. Before you start designing the schema and defining the search features, there are many factors to be considered and strategies to be in place. You might feel that some of the factors are irrelevant and so might ignore them, but that can drastically affect the user experience and the conversion rate. The following are some of the factors you should think about before getting into development.

Know the Vertical

If you are developing a vertical search engine, your first task is to understand the problem statement and then to know the domain. Most of the domains have their own unique feature requirements and bring their own challenges. For example, in a geographical search, location and proximity are crucial for computing the relevancy of documents, whereas in a biomedical domain, linkage of information across multiple resources becomes important.

Know the End User

The *end user* is the person who will ultimately use the search engine, and it's important to know his real-world needs. Along with retrieving the relevant documents, the ease of use, convenience, and navigational capabilities should also be a priority. Users generally do follow a pattern that is based on a domain or region. For example, a user might be interested in the most relevant result, such as when you search in Google, while others might need all the matching results, such a legal practitioner interested in all the matching cases. In a music discovery website, a user expects the relevant documents to appear at top in the result set; in contrast in a clothing e-commerce website a user generally browses through hundreds of matching documents. Understand the core need of the system and work toward addressing it in initial iterations.

Some of the user needs can be specific and subjective, which are generally difficult to execute and evaluate and can take a lower priority. The document ranking in such scenarios can be highly relevant to one user but irrelevant to another user. Such issues can be addressed by using techniques such as user profiling and result personalization.

Know the Content

All data is not important, and only some portion of it satisfies the information needs of the user. Unwanted data should be discarded to avoid any garbage entering the system. Also, some data needs to be enriched to fulfill the user retrieval needs. During the planning stage, it's crucial to understand the data, so that proper tools and techniques can be applied for such extraction, cleanup, enrichment, and other required text processing. The content to be searched can depend on three dimensions, very commonly addressed as the 3 Vs in the Big Data world:

> *Volume*: Some systems need to process massive volumes of data such as in a web search or social network. Facebook manages a data warehouse of more than 300 petabytes. The search engine should be scalable to support high volume, and that's what SolrCloud is for. If you are writing custom components, think in terms of SolrCloud and ensure that your features are cloud ready.

> *Variety*: Variety refers to the different forms of content. The content to be indexed can be structured or unstructured. For creating the index, data can be extracted or aggregated from multiple sources. Suppose you are building a search engine for movies, similar to IMDB. This content could be from many sources, such as a record from your primary data source, metadata provided by the content provider, reviews from a third-party application, and trending and popularity information from social media such as Twitter or YouTube. All this content integrated together would form the basis of identifying the relevance of a movie.

> *Velocity*: The speed of data processing is important if the search engine needs to process near real-time queries. Companies such as Twitter process more than 500 million tweets per day and need to stream the data in real-time. Batch processing is not a choice in such a case.

Know the Medium

The *medium* refers to the device the user will use to query the search engine. This is generally ignored, but it makes a lots of difference in information retrieval. It's difficult to type on a mobile phone, so the user is likely to write short queries that contain the important keywords and that might not be in natural language. The user may preferably use short forms of the words. Features such as autocompletion are a must have for such devices. A benefit you get with a mobile phone is that it provides additional information about the user, such as her current location, which can be used to rank localized results higher. Over the web, the search experience is supposed to be different. You get lots of space available for features such as suggestions, more-like-this, and recommendations. Most important, the user tends to write more naturally over the Web.

The medium over which the search will be consumed should not be ignored, and the features you provide should be planned accordingly.

Execute

In this step, you execute the information retrieval task planned in previous steps. You perform the text processing and retrieval techniques through several experiments and research before coming to a conclusion. While addressing the retrieval needs, other factor important for a search engine to be production ready should not be ignored. For example, if your business requires a highly distributed and scalable system, ensure that the feature is supported by SolrCloud.

Evaluate

You learned about information retrieval models and text-processing techniques to build and improve a search system. The retrieval model makes the foundation for Lucene scoring, which ranks the documents based on similarity to the user query, and the text-processing strategy plays a key role in the findability of documents. Whenever you tune a document's score, such as by applying boost, or perform any change in text processing, you generally seek to answer to some of the following questions:

- Is my search result showing the most relevant documents?

- Has any of the highly relevant document been missed?

- Does the result set contain poor or irrelevant documents?

- Have my results improved in this iteration, and how can I measure the improvement?

At times you might find that the system is missing some highly relevant documents and tune the engine to improve their ranking. This activity in turn affects the relevancy of documents for other queries, which can go unnoticed and might get discovered much later in the product life cycle. Hence, after the execute phase, it becomes crucial to examine and evaluate the search results. In this section, you will learn about the various states of a document and the evaluation concepts that apply to information retrieval.

When you perform a search, the matching documents will have any of the four states mentioned in Table 3-3. The first row in the table represents the state of the result under ideal scenarios (whether the document was correctly identified or not). The first column in the table represents your system, and whether the document matched the user query or not.

Table 3-3. *Contingency Table (2×2)*

	Identified	Rejected
Matched	True positive	False positive
Not Matched	True negative	False negative

Descriptions of all the values in the contingency table follow.

True Positive

In this scenario, the correct documents are identified for a user query. Suppose the user query is "cancer," and the application retrieves a document matching "cancer." This is an example of a true positive.

False Positive

In this scenario, a document is incorrectly identified as a match. For example, a query for "cancer disease" gets a result for cancer that refers to a crab or the astrological sign Cancer. This scenario generally occurs because of inefficient text cleansing (for example, a missed stop-word removal), which results in an irrelevant document being identified as a match. Remember the expression *garbage in, garbage out*. This scenario is also called a *false alarm* or *type I error*.

True Negative

In this scenario, a document is correctly rejected. For example, a query for "cancer disease" doesn't get a result for cancer that refers to a crab or an astrological sign. A majority of documents should fall in this category, and a true negative has no role in determining the quality of the retrieved result.

False Negative

In this scenario, a document that should have been part of the response is incorrectly rejected. For example, if the system is expected to bring semantically related results, and documents related to "neoplasm benign" are missed on the user query "cancer disease," then it's a case of a false positive. This scenario typically occurs because of improper normalization and enrichment of documents, where even an additional punctuation mark or missed lowercasing can reject a document. This type of error can be classified as a *type II error*.

The conditions *false positive* and *false negative* are undesirable and should be avoided and reduced to minimal. The false positive scenario leads to pagination of results and affects the user experience and confidence in the system. If the search engine is accessed over a medium such as Short Message Service, false positive matches are totally not acceptable. False negative scenarios can even get worse and affect the business directly; a user looking for a product in an e-commerce web site will not be able to discover the product even though it's available with the seller.

Evaluation Metrics

You need metrics to determine whether the retrieved result matches the user expectation. Also, you might be interested in comparing the result of your existing system with the result of a new and evolved system. Precision and recall are the primary metrics that are helpful in evaluating the result. Accuracy is another metric but is generally avoided due to its impractical computation.

Accuracy

Accuracy measures the effectiveness by considering both true positives and true negatives (how well the system correctly identifies or rejects a document). Here is the algorithm for evaluation:

$$\frac{TP+TN}{TP+FP+TN+FN}$$

Where,
TP is True Positive,
TN is True Negative,
FP is False Positive,
FN is False Negative

Interestingly, *accuracy* is never used to evaluate an information retrieval system, because using it as a measure can go absolutely wrong, because it considers both relevant and irrelevant documents. Suppose you have 100 documents in an index, and for a query the corpus contains only 10 relevant matches. Assume that the system is one of the poorest, and for that query it retrieves 10 documents, all of which happen to be irrelevant. The following indicates how *accuracy* would evaluate the result:

```
TP = 0 (no relevant document retrieved)
TN = 80 (out of 90 irrelevent documents, 80 were correctly rejected)
FP = 10 (10 irrelevant documents are incorrectly retrieved)
FN = 10 (10 relevant document incorrectly rejected)
```

$$\text{Accuracy} = \frac{0+80}{0+80+10+10} = 80\%$$

From this example, you can make out that even when the system retrieves 0 relevant results, you still get an accuracy of 80%. Hence, *accuracy* is generally avoided as a measure, and precision and recall are considered.

Precision and Recall

Precision and recall are two important measures for evaluating the effectiveness of the information retrieval system. *Precision* is the fraction of retrieved documents that are relevant, and *recall* is the fraction of relevant documents that are retrieved. Precision and recall can be computed using this formula:

$$\text{Precision} = \frac{Relevant \cap Retrieved}{Retrieved}$$

$$\text{Recall} = \frac{Relevant \cap Retrieved}{Relevant}$$

Suppose that your index has 20 documents related to music and 10 documents related to movies. Now, a query related to music might return 10 documents, out of which 5 are related to music and 5 are related to movies. Precision of the system will be $5/10 = 1/2$, or 50%. Recall will be $5/20 = 1/4$, or 25%.

In a nutshell, we can say that precision is a measure of quality, whereas recall is a measure of quantity. So, high recall means that an algorithm returned most of the relevant results, and high precision means that an algorithm returned more relevant results than irrelevant.

It's easier to compute *precision*, as you need to identify the relevant documents from retrieved documents. Suppose you query Solr for 10 documents, specifying rows=10. In that case, you can even manually traverse through the documents to identify the relevant ones. Because recall works on the relevant documents, which is difficult to identify among all the documents in the corpus. Its count can be huge and manual traversal would be a challenge.

Depending on the problem you are trying to solve, one of the two measures can be of more importance to you. For example, in the legal domain, you may be interested in retrieving all the relevant documents, so high recall interests you more. If you are building a web search engine, you would be interested in retrieving the most relevant documents, so you would be interested in high precision. Generally, both measures are used together to attain a trade-off, as the general goal of information retrieval is to retrieve a few relevant documents and have the most relevant document at top.

F-Measure

An *F-measure* can be used as a single measurement for the system, as it combines both precision and recall to calculate the result. It computes harmonic mean of precision and recall as follows:

$$F\ Score = \frac{2*Precision*Recall}{Precision + Recall}$$

Summary

This chapter focused on concepts and approaches related to information retrieval. You learned about the models for information retrieval and the ways to estimate the effectiveness of a search result. You also learned about the tools and resources that can be utilized to develop a more effective search engine.

The next chapter covers designing the schema, and the chapters that follow cover indexing documents and searching for results. Chapter 11 contains examples related to the text-processing concepts discussed in this chapter.

CHAPTER 4

■ ■ ■

Schema Design and Text Analysis

Search engine development in Solr initially follows four sequential steps: Solr setup, schema design, indexing documents, and searching for results. Schema design is the process of defining the structure of data and is a prerequisite for the process of indexing and searching.

This chapter covers defining fields, specifying types, and other features.

The role of text analysis is vital in information retrieval. It's the text analysis process that determines the terms (the smallest piece of information, to be used for matching and scoring of documents). This chapter covers the text analysis process, including what analyzers do, the various analyzers/tokenizers available in Solr, and chaining them together.

In this chapter, you will learn about running Solr in schemaless mode, using a managed schema, and working with REST APIs.

This chapter is divided into the following sections:

- Schema design

- Text analysis

- Going schemaless

- REST API for managing schema

- solrconfig.xml file

- Frequently asked questions

Schema Design

Schema design is one of the most fundamental steps for building an effective search engine. It is the process of defining the structure of data and applying text analysis to control the matching behavior.

Before defining the schema, you should understand the problem you are trying to solve and get your strategy in place. You should be able to answer a few questions, including these: What are you using Solr for? What search experiences will you be offering? Which portion of data should be searchable? What information is to be retrieved?

Solr is generally used to index denormalized data. If your data is normalized, you might want to flatten it and define the structure before indexing. If total denormalization is a challenge, Solr allows you to join indexes. But a join in Solr is different from database joins and has its own limitations. Solr also supports indexing hierarchical data, with parent-child relationships. Chapter 7 covers these advanced search features.

All search engines are unique in their own ways, either because of the domain, nature of data, or other factor. Searches can be on full-text or metadata. Also, Solr is not just limited to being a text search engine and is being widely used as a NoSQL datastore and for performing analytics; many new innovative use cases have been seen. A project called Lucene Image Retrieval (LIRE), for example, uses Solr for image searches.

If you are using Solr as a NoSQL datastore or want to get started quickly or don't have complete visibility of the data or are working with a data structure that's dynamic, you can choose to go schemaless and leave it to Solr to automatically detect the `fieldType` and index documents. As of release 5.0, Solr creates a core in schemaless mode by default. You'll learn more about this topic at the end of this chapter.

Documents

In Solr, each search result corresponds to a *document*. This basic unit of information is analogous to a record in a database table. When developing a search engine, the first step in schema design is to determine what makes a document for your search engine. The same data can be represented and indexed differently, and the definition of a document can be different depending on the result you expect from the engine and its purpose.

For example, in the Indian film industry, most movies have five to ten songs. If you are building a movie search engine, each movie is a document. Each document then contains multiple songs, indexed as a `multiValued` field. In contrast, if you were building a music search engine, each song name would be a unique document, and the movie name is redundant in those documents.

Similarly, if you are developing an online bookstore, each book or journal will be a document, which contains information such as ISBN, book name, author, and publisher. But if you are developing a search engine for researchers, perhaps each chapter, topic, or article of the book or journal can be a document.

schema.xml File

The `schema.xml` file defines the document structure and the fields that it contains. These fields are used when adding data to Solr or querying for results. You will learn about fields in Solr in the next section.

In Solr, `schema.xml` and `solrconfig.xml` are the two primary configuration files. Usually you will be playing with them to modify your search strategy and enhance the user experience. These files can be located in the `conf` directory of the cores in `$SOLR_HOME` or in named configsets.

The `schema.xml` file has a well-defined purpose, and the `solrconfig.xml` file is for all other configurations. The following is the list of configurations supported in `schema.xml`:

- Define `field` types and the text analysis, if supported

- Define each field and its applicable properties

- Define dynamic fields

- Specify the scoring algorithm

- Copy data from one field to another

- Specify other field-related definitions such as identification of a unique field or a default field

---

■ **Note** The `solrconfig.xml` file is discussed at the end of this chapter.

As the file extension of schema.xml states, the configuration is specified in XML format, where <schema> is the root element. This element supports two attributes: name and version. The name attribute assigns a name to the schema that can be used for display. The version attribute states the version number of supported syntax and behavior. The latest version as of Solr 5.3.1 is 1.5. The following is a sample schema.xml file:

```
<schema name="example" version="1.5">
  <field name="title" type="string" indexed="true" stored="true"/>
  <field name="isbn" type="string" indexed="true" stored="true"/>
  ..
  <fieldType name="string" class="solr.StrField" sortMissingLast="true"/>
  <fieldType name="int" class="solr.TrieIntField" precisionStep="0"
positionIncrementGap="0"/>
  ..
</schema>
```

The core should be reloaded to reflect any changes in this file. If any change has been made in the index-time processing, the documents should be reindexed after reloading the core.

Fields

Each section of information in a document (for example, ISBN, book name, author, and publisher) is a field and is analogous to a column in database tables. The following is a sample definition of a field in schema.xml:

```
<field name="title" type="string" indexed="true" stored="true"/>
<field name="isbn" type="string" indexed="true" stored="true"/>
..
```

Solr supports a set of attributes to configure the behavior of a field. Among the attributes, type defines the fieldType, which is similar to Java's data types but is much more powerful. It links the field to the chain of analysis to be performed on its data while indexing and querying.

■ **Note**   Earlier versions of Solr required fields to be defined inside the <fields> element. Recent releases have flattened the structure, and you can directly specify fields inside the <schema> element.

Field Attributes

The following are descriptions of attributes supported by a field. You can also define the attributes of fieldType in the field element, which will override the value specified in the fieldType element.

name

This mandatory parameter assigns a name to the field, which is referenced when performing any operation on it such as indexing, querying, and highlighting.

You can use only alphabetic characters, numbers, and underscores to name a field. The names are case sensitive. Names starting and ending with an underscore (such as _version_ and _root_) are reserved.

There is no other specification for naming fields, but it's advised to follow one convention—for example, keep all words in lowercase and separate them with an underscore, or follow camel casing for readability.

type

This mandatory parameter specifies the name of the fieldType. You will learn more about fieldType in the next section.

default

This parameter specifies the default value for a field when no value is provided while indexing a document.

This parameter is also useful when you want to automatically index a value for a field instead of specifying it in every document. One classical example is the index timestamp, which indicates the time that the document was added to Solr. Here is an example field definition for indexing the timestamp:

```
<field name="timestamp" type="date" indexed="true" stored="true" default="NOW" />
```

In this example, the type="date" attribute specifies the fieldType as TrieDateField, and NOW is provided as the value for the default attribute, which specifies the current timestamp.

The example also contains indexed and stored attributes, which are attributes of fieldType that have been overridden in our field definition. Some fieldType parameters are generally overridden by the field, and this occurs so frequently that you may feel that they are properties of the field instead of the fieldType.

Reserved Field Names

Solr reserves field names starting and ending with an underscore for special purposes. The following are some of the reserved field names:

> _version_: Solr uses this field for transaction logging, to support optimistic locking of documents in SolrCloud and for real-time get operations.

> _root_: This field is required to support nested documents (hierarchical data). It identifies the root document in a block of nested documents.

> _text_: This field is a predefined catchall field, to enable single field searching in schemaless mode.

fieldType

The fieldType element determines the type of value a field can hold, how the value should be interpreted, operations that can be performed on it, and the text analysis the field will go through.

The significance of the field type is critical in Solr. It's the field type and the specified analysis chain that determine the text analysis pipeline to be applied while indexing and querying documents. The matching strategy can be expressed as a sequence of analyzers, tokenizers, and token filters in the field definition. Whenever you want to tune your search for a query term to match or not match an indexed term, you will usually be changing the fieldType definition or its analysis chain.

The following is an example of a fieldType element, where name is the fieldType identifier, class is the Solr's implementation class name, and sortMissingLast is the property needed by the implementation class:

```
<fieldType name="string" class="solr.StrField" sortMissingLast="true" />
```

■ **Note** Earlier versions of Solr required field types to be defined inside the <types> element. Recent releases have flattened the structure, and field types can directly be specified inside the <schema> element.

The type of value supported, the field's behavior, and the text analysis to be performed on the field depend on three types of configuration:

- Implementation class
- Attributes
- Text analysis

Each is described next.

Implementation Class

The *implementation class* implements the features of the field type. It determines the type of values the field can hold and how the values should be interpreted. To customize the text processing, the implementation class usually supports a set of attributes, some of which are marked mandatory.

Based on the data and the type of operation to be performed on the field, you need to choose a fieldType. Suppose your data is Boolean; you will choose the implementation class solr.BoolField. If your data is of the type Integer, you might choose the implementation class solr.TrieIntField. Table 4-1 shows the data types and supported implementation classes provided by Solr.

Table 4-1. Primary Data Types Provided and Their Implementation Classes

Data	Implementation Class
String	solr.StrField solr.TextField
Boolean	solr.BoolField
Number	solr.TrieIntField solr.TrieLongField
Float	solr.TrieFloatField solr.TrieDoubleField
Date	solr.TrieDateField solr.DateRangeField
Binary data	solr.BinaryField
Spatial data	solr.LatLonType solr.PointType solr.SpatialRecursivePrefixTreeFieldType
Closed set of values	solr.EnumField
Random unique ID	solr.UUIDField
Value from external source	solr.ExternalFileField

Here are some key points to note about the implementation classes:

- The text added to solr.StrField is indexed and queried as it is. No analysis (no modification) can be applied to it. If you want to split the incoming text by whitespace or change it to lowercase, solr.StrField is not the appropriate fieldType for you. It is suitable if you want to index the text as it is—for example, in the case of a document identifier such as product SKU.

- The solr.TextField allows to you perform custom analysis on the text by applying a chain containing an analyzer or a tokenizer and list of token filters that can be applied while indexing or querying documents. While performing the analysis, you can transform the text in any desired way; for example, you can split a token, introduce a new token, remove a token, or replace a token with another token.

- solr.DateRangeField provides additional provisions for expressing date ranges in the query. Another difference from solr.TrieDateField is that the response format is String instead of Date.

Refer to the Solr official guide at https://cwiki.apache.org/confluence/display/solr/Field+Types+Included+with+Solr for a complete list of field types available in Solr.

■ **Note** Class names starting with solr refer to Java classes in a standard package (such as org.apache.solr.analysis), and you don't need to provide the complete package name.

---

fieldType Attributes

Additional attributes can be specified as part of the element while defining the fieldType. These attributes can be generic and can be applied on any fieldType, or can be specific to the implementing class.

The following is a sample fieldType definition for numeric data having a different value for the precisionStep attribute. The precisionStep attribute enables faster-range queries but increases the index size. If you need to execute range queries on a field, use the fieldType tint. Otherwise, use the fieldType int. The precisionStep="0" disables indexing data at various levels of precision.

```
<fieldType name="int" class="solr.TrieIntField"
           precisionStep="0" positionIncrementGap="0" sortMissingLast="true"/>
<fieldType name="tint" class="solr.TrieIntField"
           precisionStep="8" positionIncrementGap="0" sortMissingLast="true"/>
```

In this example, sortMissingLast is the generic attribute that can be applied on any fieldType, and precisionStep is the attribute of the implementation class TrieIntField.

The following are the primary fieldType attributes provided by Solr.

indexed

For a field to be searchable, it must be indexed. If you will be querying a field for matching documents, it must be indexed by setting the attribute indexed="true". Only when this attribute is enabled, can the generated tokens be indexed and the terms become searchable. If you set indexed="false", the query operation on this field will not fetch any result, as no terms are indexed.

You may set indexed="false" when you are adding a field for display that will never be queried upon.

stored

Only stored fields can be displayed. If you set stored="false", the data in this field cannot be displayed.

You may set stored="false" when you know that you will never return the value of this field back to the user. Also, if you are indexing the same text to multiple fields for performing different analysis, in that case, you can set all copies as indexed="true" and store only one copy of it. Whenever you need to display the value, you get it from the stored field. Here is an example schema definition for such a scenario:

```
<field name="title" type="string" indexed="true" stored="true"/>
<field name="title_ws" type="text_ws" indexed="true" stored="false"/>
<field name="title_gen" type="text_general" indexed="true" stored="false"/>
```

Suppose you want to query and display the title_gen field. In that case, query the title_gen field and display the title field. Here is a sample query for such a scenario:

```
$ curl http://localhost:8983/solr/hellosolr/select?q=user+query&qf=title_
gen&fl=title&defType=edismax
```

If possible, set stored="false", as it would provide better performance and reduced index size (size of stored information). Stored fields of larger size are even costlier to retrieve.

The following are possible combinations of indexed and stored parameters:

> indexed="true" & stored="true": When you are interested in both querying and displaying the value of a field.

> indexed="true" & stored="false": When you want to query on a field but don't need its value to be displayed. For example, you may want to only query on the extracted metadata but display the source field from which it was extracted.

> indexed="false" & stored="true": If you are never going to query on a field and only display its value.

> indexed="false" & stored="false": Ignore input values for a field. If the document being indexed or Lucene query contains a field that doesn't exist, Solr may report an exception. You can handle this exception by creating an ignored field (a field with both these attributes disabled). Now, suppose that you have an update processor that extracts metadata from a field, and you are interested in only the extracted metadata and not the value of the unstructured field. This attribute can be quite useful for ignoring such fields.

■ **Note** It's important to note that the value stored in the field is the original value received by it and not the analyzed value. If you want to transform the value before storing it, the transformation should be done using either transformers or preprocessors. Chapter 5 covers this topic.

---

required

Setting this attribute as true specifies a field as mandatory. If the document being indexed doesn't contain any value for the field, it will not be indexed. By default, all fields are set as required="false".

multiValued

This Boolean parameter specifies whether the field can store multiple values. For example, a song can have multiple singers, a journal can have multiple authors, and so forth. You might want to set the singer and author fields as multiValued="true". Here is a sample definition in schema.xml for the singer and author fields:

```
<field name="singer" type="string" indexed="true" stored="true" multiValued="true"/>
<field name="actor" type="string" indexed="true" stored="true" multiValued="true"/>
```

Because you generally index denormalized data, it's quite common to have few multiValued fields in schema.xml. If you are copying data from multiple source fields into one destination field, ensure that you define the destination field as multiValued, as Solr won't allow copying multiple values to a single valued field. If the source field is multiValued, in that case also, the destination field should be defined as multiValued. By default, all fields are single valued.

docValues

docValues is an interesting feature introduced in Solr 4.0. If this Boolean parameter is set to true, a forward index is created for the field. An inverted index is not efficient for sorting, faceting, and highlighting, and this approach promises to make it faster and also free up the fieldCache. The following is an example field definition with docValues enabled:

```
<field name="language" type="string" indexed="true" stored="false" docValues="true"/>
```

Enabling docValues requires all the documents to be reindexed.

sortMissingFirst/sortMissingLast

Both these attributes are helpful in handling a scenario in sorting, where the field being sorted doesn't contain any value for some of the documents. Specifying the sortMissingLast="true" attribute on a field sorts the documents without a value for the field last (after the documents containing a value for the field). On the contrary, specifying sortMissingFirst="true" sorts the documents without a value for the field at the top of the result set. This position is maintained regardless of the sorting order being either ascending or descending.

By default, both these attributes are set to false, and in that case sorting in ascending order places all documents with missing values first, and sorting in descending order places all documents with missing values last.

positionIncrementGap

Internally, the multiValued field is implemented by padding spaces between values (between the last token of a value and the first token of the next value). The optional attribute positionIncrementGap specifies the number of virtual spaces to put between values to avoid false phrase matching.

Suppose a document has two values, bob marley and elvis presley, for the multiValued field singer. If you specify positionIncrementGap="0", the phrase query *marley elvis* will match the document, as there is no padding and it is treated as part of the same token stream. If you specify positionIncrementGap="100", even phrases with moderate slop will not match, as *marley* and *elvis* are a hundred spaces apart.

precisionStep

This is an advanced topic for executing faster range queries on numeric and date fields. Range queries are search requests for documents with values of a field in a specified range, such as products in the price range of $500 to $1,000. Range query is covered in more detail in Chapter 6.

The default precision step specified by Solr for a numeric field is 4, which is optimal for executing faster range queries. If you don't need to execute range queries on a numeric field, specify `precisionStep="0"`, which offers more-efficient sorting. The `schema.xml` provided with Solr contains numeric fields such as int and float for general purposes, and `precisionStep="0"` and fields prefixed with *t* such as `tint`, `tfloat` with `precisionStep="8"` for numeric fields that need range queries.

Lower step values generate more tokens and speed up range queries but consume more disk space. Generally, the value should be kept between 1 and 8. Refer to the Lucene Javadoc at `http://lucene.apache.org/core/5_3_1/core/org/apache/lucene/search/NumericRangeQuery.html#precisionStepDesc` for the implementation details.

omitNorms

Fields have norms associated with them, which holds additional information such as index-time boost and length normalization. Specifying `omitNorms="true"` discards this information, saving some memory.

Length normalization allows Solr to give lower weight to longer fields. If a length norm is not important in your ranking algorithm (such as metadata fields) and you are not providing an index-time boost, you can set `omitNorms="true"`. By default, Solr disables norms for primitive fields.

omitTermFreqAndPositions

The index postings also store information such as term frequency, position information, and payloads, if any. You can disable this additional information by setting `omitTermFreqAndPositions="true"`. Disabling this attribute saves memory, reduces index size, and provides better performance. If you need to support queries such as a phrase query or span query on the field, you shouldn't disable `omitTermFreqAndPositions`, as these queries rely on position information. Query terms that are more frequent in a document are usually considered more relevant in full-text fields, and that information is maintained by term frequency. Hence, you might not want to disable it in full-text fields.

omitPosition

Specifying the Boolean attribute `omitPosition="true"` omits the position information but retains the term frequency.

termVectors

Specifying the Boolean attribute `termVectors="true"` retains the complete term vectors information. This attribute is generally used with `termPositions` and `termOffsets`. These are used by features such as highlighting and "more like this" to offer better performance; otherwise, the field would be reanalyzed by using the stored value.

termPositions

Specifying the Boolean parameter `termPositions="true"` retains the position of the term in the document.

termOffsets

Specifying the Boolean parameter `termOffsets="true"` retains the offset information of the term in the document.

termPayloads

Specifying the Boolean parameter `termPayloads="true"` retains the payload information for the term in the document. Payloads allow you to add a numeric value to a term, which you can use in scoring. This feature is useful when you want to give a high weight to a term (such as nouns or correlated words).

■ **Tip** If remembering class implementations, attributes, and the (yet-to-be-covered) text analysis seems too much to digest, don't worry! The best approach to designing your own schema is to take the full-fledged `schema.xml` provided in the Solr distribution and edit it. In Solr 5.*x*, the `schema.xml` file provided in the named configset `sample_techproducts_configs` can be the reference point for designing your schema.

Text Analysis, If Applicable

Table 4-1 introduced the field type `solr.TextField` for string data. `TextField` is a special implementation of a field type that supports analyzers with a configurable chain of a single tokenizer and multiple token filters for text analysis. Analyzers can break the input text into tokens, which is used for matching instead of performing an exact match on the whole text. In turn, `solr.StrField` performs only an exact match, and analyzers cannot be applied.

Text analysis on `TextField` is covered in more detail in an upcoming section.

copyField

You may want to analyze the same text in multiple ways or copy the text from multiple fields into a single field. The `copyField` element in `schema.xml` provides the provision to copy the data from one field to another. You specify the copy-from field name in the `source` attribute and the copy-to field name in the `dest` attribute, and whenever you add documents containing a source field, Solr will automatically copy the data to the destination fields. The following is an example of `copyField`, which copies the text of the `album` field to multiple fields for different analysis:

```
<copyField source="album" dest="album_tokenized"/>
<copyField source="album" dest="album_gram"/>
<copyField source="album" dest="album_phonetic"/>
```

If you are copying data from multiple sources to a single destination, or any of the source fields is `multiValued`, ensure that the destination field is also defined as `multiValued="true"`. Otherwise, Solr will throw an exception while indexing documents.

copyField Attributes

The following are attributes supported by `copyField`.

source

The `source` attribute specifies the field from which the data is to be copied. The source field must exist. The field name can start and end with asterisk to copy from all the source fields matching the pattern.

dest

The `dest` attribute specifies the destination field to which the data is to be copied. The destination field must exist. The field name can start and end with asterisk to copy the text to all the destination fields matching the pattern. You can specify a wildcard in the destination field only if it is specified in the source field also.

maxChars

This optional integer attribute allows you to keep a check on the field size and prevent the index from growing drastically. If the number of characters indexed to the destination field outgrows the `maxChars` value, those extra characters will be skipped.

Define the Unique Key

The element `<uniqueKey>` in `schema.xml` is analogous to a primary key in databases. This element specifies the field name that uniquely identifies a document. Here is a sample definition that specifies `isbn` of a book as a unique identifier for documents.

```
<uniqueKey>isbn</uniqueKey>
```

It's not mandatory to declare a `uniqueKey`, but defining it is strongly recommended. It's also highly likely that your application will have one. The following are rules and suggestions for defining a `uniqueKey` field:

- The field should be of type String or UUID.
- Any index-time analysis on this field might break document replacement or document routing in SolrCloud and should be avoided.
- A field with multiple tokens is not allowed as a `uniqueKey`.
- A dynamic field cannot be used to declare a `uniqueKey`.
- The value of this field cannot be populated by using `copyField`.

If you index a document and if another document already exists with the same unique key, the existing document will be overwritten. To update a document instead of replacing it, use the Atomic Update feature of Solr. Chapter 5 provides more details on atomic updates.

Dynamic Fields

Instead of declaring all the fields explicitly, Solr allows you to define dynamic fields by specifying patterns for creating fields. While indexing a document, if any of the specified fields isn't defined in `schema.xml`, Solr looks for a matching dynamic field pattern. If a pattern exists, Solr creates a new field of the `fieldType` defined in the `<dynamicField>` element.

If you want to perform a similar analysis on multiple fields, then instead of declaring them explicitly, you could define a dynamicField for that fieldType. Suppose you want to create N-grams for the fields movie name, actor, and director. Instead of explicitly defining fields for each one of them, you can create dynamic fields as shown here:

```
<dynamicField name="*_gram" type="ngrams" indexed="true" stored="false"/>
```

Similarly, if you are performing a multilingual operation, a dynamic field can be useful for storing language-specific information:

```
<dynamicField name="*_ut_en" type="ngrams" indexed="true" stored="true"/>
<dynamicField name="*_ut_fr" type="ngrams" indexed="true" stored="true"/>
<dynamicField name="*_ut_sp" type="ngrams" indexed="true" stored="true"/>
```

At times, you don't know the field type until the document is indexed—for example, while extracting metadata from a rich document. Dynamic fields are useful in such scenarios.

The dynamicField element supports the same attribute as the field definition, and all behavior remains the same.

defaultSearchField

If a search request doesn't contain the field name to be queried upon, Solr searches on the default field. This element specifies the default field to query. The following is an example query that doesn't contain a field name, and Solr uses the default field to query.

schema.xml:

```
<defaultSearchField>aggregate_text</defaultSearchField>
```

Sample query:

```
select?q=solr rocks&defType=standard // lucene
select?q=solr rocks&defType=edismax  // qf parameter is not specified
```

This element has been deprecated in Solr 3.6 and should not be used as fallback. Instead, the df request parameter should be used.

solrQueryParser

This element specifies the default operator to be used by the query parsers, if an operator is not specified in the query. A sample solrQueryParser definition is provided here:

```
<solrQueryParser defaultOperator="OR"/>
```

This element has been deprecated since Solr 3.6, and the q.op request parameter should be used instead.

Similarity

Lucene uses the Similarity class implementation for scoring a document. To use an implementation other than the default implementation, you can declare it by using this element and specifying the class name in the class attribute. Here is the specification for the default similarity in schema.xml:

```
<similarity class="solr.DefaultSimilarityFactory"/>
```

A different similarity algorithm can be applied on all the fields or on a specific field. Here is an example for specifying a different similarity on a specific field:

```
<fieldType name="text_ib">
  <analyzer/>
  <similarity class="solr.IBSimilarityFactory">
    <str name="distribution">SPL</str>
    <str name="lambda">DF</str>
    <str name="normalization">H2</str>
  </similarity>
</fieldType>
<similarity class="solr.SchemaSimilarityFactory"/>
```

Similarity implementations are covered in more detail in Chapter 8.

Text Analysis

Our discussion of schema design provided an overview of text analysis. In this section, you will learn about the process in more detail.

Analysis is the phase of converting a text stream into terms. *Terms* are the smallest unit of information used by Lucene for matching and computing the score of documents. A term is not necessarily the words in the input text; the definition of a term depends on how you analyze the text stream. A term can be the whole input text, a sequence of two or more words, a single word, or a sequence of any characters in the text stream.

Figure 4-1 depicts an example: different terms are emitted for the same input text stream because of different analysis. As you can see, the KeywordTokenizerFactory doesn't make any changes to the stream, and the emitted term is the whole input text; in contrast, the WhitespaceTokenizerFactory splits on whitespace and multiple terms are emitted. You will learn about analyzers and tokenizers later in this chapter.

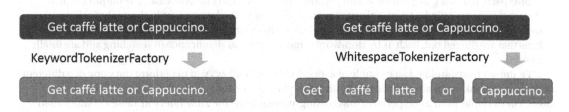

Figure 4-1. Text stream and the emitted terms

To understand the matching behavior, Table 4-2 provides few simple user queries that are searched on (or matched against) fields with this analysis. For simplicity, the table provides queries of one word, and you can assume that no analysis is being performed at query time.

Table 4-2. *Query Match Status*

Query	Tokenizer	Match Status	Description
latte	KeywordTokenizerFactory	No match	"Get caffé latte or Cappuccino." is the indexed term.
latte	WhitespaceTokenizerFactory	Match	"latte" is the indexed term.
Latte	WhitespaceTokenizerFactory	No match	The indexed term is "latte" and because of a difference in case, the terms won't match.
Cappuccino	WhitespaceTokenizerFactory	No match	The indexed term "Cappuccino." contains an additional period and so the terms are different.

If you had applied PatternReplaceCharFilterFactory to remove the special characters after tokenization, the *Cappuccino* query in Table 4-2 would have matched.

These are simple examples, and you can apply other processing (such as for lowercasing, converting to the nearest ASCII character, or removing special characters and symbols) as needed. The processing you perform depends on your matching requirements; it's not that the analysis performed using KeywordTokenizerFactory is wrong, but that it's meant for a different purpose.

Lucene uses the Boolean model (BM) and vector space model (VSM) together to determine the relevancy of documents with respect to a query. The combination works as follows: Documents matched by the BM are ranked by the VSM. The BM determines whether a term matches in a field. There the text analysis then comes into action, to control the matching behavior and determine the query terms that match the terms in the index. The analysis chain plays a crucial role in document matching.

■ **Note**   The query parser also play important roles in determining the matching documents. You will learn about it in Chapter 6.

An *analyzer* defines a chain of processes, each of which performs a specific operation such as splitting on whitespace, removing stop words, adding synonyms, or converting to lowercase. The output of each of these processes is called a *token*. Tokens that are generated by the last process in the analysis chain (which either gets indexed or is used for querying) are called *terms*, and only indexed terms are searchable. Tokens that are filtered out, such as by stop-word removal, have no significance in searching and are totally discarded.

Figure 4-1 oversimplified an example of a term in Solr. Solr allows you to perform the same or a different analysis on the token stream while indexing and querying. Query-time analysis is also needed in most cases. For example, even if you perform lowercasing at index time, the *Latte* query in Table 4-2 will lead to no match, as the query token itself starts with an uppercase letter. You generally perform the same analysis while indexing and searching, but you may want to apply some of the analysis either only while indexing or only while searching, as in the case of synonym expansion.

Figure 4-2 depicts a typical analyzer that executes a chain of analysis on the text stream. The first process in the chain receives the input stream, splits it on whitespace, and emits a set of tokens. The next process checks the tokens for non-ASCII characters; if any exist, they are converted to the nearest ASCII equivalent. The converted tokens are input to the process for removing stop words, which filters out the keywords present in the stop-words list. The next process converts all tokens to lowercase, and then the stemmer converts the tokens to their base format. Finally, the tokens are trimmed, and the terms emitted by this last process are finally indexed or used for querying.

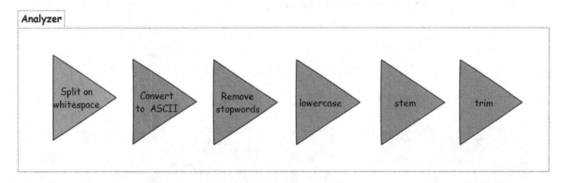

Figure 4-2. *A typical analysis chain*

The following is a sample `fieldType` definition to build the analysis chain specified in figure 4-2:

```
<fieldType name="text_analysis" class="solr.TextField" positionIncrementGap="100">
  <analyzer>
    <tokenizer class="solr.WhitespaceTokenizerFactory"/>
    <filter class="solr.AsciiFoldingFilterFactory"/>
    <filter class="solr.StopFilterFactory" ignoreCase="true" words="stopwords.txt" />
    <filter class="solr.LowerCaseFilterFactory"/>
    <filter class="solr.PorterStemFilterFactory"/>
    <filter class="solr.TrimFilterFactory"/>
  </analyzer>
</fieldType>
```

Figure 4-3 depicts an example of the text analysis of this `fieldType` definition. Suppose you are building a movie search engine that discovers movies for the user, even if the query partially matches. The system uses the preceding text analysis and indexes the movie name as *To Kill a Mockíngbird*, with the letter *í* in *Mockingbird* mistakenly having an accent, as you can see. You will see how the matching works when a user who hardly remembers the correct movie name searches *kills the mockingbird*. Also note that a majority of users, like this one, generally provide queries in lowercase. The following steps indicate how the analysis chain results in the user finding the movie *To Kill a Mockíngbird*:

1. `WhitespaceTokenizerFactory` splits the text stream on whitespace. In the English language, whitespace separates words, and this tokenizer fits well for such text analysis. Had it been an unstructured text containing sentences, a tokenizer that also splits on symbols would have been a better fit, such as for the "Cappuccino." example in Figure 4-1.

2. `AsciiFoldingFilterFactory` removes the accent as the user query or content might contain it.

3. `StopFilterFactory` removes the common words in the English language that don't have much significance in the context and adds to the recall.

4. `LowerCaseFilterFactory` normalizes the tokens to lowercase, without which the query term *mockingbird* would not match the term in the movie name.

5. `PorterStemFilterFactory` converts the terms to their base form without which the tokens *kill* and *kills* would have not matched.

6. `TrimFilterFactory` finally trims the tokens.

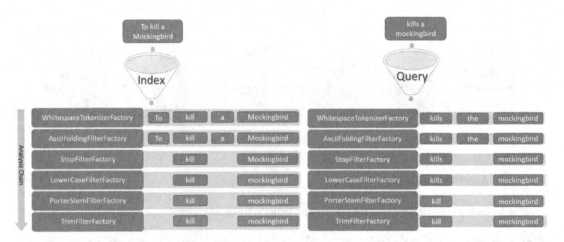

Figure 4-3. *Text analysis and term matching*

Tokens

The *token* stores the text and the additional metadata, including the start and end offset of the text, token type, position increment information, application-defined bit flag, and byte payload.

If you are writing your custom implementation for text analysis, the additional metadata should not be ignored, as some of the components require this additional information to function. The offset value is used by features such as highlighting. The position increment value identifies the position of each token in the field and plays an important role in phrase and span queries. A position increment value greater than 1 indicates a gap (a word from that position has been removed)—for instance, stop-word removal leaves a gap. A value of 0 places a token in the same position as the previous token; for example, synonym enrichment places synonyms in the same position. The default value for position increment is 1.

Terms

Terms are the output of the analysis process, each of which is indexed and used for matching. A term holds the same information as a token, except the token type and the flag.

■ **Note** The terms *token* and *term* are used interchangeably at times to refer to the emitted tokens.

Analyzers

The analysis process is defined by the analyzer, which is specified as a child element of `<fieldType>` in `schema.xml`. It analyzes the input text and optionally runs it through an analysis chain. Analyzers can perform two types of analysis, as described next.

Simple Analysis

The `analyzer` element specifies the name of the class implementing the analysis. For example:

```
<fieldType name="text_simple" class="solr.TextField">
  <analyzer class="org.apache.lucene.analysis.WhitespaceAnalyzer"/>
</fieldType>
```

The preceding `fieldType` definition for simple analysis emits terms by splitting the input token stream on whitespace. If the input stream is *Bob Marley*, the analyzed terms of a field of type `text_simple` will be Bob and Marley.

Analysis Chain

Instead of specifying the class implementing the analysis, the `analyzer` element contains a series of child elements called `tokenizer` and `filter`. These elements chained together form a pipeline for processing and analyzing the input text. The sequence in which the elements are specified in the chain matters: they should be specified in the order you want them to run. At a high level, the analysis chain can be used to perform the following operations:

- Splitting the text on whitespace, symbols, or case change
- Normalizing
- Removing the junks
- Performing enrichment

The `fieldType` definition in Figure 4-2 provides an example of an analysis chain. You will notice that the `fieldType` definition of this analyzer doesn't contain the `classname` attribute, as in the case of simple analysis. Instead it contains a set of child elements, each of which corresponds to a text analysis process in the chain.

Analysis Phases

In the preceding examples, we performed the same analysis for indexing and querying documents. Solr allows you to perform a different analysis during both phases (indexing and querying), and one phase can have even no analysis at all. For example, if you want the term *inc* to match *incorporated*, you may need to do synonym expansion, and doing it during one phase, either indexing or querying, will match both the terms.

The following are some important points about text analysis:

- The scope of the analyzer is limited to the field it is applied on. It cannot create a new field, and the terms emitted by one field cannot be copied to another field.
- `copyField` copies the stored value of the field and not the terms emitted by the analysis chain.

A description of both analysis phases follows.

Indexing

Index-time analysis applies when a document is added to Solr. Each field has a type. If the `fieldType` has an analyzer defined, the text stream is analyzed and the emitted terms are indexed along with posting information such as position and frequency. Figure 4-4 depicts an index-time analysis process. It's important to note that the analysis process affects only the indexed term, and the value stored is always the original text received by the field. The transformed text can only be queried upon and cannot be retrieved.

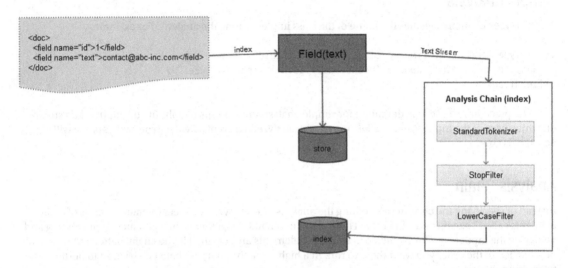

Figure 4-4. *Index-time analysis*

A different analysis can be performed at index time by specifying the analyzer element with the `type="index"` attribute, as shown here:

```
<fieldType name="text_analysis" class="solr.TextField" positionIncrementGap="100">
  <analyzer type="index">
    <tokenizer class="solr.WhitespaceTokenizerFactory"/>
    <filter class="solr.AsciiFoldingFilterFactory"/>
    ...
  </analyzer>
  <analyzer type="query">
    <tokenizer class="solr.WhitespaceTokenizerFactory"/>
    <filter class="solr.AsciiFoldingFilterFactory"/>
    ...
  </analyzer>
</fieldType>
```

■ **Note**   Any change in the index-time analyzer or its analysis chain requires a core reload and reindexing of all documents.

Querying

Query-time analysis on the field is invoked by the query parser for a user query. Figure 4-5 depicts a query-time analysis process. You can see that the analysis differs from index-time analysis.

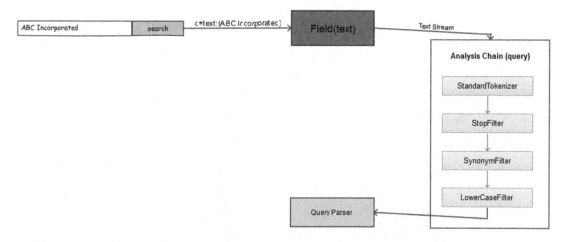

Figure 4-5. *Query-time analysis*

A different analysis can be performed at query time by specifying the analyzer element with the type="query" attribute for the fieldType.

■ **Note**   Any change in the query-time analyzer or its analysis chain requires only the core to be reloaded, and reindexing is not required.

Analysis Tools

For examining the fields and the analysis process, the following tools can be used.

Solr Admin Console

To examine the fields and fieldTypes defined in schema.xml, Solr provides the Analysis tab in the admin console. The associated page provides separate fields for index-time and query-time analysis. You need to input the text to be analyzed, select the field or fieldType, and click Analyze Values. If values are supplied in both text boxes, the process highlights the matching tokens. If you are interested only in terms emitted by the analyzer, you can disable the Verbose Output option.

On the Analysis screen, you can find a question-mark symbol beside the Analyze Fieldname drop-down list, which will take you to the Schema Browser screen. This screen allows you to view the properties of fields and examine the indexed terms. Figure 4-6 shows the Schema Browser screen for a field. It shows field properties and the top terms indexed to that field along with term frequency.

Field: abstract

Field-Type:	org.apache.solr.schema.TextField
PI Gap:	100
Docs:	5611

Flags:	Indexed	Tokenized	Stored	TermVector Stored
Properties	✔	✔	✔	✔
Schema	✔	✔	✔	✔
Index	✔	✔	✔	✔

ⓘ Index Analyzer: org.apache.solr.analysis.TokenizerChain ☒

ⓘ Query Analyzer: org.apache.solr.analysis.TokenizerChain ☒

❶ Load Term Info	5 /39264 Top-Terms: ⓘ		Histogram:
☐ Autoload	2,471 were	1	20,305
	2,302 from	2	5,161
	1,962 we	4	4,237
	1,539 which	8	3,202
	1,496 have	16	2,298
		32	1,645
		64	1,091

Figure 4-6. *Schema Browser*

Luke

The Lucene Index Toolbox (Luke) is a wonderful open source tool for examining as well as modifying the index. You should use the same version of Luke as the Lucene libraries. You can find the tool at `https://github.com/DmitryKey/luke`.

Analyzer Components

The analysis chain is specified inside the `<analyzer>` element and is composed of a combination of three types of components described next. Figure 4-7 depicts how a text stream flows through the analyzer and tokens are emitted.

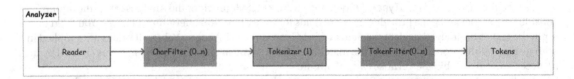

Figure 4-7. *Analyzer components chaining*

CharFilters

This component cleans up and preprocesses the characters before being processed by the tokenizer. Multiple `CharFilters` can be chained together and should always be configured before `Tokenizer`.

Tokenizers

Tokenizer accepts the text stream, processes the characters, and emits a sequence of tokens. It can break the text stream based on characters such as whitespace or symbols. An adjacent sequence of characters forms tokens. It can also add, remove, or replace characters.

Tokenizers should always be specified before `TokenFilters` and can be specified only once in an analyzer. Also, the tokenizer has no information about the field it is specified in. Table 4-3 specifies the tokenizer implementations provided by Solr.

Table 4-3. Tokenizer Implementations

Implementation	Description
KeywordTokenizerFactory	Does no tokenization. Creates a single token for the entire text. Preferred for exact matching on fields such as metadata. Input: "Bob Marley is a legendary singer." Output: "Bob Marley is a legendary singer."
StandardTokenizerFactory	Sophisticated and smart general-purpose `Tokenizer`. It splits on whitespace and punctuations, identifies sentence boundaries and URLs. It uses the Unicode standard word-boundary rule. Input: "Bob Marley is a legendary singer." Output: "Bob" "Marley" "is" "a" "legendary" "singer"
WhitespaceTokenizerFactory	It simply splits on whitespace. Input: "Bob Marley is a legendary singer." Output: "Bob" "Marley" "is" "a" "legendary" "singer."
ClassicTokenizerFactory	It supports the behavior of `StandardTokenizer` as in Solr 3.1. It recognizes e-mail IDs and keeps them intact (the current `StandardTokenizer` splits the ID because of the @ symbol). Input: "Bob's id is contact@bob.com" Output: "Bob's" "id" "is" "contact@bob.com"
LetterTokenizerFactory	It treats contiguous letters as tokens, and everything else is discarded. Input: "Bob's id is contact@bob.com" Output: "Bob" "s" "id" "is" "contact" "bob" "com"

TokenFilters

`TokenFilter` processes the tokens produced by `Tokenizer`. The important difference between `Tokenizers` and `TokenFilters` is that the `Tokenizer` input is `Reader`, whereas the `TokenFilter` input is another `TokenStream`.

`TokenFilters` should always be specified after a `Tokenizer` and can be specified any number of times. Also, the `TokenFilter` has no information about the field it is processing for.

Solr provides a wide range of token filter factories. The next section covers the primary filter factories. Refer to the Solr official reference guide at `https://cwiki.apache.org/confluence/display/solr/Filter+Descriptions` for a complete list of filters provided by Solr.

Common Text Analysis Techniques

Solr out-of-the-box provides a wide variety of analyzers, tokenizers and token filters to quickly and easily build an effective search engine. In this section, you will learn about the text processing techniques which can be applied using these field analyzers to achieve the desired search behavior.

Synonym Matching

Before exploring synonym matching, let's consider an example. Synonyms for the word *define* include *describe, detail, explain, illustrate,* and *specify.* Before performing a search, the end user thinks about which keywords to use to express the intent and formulate the query. Suppose the user is looking for the definition of the word *synonym*; his query could be *define synonym, describe synonym,* or any other synonym for the word *define.* Hence, it's really crucial to maintain synonyms for terms. Otherwise, even if your corpus contains the information the user is looking for, the system will fail to retrieve it.

Solr provides SynonymFilterFactory to perform dictionary-based synonym matching. Synonyms can be configured in a text file with a list of keywords and their matching synonyms. The following is a sample definition of SynonymFilterFactory in schema.xml:

```
<fieldType name="text_synonyms" class="solr.TextField">
  <analyzer>
    <tokenizer class="solr.WhitespaceTokenizerFactory"/>
    <filter class="solr.SynonymFilterFactory" synonyms="synonyms.txt"
     ignoreCase="true" expand="false"/>
  </analyzer>
</fieldType>
```

Refer to the sample synonyms.txt file provided in the named configsets for the file format.

Parameters

The following parameters are supported by SynonymFilterFactory:

> synonyms: Specifies the name of the external text file that contains the synonym mapping.

> ignoreCase: If set to true, the case of keywords will be ignored during lookup.

> expand: If true, the tokens will be expanded. If false, the synonyms will collapse to the keyword.

Given the need of having a generic synonym (applicable to the language) and specific synonym (specific to your domain), you can configure multiple SynonymFilters in an analysis chain. Basically, any TokenFilter can be configured multiple times, if needed.

SynonymFilterFactory can be applied at both index time and query time, but is usually applied at either of the two. Index-time synonym expansion results in a bigger index size, and any change in the list requires reindexing. But it also has benefits. The expanded tokens will contribute to inverse document frequency (IDF), which gives higher importance to rarer words.

The query-time synonym expansion doesn't increase the index size and saves you from reindexing after changing the synonym list, but it increases the query response time. The problem in query-time expansion is with synonyms containing multiple words, such as *movie star*. Such words are already tokenized by the QueryParser into *movie* and *star* before being processed by the analyzer. Another problem is with phrase queries: the tokens in the phrase would get expanded, which results in the phrase having multiple tokens that could end up being a no-match. For example, *movie star* can expand to `"(movie | cinema) (star | actor | cast)"` and end up not matching documents containing *movie star*.

Phonetic Matching

Phonetic matching algorithms are for matching words that sound alike and are pronounced similarly. Edit distance and N-grams are particularly suitable when words are misspelled, but phonetics is suitable when a word is written differently but is always pronounced the same.

Name matching is a typical example: a name can have multiple spellings but be pronounced the same. For matching a person's name, phonetic algorithms become even more crucial, as there is no standard definition or dictionary for names. A name can have multiple variations that are pronounced the same. For example, *Christy* and *Christie* are phonemes for the same name, and both are correct.

Phonetic matching may not work well for typographical errors, which are unintentional and typically include letters in the wrong order (for example, *good* typed as *godo*). However, phonetic matching can be effective if the error is intentional, as in the case of tweets or short messages where the user might replace *good* with *gud*, or *you* with *u*.

The purpose of phonetic matching is to increase recall and ensure that no terms are missed that could have matched. It's advised to give low boost to the phonetic field, as this may end up matching totally unrelated words either due to words being phonetically similar but representing different concepts or due to the limitations of the algorithm.

Phonetics are highly language specific, and most of the algorithms are developed for English. The algorithms encode the tokens and are supposed to be the same for phonetically similar words. Table 4-4 provides a list of phonetic algorithms supported by Solr and sample definitions.

Table 4-4. *Phonetic Algorithms*

Algorithm	Definition
Beider-Morse Phonetic Matching (BMPM)	Provides much better codes for first name and last name.
	Configuration:
	`<filter class="solr.BeiderMorseFilterFactory" nameType="GENERIC" ruleType="APPROX" concat="true" languageSet="auto"/>`
Soundex	Developed to match phonetically similar surnames. It generates codes of four characters, starting with a letter and followed by three numbers.
	Configuration:
	`<filter class="solr.PhoneticFilterFactory" encoder="Soundex"/>`
Metaphone	It is used generally for matching similar-sounding words and is not limited to surnames.
	Configuration:
	`<filter class="solr.PhoneticFilterFactory" encoder="Metaphone"/>`

(continued)

Table 4-4. (*continued*)

Algorithm	Definition
Double Metaphone	This extension of Metaphone addresses peculiarities in languages other than English.
	Configuration:

	```<filter class="solr.DoubleMetaphoneFilterFactory"/>```
	```<filter class="solr.PhoneticFilterFactory"```
	```encoder="DoubleMetaphone"/>```

Refined Soundex	Refined version of Soundex, which matches fewer names to the same code.
	Configuration:
	```<filter class="solr.PhoneticFilterFactory"``` ```encoder="RefinedSoundex"/>```
Daitch-Mokotoff Soundex	Refinement of Soundex. It provides high accuracy for matching names, especially Slavic and European. It generates codes of six numeric digits.
	Configuration:
	```<filter class="solr.DaitchMokotoffSoundexFilterFactory"``` ```inject="true"/>```
Caverphone	Optimized for accents in New Zealand.
	Configuration:
	```<filter class="solr.PhoneticFilterFactory" encoder="Caverphone"/>```
Kölner Phonetik (a.k.a. Cologne Phonetic)	It is suitable for German words.
	Configuration:
	```<filter class="solr.PhoneticFilterFactory"``` ```encoder="ColognePhonetic"/>```
New York State Identification and Intelligence System (NYSIIS)	Provides a better result than Soundex, using a more sophisticated rule for code generation.
	Configuration:
	```<filter class="solr.PhoneticFilterFactory" encoder="Nysiis"/>```

N-Grams

N-Gram breaks the input token into multiple subtokens called *grams*. For example, grams for the input token *hellosolr* of size 4 will be *hell*, *ello*, *llos*, *loso*, *osol*, and *solr*. If the user query is *solr*, you can see that the last gram generated will match.

N-grams are useful for matching substrings and misspelled words. It is also useful for features such as autocompletion, prefix and postfix queries, and wildcard searches. N-grams increase the recall and match tokens that would otherwise be missed.

Solr provides Tokenizers as well as TokenFilters for N-grams. If you want to generate grams on the tokenized text, you can use TokenFilter; otherwise, the Tokenizer can be used. Table 4-5 lists the implementations provided by Solr for N-gram.

Table 4-5. *N-Gram Implementations*

Implementation	Definition	Example

`NGramTokenizerFactory` `NGramFilterFactory`	Generates N-grams from all character positions and of all sizes in the specified range
	
	Attributes:
	
	minGramSize: Minimum gram size
	maxGramSize: Maximum gram size
	
	Configuration:
	
	`<tokenizer class="solr.`
	`NGramTokenizerFactory" minGramSize="3"`
	`maxGramSize="4"/>`
	`<filter class="solr.NGramFilterFactory"`
	`minGramSize="3" maxGramSize="4"/>`
		Input: hellosolr
		Output: hel, ell, llo, los, oso, sol, olr, hell, ello, llos, loso, osol, solr

`EdgeNGramTokenizerFactory` `EdgeNGramFilterFactory`	Generates N-grams from the specified edge and of all sizes in the specified range
	Attributes:
	
	minGramSize: Minimum gram size
	maxGramSize: Maximum gram size
	
	side: Edge from which grams should be generated. Value can be front or back. Default is front.
	
	Configuration:
	
	`<tokenizer class="solr.`
	`EdgeNGramTokenizerFactory"`
	`minGramSize="4" maxGramSize="5"/>`
	`<filter class="solr.`
	`EdgeNGramFilterFactory" minGramSize="4"`
	`maxGramSize="5" side="front"/>`
		Input: hellosolr
		Output: hell, hello

The edge N-gram generates fewer tokens and provides better performance than N-gram. N-gram offers better recall but should be used carefully, as it can lead to overmatching.

If you keep the `minGramSize` small, lots of tokens will be generated and the index size and indexing time will increase and will have performance implications. You should generate N-grams only for a few fields and try to keep the `minGramSize` high and `maxGramSize` low.

Shingling

Shingling generates grams on the basis of words instead of on the basis of characters. For the input stream *apache solr rocks*, the shingles generated would be *apache solr* and *solr rocks*.

Shingling provides a mechanism to improve relevance ranking and precision, by allowing you to match subphrases. Phrase queries match the entire sequence of tokens, token-based matching matches an emitted term, and shingles fit between both. Shingling provides better query-time performance than phrases with a trade-off of additional tokens generated.

Shingles are generally applied while indexing, but can be applied both while indexing and querying. Also, the shingle fields are usually given a high boost.

The following is a sample definition of SynonymFilterFactory in schema.xml:

```
<fieldType name="text_shingles" class="solr.TextField">
  <analyzer>
    <tokenizer class="solr.WhitespaceTokenizerFactory"/>
    <filter class="solr.ShingleFilterFactory" minShingleSize="2" maxShingleSize="3"
outputUnigrams="false"/>
  </analyzer>
</fieldType>
```

Parameters

The following parameters are supported by ShingleFilterFactory:

> minShingleSize: The minimum number of tokens per shingle. The default value is 2.

> maxShingleSize: The maximum number of tokens per shingle. The default value is 2.

> outputUnigrams: This Boolean parameter specifies whether the individual tokens should be generated. By default, this is set to true. If this parameter is true and you are giving a high boost to the field, evaluate that the boost doesn't adversely affect the relevancy, as your general intention would be to give higher boost to shingles constituted of multiple tokens.

> outputUnigramsIfNoShingles: This Boolean parameter specifies whether individual tokens should be generated if no shingle is generated. By default, this is set to false.

> tokenSeparator: This specifies the separator for joining the tokens that form the shingles. The default value is " ".

Stemming

Stemming is the process of converting words to their base form in order to match different tenses, moods, and other inflections of a word. The base word is also called a *stem*. It's important to note that in information retrieval, the purpose of stemming is to match different inflections on a word; stems are not necessarily the morphological root.

Stemmers are generally language specific. A wide range of stemmers are available for English. For other languages, stemmers are also available. Table 4-6 specifies the primary stemmers supported in Solr.

Table 4-6. *Stemming Algorithms*

Stemmer	Factory Class	Features	Language
Porter Stem	`solr.PorterStem FilterFactory`	Algorithm based. Fast algorithm.	English
KStem	`solr.KStem FilterFactory`	Similar to Porter Stem but less aggressive and faster.	English
Snowball	`Solr.SnowballPorter FilterFactory`	Algorithm based. Slower than Porter Stem. More aggressive.	Multiple languages
Hunspell	`solr.HunspellStem FilterFactory`	Combination of dictionary- and rules-based stemmer. Uses same dictionary as in Apache OpenOffice.	Supports 99 languages
English Minimal Stem	`solr.EnglishMinimalStem FilterFactory`	Less aggressive. Suitable for light stemming and cases like plural-to-singular conversion.	Multiple languages

Figure 4-8 shows the result of stemming for words whose base is *travel*. We applied `PorterStemFilter` at index time and `EnglishMinimalStemFilter` at query time, to illustrate the difference in results and level of aggressiveness of both algorithms. `PorterStemFilter` is more aggressive and converts all inflections of travel to its base word, while `EnglishMinimalStemFilter` does it only for a few inflections.

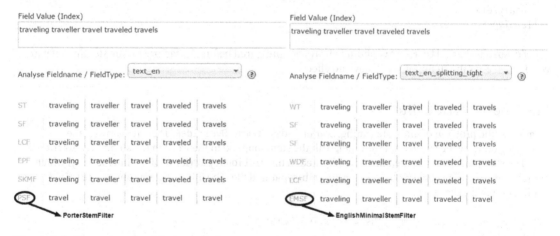

Figure 4-8. *Stemming algorithm comparison*

■ **Caution**   In Figure 4-8, a different stemmer has been configured at index time and query time for comparison. Rarely will there be a scenario where you would want to configure this way.

While stemming the tokens, the problem of overstemming and understemming can occur, so the stemming algorithm should be chosen considering these error measurements. In *overstemming*, two totally unrelated words are stemmed to the same root, though they shouldn't be (a false positive). In *understemming*, two related words are not stemmed to the same root, though they should be (a true negative). For example, `EnglishMinimalStemFilter` not stemming *traveling* to *travel* is a case of understemming, and `PorterStemFilter` stemming *university* and *universe* both to *univers* is a case of overstemming.

Stemming should generally be applied both while indexing and querying. Stemming doesn't increase the size of the index.

Solr provides provisions to solve the problem of overstemming and understemming with `KeywordMarkerFilter` and `StemmerOverrideFilter`, respectively.

KeywordMarkerFilter

`KeywordMarkerFilter` prevents words from being stemmed, by specifying the protected words in a file. The filename should be specified in the `protected` attribute of the filter factory.

`KeywordMarkerFilter` makes an effective solution for blacklisting words that result in false positives due to overstemming. In the previous example, you saw *university* being overstemmed. Suppose you don't want a term to be stemmed; you can add it to the protected words file and configure `KeywordMarkerFilter`. The following is a sample `fieldType` configuration in `schema.xml`:

```
<fieldType name="text_stem" class="solr.TextField">
  <analyzer>
    <tokenizer class="solr.WhitespaceTokenizerFactory"/>
    <filter class="solr.KeywordMarkerFilterFactory" protected="protwords.txt" />
    <filter class="solr.PorterStemFilterFactory" />
  </analyzer>
</fieldType>
```

`KeywordMarkerFilterFactory` should always be configured before the factory for the stemmer. If you configure it after the stemmer, it will have no effect.

StemmerOverrideFilter

To address the problem of understemming, Solr provides `StemmerOverrideFilter`. It overrides the stemming done by the configured stemmer, with the stem mapped to the word in the stemming override file.

The stemming override filename is configured in the `dictionary` attribute of the filter factory, which contains the mapping of words to its stems in a tab-separated file. The following is a sample `fieldType` configuration in `schema.xml`:

```
<fieldType name="text_stem" class="solr.TextField">
  <analyzer>
    <tokenizer class="solr.WhitespaceTokenizerFactory"/>
    <filter class="solr.StemmerOverrideFilterFactory" dictionary="stemdict.txt" />
    <filter class="solr.PorterStemFilterFactory" />
  </analyzer>
</fieldType>
```

`StemmerOverrideFilterFactory` should always be configured before the factory for the stemmer. If you configure it after the stemmer, it will have no effect.

Blacklist (Stop Words)

Some of the terms are of no importance to your search engine. For example, words such as *a, an,* and *the* add to the bag of words and end up increasing the false positives. You might want to stop such words from being indexed and queried. Solr provides StopFilterFactory to blacklist and discard the words specified in the stop-words file from the field tokens. Here is an example configuration:

```
<analyzer>
  <tokenizer class="solr.WhitespaceTokenizerFactory"/>
  <filter class="solr.StopFilterFactory" words="stopwords.txt"/>
</analyzer>
```

Figure 4-9 illustrates stop-word removal with an example of a movie search engine; the word *movie* is assumed to be a stop word. We added the keyword *movie* to the stop-words file and analyzed the text *review of movie shawshank redemption*. The stop-words filter removes the token *movie* from the token stream. Also, it creates a gap in the stream that can be determined by the token metadata, such as the position and start and end offsets.

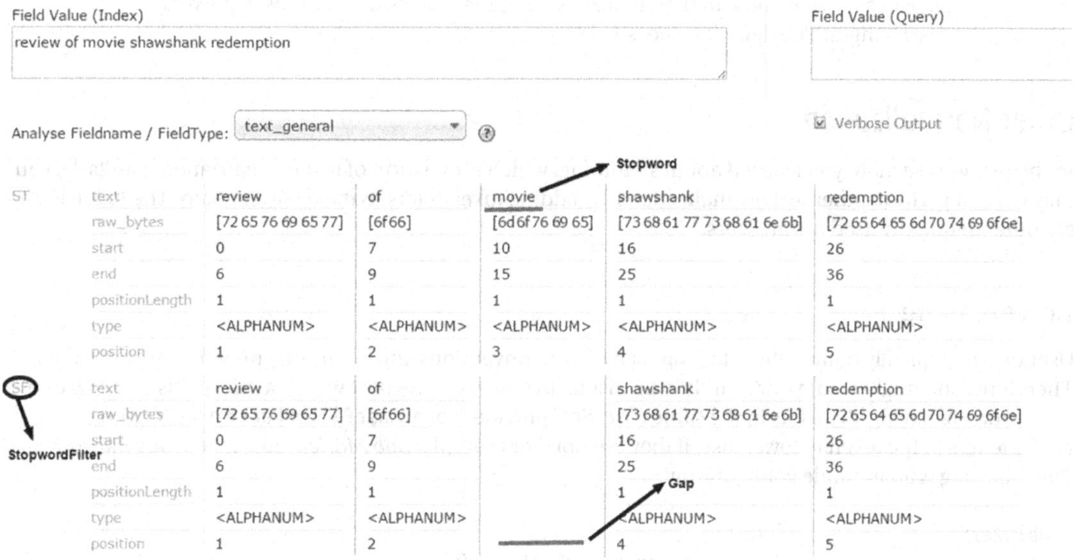

Figure 4-9. *Stop-words removal*

The stopwords.txt file provided in the sample_techproducts_configs configset is blank and it contains no entries. Common English words such as *a, an,* and *the* generally make good candidates for the stopwords.txt file. To find stop words specific to your content, the Schema Browser in the Solr admin console is a good place to start. You can select a field and load the terms with highest frequency by clicking the Load Term Info button. You can then review these high-frequency terms to determine whether some of them can be stop words.

Whitelist (Keep Words)

Whitelisting is the opposite of stop-word removal or blacklisting. This allows only those tokens to pass through that are present in the specified list, and all other tokens are discarded. Suppose your application supports a specified set of languages; in that case, you might want to apply a filter that keeps only the supported language and discards all other text.

You can achieve this in Solr by using the KeepWordFilterFactory class. This filter is generally applied while indexing. The following is an example configuration:

```
<analyzer>
  <tokenizer class="solr.WhitespaceTokenizerFactory"/>
  <filter class="solr.KeepWordFilterFactory" words="keepwords.txt"/>
</analyzer>
```

The following are the supported parameters:

words: Path of the text file containing the allowed words. The file-definition rule is the same as the stop-words file.

ignoreCase: This Boolean parameter, if set to true, makes the filter insensitive to case changes. The default value is false.

Other Normalization

In the previous section, you learned about stemming, which is one form of text normalization. Similarly, you may need to perform other text normalizations, by adding token filters to the analysis chain. The following are other frequently used normalizers.

Lowercasing

User queries typically don't adhere to language casing conventions and are mostly provided in lowercase. Therefore,, you might want your search to be insensitive to case. The best way to achieve this is follow one convention of having all tokens in the same case. Solr provides LowerCaseFilterFactory to convert all the letters in the token to lowercase, if they are not. For example, *Bob Marley* must match *bob marley*. The following is an example configuration:

```
<analyzer>
  <tokenizer class="solr.WhitespaceTokenizerFactory"/>
  <filter class="solr.LowerCaseFilterFactory"/>
</analyzer>
```

This is generally applied both while indexing and querying.

Convert to Closest ASCII Character

If you want your search experience to be insensitive to accents, so that both accented and nonaccented characters match the same documents, you should add ASCIIFoldingFilterFactory to the analysis chain. This filter converts Unicode characters to their closest ASCII equivalents, if available. For example, *Bełżec* should match *Belzec*. Here is an example configuration:

```
<analyzer>
  <tokenizer class="solr.WhitespaceTokenizerFactory"/>
  <filter class="solr.ASCIIFoldingFilterFactory"/>
</analyzer>
```

This is generally applied both while indexing and querying.

Remove Duplicate Tokens

After performing a series of operations on the text, the chain might end up generating duplicate tokens, such as performing enrichments or synonym expansion followed by stemming. Solr provides the RemoveDuplicatesTokenFilterFactory implementation to remove the duplicate tokens at the same position. The following is an example configuration:

```
<analyzer>
  <tokenizer class="solr.WhitespaceTokenizerFactory"/>
  <filter class="solr.RemoveDuplicatesTokenFilterFactory"/>
</analyzer>
```

This is generally applied while indexing.

Multilingual Support

The text analysis you perform depends a lot on the language you need to support. You may be developing a search engine for a specific language or you may need to support multiple languages. To support a specific language, you can define all fieldTypes as per the linguistics of that language. If you need to support multiple languages, you can define different fieldTypes for each language and copy the text to the corresponding field. The named configsets provided by Solr contain fieldType definitions for a wide range of languages, a sample of which is provided here:

```
<!-- German -->
<fieldType name="text_de" class="solr.TextField" positionIncrementGap="100">
  <analyzer>
    <tokenizer class="solr.StandardTokenizerFactory"/>
    <filter class="solr.LowerCaseFilterFactory"/>
    <filter class="solr.StopFilterFactory" ignoreCase="true"
words="lang/stopwords_de.txt" format="snowball" />
    <filter class="solr.GermanNormalizationFilterFactory"/>
    <filter class="solr.GermanLightStemFilterFactory"/>
    <!-- less aggressive: <filter class="solr.GermanMinimalStemFilterFactory"/> -->
    <!-- more aggressive: <filter class="solr.SnowballPorterFilterFactory"
language="German2"/> -->
  </analyzer>
</fieldType>
```

The preceding `fieldType` definition is for the German language. You can see that Solr provides factories specific to it. Among the provided factories, it offers multiple implementations for stemmers, and you can use the one that works well for your needs.

The alphabets of many languages use diacritical marks, such as French scripts, to change the sounds of letters to which they are added. A simple way to normalize is to use `ASCIIFoldingFilterFactory`, which we discussed in the previous section, to convert words with accents to the closest ASCII character. But this doesn't work for languages such as Arabic, whose diacritics cannot be converted to ASCII characters.

For some languages, Solr provides specific tokenizers and filter factories such as `ElisionFilterFactory` to handle the elision symbol that applies to a selected language. Also, some filter factories accept a different input file that contains the content specific to that language. For example, stop words in English are different from those in Bulgarian. Solr provides a `lang` subdirectory in `conf` that contains a list of language-specific files that can be used by the factories.

In a language like English, you can easily identify the words on the basis of whitespace, but some languages (for example, Japanese) don't separate words with whitespace. In these cases, it's difficult to identify which tokens to index. The following is an example of Japanese script for the sentence, "What will you have, beer or coffee?"

あなたは、ビールやコーヒーを何を持っているのだろうか？

Solr provides `CJKTokenizerFactory`, which breaks Chinese, Japanese, and Korean language text into tokens. The tokens generated are *doubles*, overlapping pairs of CJK characters found in the text stream. It also provides `JapaneseTokenizerFactory` and other filters for Japanese language, which are defined in the `fieldType` `text_ja` in the `schema.xml` file bundled with Solr. The example in Figure 4-10 shows the analysis performed by `text_ja` for text in the Japanese language.

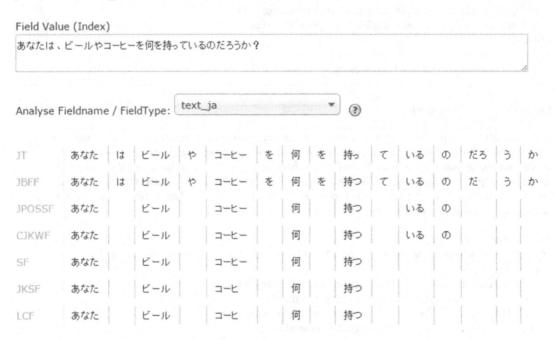

Figure 4-10. *Text analysis example for Japanese language*

You can refer to the official guide at `https://cwiki.apache.org/confluence/display/solr/Language+Analysis` for the complete list of language-specific factories provided by Solr.

Going Schemaless

Schemaless mode is the quickest way of getting started with Solr. It allows you to start Solr with zero schema handcrafting and simply index documents without worrying about field definitions. In schemaless mode, you can initially bypass whatever you read early in this chapter. If you want finer control over field definitions or other schema configurations, you can use a managed schema and REST APIs.

Schemaless mode is essentially the proper packaging of a set of Solr features that enables easy setup and creating fields on-the-fly. The following are the features that can be used together to support such a dynamic schema.

- Automatic field type identification

- Automatic field creation

- Managed schema and REST APIs

- Dynamic fields

Schemaless mode is useful if you are new to Solr or you don't know the document structure or the structure changes frequently.

Solr bundles an example configset for schemaless mode. You can test it by running the Solr script as follows:

```
$ ./solr start -e schemaless
```

If you want to create a schemaless core, you can either create a core/collection without any configuration information or specify the prebundled configset data_driven_schema_configs. Here is an example for creating a schemaless core:

```
$ ./solr create -c schemaless -d data_driven_schema_configs
$ ./solr create -c schemaless // by default uses data_driven_schema_configs
```

What Makes Solr Schemaless

As you learnt, Solr goes schemaless by bundling a set of features together. The following are features that can be leveraged to go schemaless.

Automatic Field Type Identification

Whenever Solr encounters a new field that is not defined in the schema, it run a set of parsers on the field content, to identify the field type. Currently, Solr provides field type guessing only for the primitive fieldTypes: Integer, Long, Float, Double, Boolean, and Date.

Remember, the field type guess using a dynamic field is based on the field name pattern, but here it is based on field content. Solr implements this feature by providing the update processor factories starting with name Parse*, which identifies the field type while preprocessing. You will read about update processor factories in more detail in Chapter 5.

Automatic Field Addition

For unknown fields, if Solr successfully guesses the fieldType, it adds that field to the schema. The field addition is handled by AddSchemaFieldsUpdateProcessorFactory configured subsequent to the processor for field-type guessing.

Managed Schema and REST API

Automatic field type identification and field addition is limited to primitive field types. If you want to specify a fieldType for any field or define text analysis on it, you might want to add a field and/or fieldType. You can do this on-the-fly by using the managed schema and REST APIs. We discuss this in more detail in the next section.

Dynamic Fields

A dynamic field is supported in Solr since early releases and supports a limited yet powerful schemaless capability. It allows you to assign a complex fieldType to a new field that matches the field-naming pattern.

Configuration

This section specifies the steps that configure Solr to go schemaless. If you are creating a core using the data_driven_schema_configs configset, Solr has the configurations already in place, and you just need to start indexing documents. If you want to manually define or modify the existing schemaless core, the following are the steps to be followed:

1. Define the following updateRequestProcessorChain with the update processor factories specified in sequence in solrconfig.xml. All the defined factories starting with Parse* perform the fieldType identification. The AddSchemaFieldsUpdateProcessorFactory is responsible for creating fields automatically, and the UUIDUpdateProcessorFactory generates unique identifiers for the document. The RemoveBlankFieldUpdateProcessorFactory and FieldNameMutatingUpdateProcessorFactory are for normalization of a field and its value.

```
<updateRequestProcessorChain name="add-unknown-fields-to-the-schema">
    <!-- UUIDUpdateProcessorFactory will generate an id if
none is present in the incoming document -->
    <processor class="solr.UUIDUpdateProcessorFactory" />

    <processor class="solr.LogUpdateProcessorFactory"/>
    <processor class="solr.DistributedUpdateProcessorFactory"/>
    <processor class="solr.RemoveBlankFieldUpdateProcessorFactory"/>
    <processor class="solr.FieldNameMutatingUpdateProcessorFactory">
      <str name="pattern">[^\w-\.]</str>
      <str name="replacement">_</str>
    </processor>
    <processor class="solr.ParseBooleanFieldUpdateProcessorFactory"/>
    <processor class="solr.ParseLongFieldUpdateProcessorFactory"/>
    <processor class="solr.ParseDoubleFieldUpdateProcessorFactory"/>
    <processor class="solr.ParseDateFieldUpdateProcessorFactory">
```

```
        <arr name="format">
          <str>yyyy-MM-dd'T'HH:mm:ss.SSSZ</str>
          <str>yyyy-MM-dd'T'HH:mm:ss,SSSZ</str>
          <str>yyyy-MM-dd'T'HH:mm:ss.SSS</str>
          <str>yyyy-MM-dd'T'HH:mm:ss,SSS</str>
          <str>yyyy-MM-dd'T'HH:mm:ssZ</str>
          <str>yyyy-MM-dd'T'HH:mm:ss</str>
          <str>yyyy-MM-dd'T'HH:mmZ</str>
          <str>yyyy-MM-dd'T'HH:mm</str>
          <str>yyyy-MM-dd HH:mm:ss.SSSZ</str>
          <str>yyyy-MM-dd HH:mm:ss,SSSZ</str>
          <str>yyyy-MM-dd HH:mm:ss.SSS</str>
          <str>yyyy-MM-dd HH:mm:ss,SSS</str>
          <str>yyyy-MM-dd HH:mm:ssZ</str>
          <str>yyyy-MM-dd HH:mm:ss</str>
          <str>yyyy-MM-dd HH:mmZ</str>
          <str>yyyy-MM-dd HH:mm</str>
          <str>yyyy-MM-dd</str>
        </arr>
      </processor>
      <processor class="solr.AddSchemaFieldsUpdateProcessorFactory">
        <str name="defaultFieldType">strings</str>
        <lst name="typeMapping">
          <str name="valueClass">java.lang.Boolean</str>
          <str name="fieldType">booleans</str>
        </lst>
        <lst name="typeMapping">
          <str name="valueClass">java.util.Date</str>
          <str name="fieldType">tdates</str>
        </lst>
        <lst name="typeMapping">
          <str name="valueClass">java.lang.Long</str>
          <str name="valueClass">java.lang.Integer</str>
          <str name="fieldType">tlongs</str>
        </lst>
        <lst name="typeMapping">
          <str name="valueClass">java.lang.Number</str>
          <str name="fieldType">tdoubles</str>
        </lst>
      </processor>
      <processor class="solr.RunUpdateProcessorFactory"/>
    </updateRequestProcessorChain>
```

2. For the chain to be usable, UpdateRequestProcessorChain should be registered in the update handler that gets invoked for indexing the documents:

```
<initParams path="/update/**">
  <lst name="defaults">
    <str name="update.chain">add-unknown-fields-to-the-schema</str>
  </lst>
</initParams>
```

3. Enable support for the managed schema in `solrconfig.xml`:

```
<schemaFactory class="ManagedIndexSchemaFactory">
  <bool name="mutable">true</bool>
  <str name="managedSchemaResourceName">managed-schema</str>
</schemaFactory>
```

4. After making the preceding changes, you are all set to index documents without worrying about whether the field is defined in `schema.xml`.

Limitations

Running Solr in full schemaless mode has limitations. The following are the important ones to be noted:

- A limited set of Primitive `fieldTypes` is supported by automatic field addition and doesn't allow you to apply an `analyzer` or perform a specific set of text analysis.

- `Field Type` identification can lead to wrong `fieldType` guessing, as Solr cascades through the processors to identify the `fieldType`. If the document being indexed contains a number, Solr will create a field of type `TrieIntField`. Now, if the next document contains a floating-point number, Solr would fail to index this document because it has already defined the `fieldType` of this field as `TrieIntField`, and a field once defined cannot be changed automatically.

- While defining a field, you may want to fine-tune it by specifying additional attributes such as `precisionStep`. An automatic `fieldType` definition ignores that perspective.

■ **Tip** The schema should not be manually modified when running Solr in schemaless mode.

REST API for Managing Schema

Before discussing schemaless mode, we used `schema.xml`, to define the schema. Any changes in the schema require you to manually edit `schema.xml` and reload the core. Since the inception of Solr, this is the way `schema.xml` has been used. But recent releases of Solr allow you to manage the schema through REST APIs. Solr provides REST APIs to read, add, remove, and update elements for managing `field`, `fieldType`, `copyField`, and `dynamicField` elements.

Solr provides two implementations of the base class `IndexSchemaFactory` to manage schema. You need to define the implementation class in the `schemaFactory` element in `solrconfig.xml`:

- `ClassicIndexSchemaFactory`: This is the default implementation, in which you define the schema manually. The `schema.xml` file must be present in the `conf` directory and should be manually modified. This implementation doesn't support managing the schema through REST APIs.

- `ManagedIndexSchemaFactory`: This is the implementation to manage a schema through REST APIs.

Configuration

The following are the steps to configure a managed schema for using the REST APIs.

1. Define the schemaFactory element in solrconfig.xml and provide the implementation class as ManagedIndexSchemaFactory:

```
<schemaFactory class="ManagedIndexSchemaFactory">
  <bool name="mutable">true</bool>
  <str name="managedSchemaResourceName">managed-schema</str>
</schemaFactory>
```

In Solr 5.x, if you create a core without specifying the configuration directory, it will by default use the data_driven_schema_configs configset, which creates a managed schema to support REST calls. The data_driven_schema_configs configset is provided with the Solr distribution and can be located in the $SOLR_DIST/server/solr/configsets directory.

The following is the schemaFactory element in solrconfig.xml for the traditional approach to a schema definition:

```
<schemaFactory class="ClassicIndexSchemaFactory"/>
```

2. The default file for a managed schema definition is managed-schema. You can change the filename by modifying the managedSchemaResourceName parameter. On creating a core, if the schema.xml exists but the managed-schema file doesn't exist, in that case Solr will copy schema.xml to the managed-schema file and rename schema.xml to schema.xml.bak. Solr doesn't allow you to change the name of managed schema file to schema.xml. The following is the property to be set for specifying the managed schema file name:

```
<str name="managedSchemaResourceName">managed-schema</str>
```

3. If your schema is finalized, you may be interested in disallowing all future edits. To limit the REST APIs to support only read access, set the mutable Boolean parameter to false:

```
<bool name="mutable">false</bool>
```

It's good to disable the mutable setting in production.

REST Endpoints

Once you have managed-schema set up, you can start performing read and write operations using the REST API. All write requests automatically trigger core reload internally, and so should not be invoked by you in order for the changes to reflect. Table 4-7 lists the operations supported over the REST API, the endpoints to invoke, and the examples.

Table 4-7. *REST Endpoints for Managing Schema*

Operation	Endpoints & Commands	Example
Read schema	`GET /core/schema`	`curl http://localhost:8983/solr/core/` `schema?wt=json`
Read field(s)	`GET /core/schema/fields` `GET /core/schema/fields/` `fieldname`	`curl http://localhost:8983/solr/core/` `schema/fields?wt=json`

Modify field	`POST /core/schema`
	
	Commands:
	
	`add-field`
	`delete-field`
	`replace-field`
		`curl -X POST -H 'Content-type:application/` `json' --data-binary '{` `"add-field":{` `"name":"title",` `"type":"text_general",` `"stored":true }` `}' http://localhost:8983/solr/core/schema`

Read field type	`GET /core/schema/fieldtypes` `GET /core/schema/fieldtypes/` `name`	`curl http://localhost:8983/solr/core/` `schema/fieldtypes?wt=json`

Modify field type	`POST /core/schema`
	
	Commands:
	
	`add-field-type`
	`delete-field-type`
	`replace-field-type`
		`curl -X POST -H 'Content-type:application/` `json' --data-binary '{` `"add-field-type" : {` `"name":"text_ws",` `"class":"solr.TextField",` `"positionIncrementGap":"100",` `"analyzer" : {` `"tokenizer":{` `"class":"solr.WhitespaceTokenizerFactory"` `}}}` `}' http://localhost:8983/solr/core/schema`

Read dynamic field(s)	`GET /core/schema/` `dynamicfields` `GET /core/schema/` `dynamicfields/name`	`curl http://localhost:8983/solr/core/` `schema/dynamicfields?wt=json`

Modify dynamic field	`POST /core/schema`
	
	Commands:
	
	`add-dynamic-field`
	`delete-dynamic-field`
	`replace-dynamic-field`
		`curl -X POST -H 'Content-type:application/` `json' --data-binary '{` `"add-dynamic-field":{` `"name":"*_en",` `"type":"text_general",` `"stored":true }` `}' http://localhost:8983/solr/core/schema`

Read copy fields	`GET /core/schema/copyfields`	`curl http://localhost:8983/solr/core/` `schema/copyfields?wt=json`

Modify copy field	`POST /core/schema`
	
	Commands:
	
	`add-copy-field`
	`delete-copy-field`
	`replace-copy-field`
		`curl -X POST -H 'Content-type:application/` `json' --data-binary '{` `"add-copy-field":{` `"source":"title",` `"dest":[ "title_ut", "title_pn" ]}` `}' http://localhost:8983/solr/core/schema`

Other Managed Resources

Solr offers provisions to manage other resources such as stop words and synonyms using the REST APIs.

Usage Steps

The following are the steps for managing stop words and synonyms using the REST APIs.

1. Add the implementing filter factory to the analysis chain

```
<filter class="solr.ManagedStopFilterFactory" managed="product" /> // stopwords
<filter class="solr.ManagedSynonymFilterFactory" managed="product" /> // synonyms
```

2. Assign a name to the managed resource

The managed attribute assigns a name to the resource, as shown in the preceding example. This is useful if you want to support multiple stop words or synonyms, such as for the domain, feature, or language.

3. Access the resource over REST endpoint

```
/core/schema/analysis/stopwords/<name> // syntax
/core/schema/analysis/stopwords/product // example
```

Refer to the Solr manual at https://cwiki.apache.org/confluence/display/solr/Managed+Resources for its complete list of REST endpoints and the usage information.

solrconfig.xml File

Solr supports innumerable features and allows a wide set of customization and control over those features. You can use solrconfig.xml to define and configure the features you want to offer in your search solution and manage its behavior and properties by changing the XML. The important features that can be configured in solrconfig.xml are as follows:

- Define the request handler that specifies the REST endpoint and the corresponding Solr feature to expose over it. For example, all requests to the /select endpoint handle the search request, and the /update endpoint handles the indexing requests.

- Define the search components, update request processors, and query parsers, and configure them to a handler or other component that they can be chained with. Suppose you want to enable the hit-highlighting feature in your search engine. You can do this by defining the highlighting component, configuring the parameters to achieve the desired behavior, and finally chaining it to the search handler.

- Configure paths and files used by the Solr core, such as name of the schema file.

- Configure other core-level properties such as caching, included libraries, auto commit, index merging behavior, and replication.

solrconfig.xml provides a high degree of flexibility in defining and exposing a feature. You define and configure the components provided by Solr or the custom components you developed by extending the Solr base classes, and then you assemble them together to quickly expose a feature.

■ **Note** No single chapter is dedicated to the definitions and configurations supported by `solrconfig.xml`. Instead, you will learn about them as and we discuss a feature or search capability offered by Solr.

Frequently Asked Questions

This section provides answers to some of the questions that developers often ask while defining `schema.xml`.

How do I handle the exception indicating that the _version_ field must exist in the schema?

The `_version_` field is required for optimistic concurrency in SolrCloud, and it enables a real-time get operation. Solr expects it to be defined in `schema.xml` as follows:

```
<field name="_version_" type="long" indexed="true" stored="true" />
```

It's recommended to have this field in `schema.xml`, but if you still want to disable it, you can comment out the `updateLog` declaration in the `updateHandler` section in `solrconfig.xml`.

```
<!--updateLog>
  <str name="dir">${solr.ulog.dir:}</str>
  <int name="numVersionBuckets">${solr.ulog.numVersionBuckets:65536}</int>
</updateLog-->
```

Why is my Schema Change Not Reflected in Solr?

For the changes in `schema.xml` to be reflected, the core should be reloaded. If any change has been made in index-time processing of a field, all the documents should also be reindexed.

I Have Created a Core in Solr 5.0, but Schema.xml is Missing. Where Can I find it?

By default, the core created by Solr 5.0 is schemaless. It uses `managed-schema` for all schema definitions. If you want to create a core that contains `schema.xml` for manual handcrafting, do it as follows:

```
solr create -c corename -d sample_techproducts_configs
```

Summary

Good schema design is one of the fundamental steps in building a search engine that really works. If you know the structure of your data, schema design should always precede the indexing process. Though you may need to come back and tune the schema later as your search engine evolves, it's always good to get it right the first time.

Solr provides a set of fieldTypes that work for most cases, but we all have our unique challenges and that may require us to configure our own analysis chains. As you have seen, configuring a process to the chain is simple, as all Solr configurations are defined in XML files and you need to only add new elements and map them appropriately.

Some of the text analysis process is costly, both in terms of processing time and index size, so chains should be defined carefully. Also, whenever you make a change to the index-time processing for a field, reindexing is mandatory for the changes to reflect.

This chapter focused primarily on designing schema and text analysis. You looked at various analysis processes, their uses, and scenarios where they can be used. Going schemaless was covered in a separate section.

With this chapter, you are good to dive into the much awaited concepts of indexing and searching. The next chapter covers the indexing process, and then the following chapters take up searching along with advanced capabilities.

CHAPTER 5

■ ■ ■

Indexing Data

As you know, Solr creates an inverted index of the data you ingest, so the process of adding data to Solr is called *indexing*. Primarily what you do in Solr is index and search, and for data to be searchable, it must be indexed.

In Chapter 2, you indexed sample documents by using the Solr admin console. In this chapter, you will learn about the indexing process in depth and width. By *depth*, I mean getting a detailed understanding of the process. I refer to *width* in terms of the variety of decisions you need to make before indexing a document, such as the document format, indexing tool, the frequency of indexing, document preprocessing, and text analysis. The preceding chapter covered text analysis, so this chapter covers the other aspects.

You might be in a hurry to learn about the search process, as it is the ultimate goal of developing a search engine, and you might want to flick through this chapter. If you are not new to Solr, you can do this and come back to read in detail after getting the search process in place. But if you are working toward taking the system to production, the indexing process should not be overlooked. Indexing is not just a necessary prerequisite. You must remember that if you put garbage in, you will get garbage out.

The indexing process can be as simple as adding documents to make the contents searchable, but you should not limit your application to that. The full potential of Solr and other complementing technologies for data cleanup, enrichment, and metadata extraction should be utilized. You will learn about these approaches in this chapter. Additionally, Chapter 11 presents some advanced approaches for extracting the gold nuggets hidden in unstructured data. You can follow an iterative and incremental model to bring in these capabilities.

This chapter covers the following topics:

- Tools to index documents

- Indexing operations

- Indexing text documents such as XML, JSON, and CSV

- Indexing binary documents and extracting metadata

- Importing data from databases

- Preprocessing and document enrichment

- Indexing performance

- Writing a custom processor

- Understanding frequently occurring problems

Indexing Tools

Solr exposes a RESTful service over HTTP, so any REST client can search and index documents. All you need to know is the right endpoint and the applicable parameters. The client accessing the service could simply be your favorite browser, such as Chrome or Firefox, or even the Wget tool. The browser and Wget tool work well for evaluation and simple requests, but you generally need something more sophisticated.

The tool you choose depends on your indexing needs, data source, document format, and performance requirements. Solr supports a variety of document formats including XML and JSON, and some tools support a specific set of document formats or data sources. This section describes some frequently used indexing tools.

Post Script

Solr 5.0 introduced a bash script that can be executed in a *nix environment for indexing documents. This script can index documents in Solr's native format (the format specified and understood by Solr for XML and JSON), can index CSV documents, and can even perform simple web crawling. It also allows you to specify the directory path containing the documents. This script exists in the Solr distribution's `bin` directory, and you can find its usage details by running it with the `-help` option:

```
$ bin/post -help
```

The following is an example that indexes the `money.xml` file from the `example/exampledocs` directory to the `hellosolr` core:

```
$ bin/post -c hellosolr ../example/exampledocs/money.xml
```

SimplePostTool

If you are running a version earlier than Solr 5.0 or your platform is Windows, you need not worry. You can rely on the `SimplePostTool` bundle provided as `post.jar`, a Java executable file, in the `example/exampledocs` directory. The preceding `bin/post` script internally uses this JAR to provide convenient methods for indexing documents. You can find usage details by running the JAR as follows:

```
$ java -jar example/exampledocs/post.jar -h
```

Let's index the same document as before, using the SimplePostTool:

```
java -Dc=hellosolr -jar post.jar money.xml
```

In this example, we don't provide the relative path of `money.xml`, as `post.jar` exists in the same directory.

curl

Another powerful way of indexing documents is the `curl` utility. You will use curl throughout this book to index documents. Refer to the curl usage details at `http://curl.haxx.se/docs/manpage.html` or in *nix manual:

```
$ man curl
```

SolrJ Java Library

Solr provides a SolrJ Java client to access the server from your program. It provides methods to create documents, index them, form queries, perform searches, and iterate through the results. For indexing, if you are reading data from a primary datasource such as a content management system (CMS), you may prefer to use SolrJ. For importing data from a relational database, the Solr DataImportHandler contrib module makes a good starting point. However, because it is single-threaded, people do use SolrJ for writing custom import programs to process large volumes of data.

■ **Note**   Each release of Solr comes bundled with the SolrJ library, which is updated with new features provided by Solr. When using SolrJ, make sure you are using the matching version of the library as the server.

Other Libraries

Apart from SolrJ, other client libraries are available for Java. If your Java application uses the Spring Framework, you can even give Spring Data Solr a try. Client libraries are available for other languages also. Python has more than a dozen client libraries. You can refer to the Solr wiki, https://wiki.apache.org/solr/IntegratingSolr, for a complete list of client libraries.

Indexing Process

The indexing process can be simple if the data is structured and well formatted, but a bit complicated if it is unstructured and available in diverse formats and datasources. For example, indexing documents in a CSV file is just a matter of triggering an upload button or posting the text stream.

Solr supports multiple document formats including XML and JSON as input for indexing: you format the data in a structure specified by Solr or even random format and post it. The structured file you define will contain a set of documents, each specifying the fields and the content that should be indexed to that field. The field name in the input file should map to the field name defined in schema.xml.

Interestingly, you may have an XML document, but the structure and elements might be different from the native Solr format. For such a scenario, the DataImportHandler contrib module allows you to define the mapping between XML elements and Solr fields, and you can start the indexing process just by invoking the handler endpoint.

Also, the data can be available in any of the diverse data sources (for example, the local file system, database, or web page). The following steps will help you understand and develop the indexing process as per your indexing needs:

1. Text extraction: In this process, you extract the text for indexing. The text can be acquired, for example, by reading files, querying databases, crawling web pages, or reading RSS feeds. Extraction can be performed by your Java client application or Solr components. DataImportHandler is a contrib module that can be used for reading data from databases or XML files, for example. The Solr Cell framework, built on Apache Tika, can directly extract data from files in Office, Word, and PDF formats, as well as other proprietary formats.

2. Document preparation: The extracted text should be transformed into a Solr document for ingestion. The prepared document should adhere to the native format specified, for example, for XML or JSON. As a better alternative, you can use the SolrJ client to create a document for ingestion. If data is directly ingested using one of the Solr frameworks having support for automatic transformation, this step might not be required.

3. Post and commit: During this process, you post the document to the appropriate Solr endpoint with required parameters. Solr-provided extraction capabilities are performed based on the endpoint you invoke. You may optionally like to trigger a commit to persist the added documents immediately.

4. Document preprocessing: You might want to do cleanup, enrichment, or validation of text received by Solr. Solr provides a large number of UpdateRequestProcessor implementations for performing these tasks. It prebundles the processor implementation for common tasks such as deduplication and language detection, and allows you to write custom processors. You can even do the custom processing in the client program during document preparation, if you are not interested in writing Solr plug-ins.

5. Field analysis: Field analysis converts the input stream into terms. This step refers to the analysis chain of analyzers, tokenizers and token filters that are applied on the fieldType definition, which you read about in the previous chapter.

6. Index: The terms output from field analysis are finally indexed; the inverted index is created. These indexed terms are used for matching and ranking in search requests. After you trigger the post operation (mentioned in Step 3), the preprocessing and field analysis defined in Solr will be triggered automatically and documents will be indexed.

Figure 5-1 depicts the indexing steps. You can see that the data can be indexed directly or by using a client application.

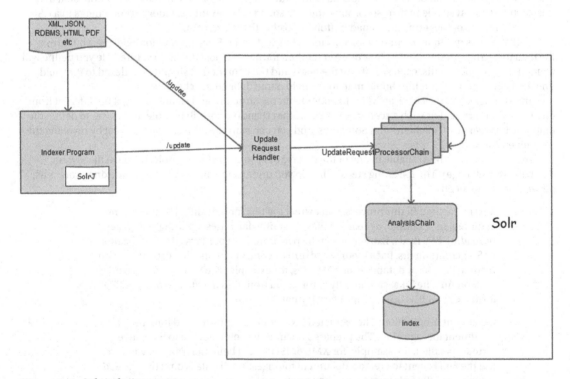

Figure 5-1. Solr indexing process

Now let's understand the index process and associated Solr components in bit more detail. Suppose you want to index an XML document. To index it, you make a request to the /update endpoint. If you go through solrconfig.xml, you will find that it is mapped to UpdateRequestHandler:

```
<requestHandler name="/update" class="solr.UpdateRequestHandler" />
```

Any request to /update is handled by UpdateRequestHandler. Similarly, other handlers are used for handling different types of content streams—for example, DataImportHandler for importing data from databases, custom XML, RSS, and atom feeds; ExtractingRequestHandler for extracting data from binary documents; and so on. Each endpoint is mapped to a specific handler, as /update is mapped to UpdateRequestHandler. You can even write your own handler by extending ContentStreamHandlerBase.

When you make a request to UpdateRequestHandler, you send the XML as a content stream, along with other parameters to process the request. Now, let's explore UpdateRequestHandler.

UpdateRequestHandler

UpdateRequestHandler supports indexing documents in XML, JSON, CSV, and javabin format. With each update request, you specify the content type. Based on this information, UpdateRequestHandler parses the document by calling the respective loader and then indexes it by invoking the processors registered in the update chain.

You can inform UpdateRequestHandler about the format of the document by providing the MIME Content-Type or by passing the request parameter update.contentType. If any of this information is not provided, the handler tries to identify the content type automatically. If it detects the content to be XML or a JSON document, it processes forward. Otherwise, it throws an exception. Based on the format of your document, you need to specify the corresponding content type, shown in Table 5-1.

Table 5-1. *Document Formats and Corresponding Content Type*

Document Format	Content Type	Features
XML	application/xml, text/xml	Accepts Solr-defined and arbitrary-format XML. Full-featured.
JSON	application/json, text/json	Accepts Solr-defined and arbitrary-format JSON. Full-featured. Comments not allowed.
CSV	application/csv, text/csv	Standard CSV format. Limited capability.
Javabin	application/javabin	Faster.

The response of the index operation is by default in same format as the content type of the document. If you want to get the response in a different format, you need to provide the response format by using the wt parameter.

UpdateRequestProcessorChain

Solr provides provisions to modify a document before it gets indexed. You can perform any processing on the text such as cleanup, enrichment, and validation. Solr allows you to modify the value of a field (for example, to set the default value, if missing), create a new field altogether (for example, to add the current timestamp), remove a field, or even filter the document from being indexed (for example, in the case of a duplicate document).

These operations are performed by UpdateRequestProcessorFactory instances, which can be chained together and configured in the update handler. Whenever an update request comes to the handler, it executes the chain, which runs all the configured processors and then indexes the document. Multiple chains can be defined in solrconfig.xml, but only one can be assigned to a handler for execution.

Apart from UpdateRequestProcessor, which is part of core Solr, some processors are also available as a contrib module, as for UIMA. You can even write your own processor implementation that will modify the document based on your custom requirements. The following is an example of how to register processors to the update handler:

```
<updateRequestProcessorChain name="mychain" default="true">
  <processor class="solr.TimestampUpdateProcessorFactory">
   <str name="fieldName">timestamp</str>
  </processor>
  <processor class="solr.CustomUpdateRequestProcessorFactory">
    <lst name="name">
      <str name="name1">value</str>
      <str name="name2">value</str>
    </lst>
  </processor>
  <processor class="solr.LogUpdateProcessorFactory" />
  <processor class="solr.RunUpdateProcessorFactory" />
 </updateRequestProcessorChain>
```

So what does this updateRequestProcessorChain do? This chain runs the registered processors in sequence. It runs TimestampUpdateProcessorFactory, which sets the current timestamp as the default value for the timestamp field. The output of this factory is input to CustomUpdateRequestProcessorFactory. Assuming this is your custom processor, it does some processing and updates the document based on the configuration. This is followed by LogUpdateProcessorFactory to update the log with update information. And what should always run in the end is RunUpdateProcessorFactory, as it finally updates the inverted index.

■ **Note** If RunUpdateProcessorFactory is not registered in your chain, no index update will happen. If it's not registered as the last component, the processors following it will have no effect.

To perform any preprocessing, the chain must be registered in the update handler. If you want to run the processing for each request, you can set it in solrconfig.xml as shown here:

```
<requestHandler name="/myupdate " class="solr.UpdateRequestHandler">
  <lst name="defaults">
    <str name="update.chain">mychain</str>
  </lst>
 </requestHandler>
```

You can also register the chain for a specific request by passing its name with the update.chain parameter, as follows:

```
$ curl http://localhost:8983/solr/hellosolr/update?update.chain=mychain
```

> ■ **Note** An extensive list of UpdateRequestProcessors provided by Solr can be found at the Solr-Start project, www.solr-start.com/info/update-request-processors/. You can also refer to the Solr Javadoc at http://lucene.apache.org/solr/5_3_1/solr-core/org/apache/solr/update/processor/ UpdateRequestProcessorFactory.html.

UpdateRequestProcessor vs. Analyzer/Tokenizer

In the previous chapter, you learned about analyzers and tokenizers. But if UpdateRequestProcessor does work similar to the index-time analyzer, you might be wondering why two features are needed. The next few paragraphs will bring out the key differences between them and explain why we need both.

The idea behind an analyzer is to modify the input stream to generate terms that are used for matching (such as lowercasing and stemming), as it provides finer control by maintaining position and offset information of tokens. It can be applied at both index and query time. UpdateRequestProcessors are implemented for preprocessing the document being indexed such as for cleanup, enriching information in new fields, and validation. It is applied only while indexing the document and plays no role at search time.

Before discussing the next difference, let's review how text is indexed and stored in Solr.

In schema.xml, you define a field as follows:

```
<field name="title" type="string" indexed="true" stored="true" />
```

In this field definition, indexed="true" means that an inverted index should be created for the field, and stored="true" means that the field text should be stored in the index literally, in a noninverted manner. Only the stored fields can be retrieved for display.

Getting back to the difference, an analyzer come into picture, after the document is submitted for indexing by RunUpdateProcessorFactory. It can transform only the text being indexed, and not the text being stored (the noninverted literal value remains unmodified). But an UpdateRequestProcessor receives the SolrInputDocument, and its modification applies to both indexed and stored text. If you put the same logic in both the components and index and retrieve some text, the analyzer's retrieved text will be unmodified while that of UpdateRequestProcessor will be modified. For example, if you write an algorithm to rate the popularity of a product based on the number of units sold, the analyzer will index the popularity for searching, executing function queries and getting range facets; but if you want to view the popularity (display it to the user), you will need to write UpdateRequestProcessor.

An analyzer is applied on a per field basis. It doesn't allow you to fetch data from one field and add it to another. Yes, to some degree you can achieve it by using copyField, but still the flexibility is limited. Also, analyzers cannot be applied on nontext primitive fields.

Indexing Operations

By now, you have a good understanding of document formats supported by Solr. In this section you will index documents in different formats. This section covers all the indexing operations for XML documents. For other formats, it gives you sufficient information to help you manage indexing.

XML Documents

In this section, you will learn how to add, delete, and update documents using Solr's native XML format. By Solr's *native format*, I mean the set of tags and attributes defined by Solr. To index documents using XML native format, you need to prepare the document in the format specified by Solr and post those documents to the server.

Any changes made to the index will be visible only after a commit has been triggered, which finalizes the operation. Let's have a look at each of the operations.

Add

You have already seen an example of adding documents to Solr in Chapter 2. The add command indexes the provided set of documents to Solr. As a reminder, each document can be compared to a tuple in your relational database. Here is a sample request to index an XML document:

```
$ curl http://localhost:8983/solr/hellosolr/update
-H "Content-Type: text/xml"
--data-binary '<add commitWithin="5000" overwrite="true">
  <doc>
    <field name="id">apl1001</field>
    <field name="product">iPad</field>
    <field name="model">nano</field>
    <field name="manufacturer">apple</field>
  </doc>
  <doc boost="2.0">
    <field name="id">apl1002</field>
    <field name="product">iPhone</field>
    <field name="model" boost="2.0">iPhone 6</field>
    <field name="manufacturer">apple</field>
    <field name="color">gold</field>
    <field name="color">silver</field>
  </doc>
</add>'
```

The following are the XML elements and attributes supported by Solr, to index documents using its native format.

- add: This root tag defines the operation of adding documents to Solr. It can constitute one or more documents to be added.

  - commitWithin: If you want to ensure that the commit is triggered automatically within a specified time, set the value of this attribute in milliseconds. Alternatively, you can invoke a commit as a request parameter.

  - overwrite: An optional attribute, by default set to true, overwrites the existing documents with the same uniqueKey. If you don't want the existing documents to be overwritten, set it to false, and those documents will be ignored.

- doc: This tag defines a Solr document and constitutes a set of fields.

  - boost: Use this optional attribute to give an index-time boost to the document.

- field: This defines a Solr field. For a multivalued field, add it to the document multiple times.

  - name: This mandatory attribute should correspond to a field name or dynamic field in schema.xml, unless you are running schemaless.

  - boost: This optional attribute gives an index-time boost to the field.

In this example, we have defined the `color` field twice for document ID `apl1002`. This is how you add value to a multivalued field. If this field is not defined as multivalued in `schema.xml`, Solr will throw an exception.

Update

What if you add a document that already exists? If `overwrite="true"` is specified, the document will be overwritten; otherwise, the new document will be ignored. The overwrite operation indexes a new document, deleting the old one. What if you want to update the value of a particular field and retain values of other fields, or you want to add a value to the existing values of a field?

Internally, Lucene has no provision to update a document. If you want to update the value of a field, you need to delete the document and add it back. If you add a document with only a specific field, the values of other fields will be deleted. To update a field, you need to get the value of all other fields either from Solr or your primary datasource, prepare a new document, and add it.

But don't worry; the Atomic Update feature of Solr takes away the pain of preparing documents by fetching the existing values. You need to do the following to perform an atomic update:

- In `schema.xml`, set all the fields as `stored="true"`, so that Solr can internally perform a fetch and prepare a new document. All the fields populated using `copyField` can remain unstored.

- In `solrconfig.xml`, register `<updateLog/>`. With this setting, the atomic update ensures that it gets the latest version of the indexed document.

- While indexing a document, pass an additional attribute, `update`. Its value can be any one of the following:

  - `set`: Sets the value of a field. If an older value exists, it will be overwritten. Set the value as `null` if you want to remove the existing value.

  - `add`: Adds a new value to the existing values for a field. The field should be multivalued.

  - `remove`: Removes the specified value from a field. The field should be multivalued.

  - `removeregex`: Removes all the values that match the specified regex pattern. The field should be multivalued.

  - `inc`: Increments the value of a numeric field by the value supplied. The field should be single valued and numeric.

The following example sets the value of the `product` field to `iPod` and adds the colors silver, gold, and pink to the index, for a document with the unique ID `apl1001`:

```
<add>
  <doc>
    <field name="id">apl1001</field>
    <field name="product" update="set">iPod</field>
    <field name="color" update="add">silver</field>
    <field name="color" update="add">gold</field>
    <field name="color" update="add">pink</field>
  </doc>
</add>
```

Delete

The delete command marks a document for deletion. On the next commit, these documents will be permanently removed from the index and will no longer be searchable. You can mark the documents for deletion either by specifying the unique ID of the documents or by specifying a query. The following are examples for deleting documents in Solr.

Delete by ID: deletes the documents with id apl1001 and apl1002

```
<delete>
  <id>apl1001</id>
  <id>apl1002</id>
</delete>
```

Delete by query: deletes all the documents that contain iPad as the product name

```
<delete>
  <query>product:iPad</query>
</delete>
```

Delete by ID and query combined: deletes the document with id apl1001 and all the products of type iPad

```
<delete>
  <id>apl1001</id>
  <query>product:iPad</query>
</delete>
```

Just as you can select all documents by using *:* at the time of searching, you can delete all the documents in the same way.

Delete all the documents in 'hellosolr' core

```
$ curl http://localhost:8983/solr/hellosolr/update
-H "Content-Type: text/xml"
--data-binary '<delete><query>*:*</query></delete>'
```

Commit

In SQL databases, you perform commit after updates. Similarly, Solr also requires a commit, and the changes are searchable only after the commit has been triggered on that core. You can perform a commit as follows:

```
$ curl http://localhost:8983/solr/hellosolr/update -H "Content-Type: text/xml"
--data-binary '<commit/>'
```

Also, you can trigger a commit by passing an additional commit parameter to the update handler:

```
$ curl http://localhost:8983/solr/hellosolr/update?commit=true
```

Solr supports two types of commits: hard and soft.

Hard Commit

A *hard commit* makes your data searchable and persists the changes to disk. The preceding commands trigger a hard commit. You can also configure `solrconfig.xml` to commit documents automatically after a specified duration (in milliseconds) or when a specified number of documents are added to the core.

Perform hard commit when 50,000 documents are added or every 5 minutes, whichever occurs earlier

```
<autoCommit>
  <maxDocs>50000</maxDocs>
  <maxTime>300000</maxTime>
</autoCommit>
```

Soft Commit

Because a hard commit persists the documents to secondary storage, the operation is costly. Solr 4.0 introduced the concept of a *soft commit*, which makes the added documents searchable instantly but relies on the hard commit for persistence. A soft commit helps you achieve near real-time searches but comes with a trade-off that if the system crashes before the next hard commit, the changes will be lost. You can configure the soft commit as follows:

Perform soft commit when 5,000 documents are added or every 5 seconds, whichever occurs earlier

```
<autoSoftCommit>
  <maxDocs>5000</maxDocs>
  <maxTime>5000</maxTime>
</autoSoftCommit>
```

You will generally prefer to perform soft commits more frequently, but ensure that they're not so frequent that the other commit starts before the first commit completes. You should perform hard commits less frequently, but the duration shouldn't be too high because a crash can lead to data loss. The values should be set adequately and will depend on your requirements.

Optimize

A Lucene index is composed of a smaller chunks called *segments*. In the process of adding a document, Solr creates new segments on each hard commit and merges them at times. When the number of segments increases, querying takes more time; performing merges speeds ups the query, but it is a costly operation that requires lots of disk swaps. Lucene merges the segments automatically based on the merge policy, but if you want to force-merge, you can call `optimize`. It performs a hard commit and then merges the segments into one. Because this is a costly operation, it should be performed less frequently (for example, as a nightly job).

```
$ curl http://localhost:8983/solr/hellosolr/update?optimize=true
$ curl http://localhost:8983/solr/hellosolr/update
-H "Content-Type: text/xml" --data-binary '<optimize/>'
```

Instead of calling optimize, you can consider setting the merge factor to a lower value in `solrconfig.xml`:

```
<mergeFactor>10</mergeFactor>
```

Rollback

Similar to databases, you can roll back the uncommitted changes:

```
$ curl http://localhost:8983/solr/hellosolr/update?rollback=true
$ curl http://localhost:8983/solr/hellosolr/update
-H "Content-Type: text/xml" --data-binary '<rollback/>'
```

JSON Documents

Solr enables you to index JSON documents in a Solr-specified structure as well as your custom structure. The process of indexing documents in a Solr-specified JSON structure is the same as the process described previously for XML documents. All you need to do is specify the content type as application/json or text/json and provide the JSON data.

Here we index the JSON document with the same data as in the preceding XML document:

```
$ curl http://localhost:8983/solr/hellosolr/update -H "Content-Type: application/json"
--data-binary '[
  {
    "id": "apl1001",
    "product": "iPad",
    "model":"nano",
    "manufacturer":"apple"
  },
  {
    "id": "apl1002",
    "product": "iPhone",
      "model": {
                "value": "iPhone 6",
                "boost": 2.0
      },
      "color": ["gold", "silver"]
  }
]'
```

Similarly, you can perform other operations such as a delete or commit, as shown here:

```
$ curl -X POST -H 'Content-Type: application/json' 'http://localhost:8983/solr/hellosolr/
update' --data-binary '
{
  "commit": {},
  "delete": { "query":"*:*" }
}'
```

If the JSON data is not in a Solr-specified style and follows an arbitrary structure, it can be indexed by passing additional mapping parameters with the update request. Refer to the Solr official document at https://cwiki.apache.org/confluence/display/solr/Uploading+Data+with+Index+Handlers for details of the additional parameters.

CSV Documents

If you have your data in CSV format, it is pretty simple to index. You don't need to adhere to a format specified by Solr, as the values are just separated by a comma. You can index a simple CSV file in two steps:

1. Map the values to Solr fields either by specifying comma-separated field names on the first line of the file or by specifying the comma separated names as the value of the `fieldnames` parameter in the request.

2. Set the content type as `text/csv` or `application/csv`. Alternatively, you can make a request without passing content-type information, if you call `/update/csv` handler instead of `/update`.

The following is a sample request to index `books.csv`, which comes along with the Solr bundle:

```
$ curl http://localhost:8983/solr/hellosolr/update/csv
--data-binary @books.csv -H 'Content-Type:text/plain'
```

The following are important parameters, which you can pass along with the request:

`separator`: If a comma is not your default separator, pass this additional parameter with the applicable separator.

`skip`: If you don't want to index all the fields in CSV, specify the comma-separated list of fields to skip.

`skipLines`: Specify the number of first lines you don't want to index.

`encapsulator`: It's quite common that text of a field contains a comma, which is also the default delimiter. You can specify an encapsulator for the file and surround the value with it. Also, you can specify a field-specific encapsulator.

`split`: For indexing data to a multivalued field, the `split` Boolean parameter is needed. Specify `split=true` to enable a split on all `multiValued` fields, and `f.<fieldname>.split=true` to apply a split on specific fields. Also, you need to provide the separator, which you can do using a field-specific separator.

The following is an almost full-fledged CSV request, which indexes the same data that we used for XML and JSON but in CSV format:

```
$ curl http://localhost:8983/solr/hellosolr/update?commit=true&split=true&f.color.
separator=,&f.color.encapsulator="
-H "Content-Type: text/xml"
--data-binary '
id,product,model,manufacturer,color
apl1001,iPad,nano,apple,
apl1002,iPhone,Person,iPhone 6,apple,"gold,silver"'
```

Index Rich Documents

If you have a business requirement for indexing books, periodicals, or journals it's highly likely that the documents are available in PDF or Word format. Solr provides a framework called Solr Cell (earlier known as the Content Extraction Library) that extracts text and metadata from files in binary format. This framework is exposed by a handler called `ExtractingRequestHandler`.

While indexing rich documents, you need to specify the MIME type. If the information is not provided, Solr will try to automatically detect the document type. It uses a Tika parser for document-type identification and extraction of content and metadata. The extracted content is added to the content field, and the metadata to fields defined according to specifications such as Dublin Core.

Apache Tika is a project focused on detection and extraction of metadata and text from over a thousand file types. The project home page at `https://tika.apache.org/` provides more details.

Following are the steps to index a PDF file:

1. Add dependencies to `lib` directives in `solrconfig.xml`:

```
<lib dir="../../../contrib/extraction/lib" regex=".*\.jar" />
<lib dir="../../../dist/" regex="solr-cell-\d.*\.jar" />
```

2. Configure the `ExtractionRequestHandler` in `solrconfig.xml`:

```
<requestHandler name="/update/extract"
class="org.apache.solr.handler.extraction.ExtractingRequestHandler">
  <lst name="defaults">
    <str name="lowernames">true</str>
    <str name="uprefix">others_</str>
    <str name="captureAttr">true</str>
    <str name="fmap.a">url</str>
    <str name="fmap.div">others_</str>
  </lst>
</requestHandler>
```

The following points describe the specified parameters:

`lowernames`: Setting this Boolean parameter to true, maps the field names to names with lowercase and underscores, if required. For example, "`Author-Name`" will be mapped to "`author_name`".

`uprefix`: The fields that are undefined in Solr are prefixed with the value specified here. You can define a dynamic field with the same pattern to handle the contents appropriately. The next step, demonstrates a dynamic field to ignore the undefined fields.

`captureAttr`: Setting this Boolean parameter to true will even index the values of attributes extracted from XHTML elements.

`fmap.<source_field>`: This parameter allows you to rename the field. The specified source field gets renamed to the value of the parameter. In this configuration, a field with name "a" will get renamed to "url", for example.

3. Define appropriate fields in `schema.xml`:

```
<field name="id" type="string" indexed="true" stored="true"
required="true"/>
<field name="content" type="string" indexed="true" stored="true"
multiValued="true"/>
<field name="author" type="string" indexed="true" stored="true"
multiValued="true"/>
<field name="title" type="text" indexed="true" stored="true"/>

<dynamicField name="others_*" type="ignored" />
```

4. Index the document:

```
$ curl 'http://localhost:8983/solr/hellosolr/update/extract?literal.
id=doc1&commit=true'
-F myfile=@example/exampledocs/solr-word.pdf
```

DataImportHandler

DataImportHandler is a contrib module that allows you to import data from varied sources. If RDBMS is your primary datastore or you need to import data from arbitrary XML, DataImportHandler is a good starting point. You can get everything in place, just with XML configurations.

For databases, you can import data from multiple tables by performing joins and flattening the result to index it as a Solr document. You can also nest queries to execute the sub-query for each row fetched by the parent query. Once a row is fetched, you can apply a transformer to modify the document before indexing it. DataImportHandler allows you to perform the following two types of updates:

Full import: A full import is like a full dump that extracts all the records from the table and indexes it.

Delta import: This performs an incremental update, which fetches only those documents that have been added/modified since the last import.

DataImportHandler is not limited to databases. With it, you can index documents in any of the following formats:

Arbitrary XML: Uses XSLT for transformation.

E-mail messages: Uses the JavaMail API.

Word/PDF documents: Uses Apache Tika. This is an alternative to indexing documents by using Solr Cell.

Import from RDBMS

Before proceeding any further, you need to understand the important elements of a data import:

dataSource: dataSource defines which source to read data from and how to connect.

entity: It's the entity that generates documents. For example, you can create an entity that reads each row from a table and creates a document.

processor: This extracts the content from a data source and adds it to the index after the transformation, if any. Default is SqlEntityProcessor, which works with relational databases. The entity element supports the processor attribute that allows you to specify the applicable processor name.

transformer: Allows you to transform the document (for example, split the data or strip the HTML).

Here are the steps to import data from the items table in HSQLDB:

1. Add dependencies to the `lib` directives in `solrconfig.xml`:

```
<lib dir="../../../dist/" regex="solr-dataimporthandler-.*\.jar" />
```

2. Define a handler in `solrconfig.xml`:

```
<requestHandler name="/dataimport"
class="org.apache.solr.handler.dataimport.DataImportHandler">
    <lst name="defaults">
      <str name="config">data-config.xml</str>
    </lst>
</requestHandler>
```

`data-config.xml` contains all the information regarding which source to read the data from, how to read the data, and how to map it with Solr fields and apply any transformation to the document, if needed.

3. Create `data-config.xml` in the `conf` directory:

```
<dataConfig>
<dataSource driver="org.hsqldb.jdbcDriver"
url="jdbc:hsqldb:example/example-DIH/hsqldb/ex"
user="sa" batchSize="10000"/>
    <document name="products">
        <entity name="item" query="select * from item">
            <field column="ID" name="id" />
            <field column="NAME" name="name" />
            <entity name="feature"
query="select description from feature where item_id='${item.ID}'">
                <field name="features" column="description" />
            </entity>
            <entity name="item_category"
query="select CATEGORY_ID from item_category where item_id='${item.ID}'">
                <entity name="category"
query="select description from category
where id = '${item_category.CATEGORY_ID}'">
                    <field column="description" name="cat" />
                </entity>
            </entity>
        </entity>
    </document>
</dataConfig>
```

4. Define the fields in `schema.xml`:

```
<field name="id" type="string" indexed="true" stored="true"
required="true"/>
<field name="name" type="string" indexed="true" stored="true"
multiValued="false"/>
<field name="features" type="string" indexed="true" stored="true"
```

```
multiValued="true"/>
<field name="description" type="string" indexed="true" stored="true"
multiValued="true"/>
```

5. Trigger the data import:

    ```
    $ curl http://localhost:8983/solr/hellosolr/dataimport?command=full-import
    ```

Document Preprocessing

As you already know, an UpdateRequestProcessor can modify or delete a field, create a new field, or even skip a document from being indexed. In this section, you will look at some of the important UpdateRequestProcessors that can be used for modifying and enriching documents. The section presents a problem or need and then explains the update processor you would use in that instance. To use a processor, it must be registered in the updateRequestProcessorChain, as shown here:

```
<updateRequestProcessorChain name="customchain">
  <!--
    Your custom processor goes here.
  -->
  <processor class="solr.LogUpdateProcessorFactory" />
  <processor class="solr.RunUpdateProcessorFactory" />
</updateRequestProcessorChain>
```

Remember that RunUpdateProcessorFactory should always be your last processor to be registered in the chain.

This updateRequestProcessorChain must be added to the update chain of the handler, or the update.chain parameter should be provided per request. You can add it to the request handler as shown here:

```
<requestHandler name="/update" class="solr.XmlUpdateRequestHandler" >
  <lst name="defaults">
    <str name="update.chain">customchain</str>
  </lst>
</requestHandler>
```

Language Detection

Multilingual data is common, and the language detection contrib module comes in handy here. It helps to detect the language of the input document and allows you to store the language information in a separate field. Solr provides two implementations of updateRequestProcessorChain:

- TikaLanguageIdentifierUpdateProcessorFactory uses Apache Tika.

- LangDetectLanguageIdentifierUpdateProcessorFactory uses the language-detection project available at https://github.com/shuyo/language-detection.

In this section, you will see how to configure language detection by using the LangDetect project. Here are the steps:

1. Add dependencies to the lib directives in solrconfig.xml:

```
<lib dir="../../../contrib/langid/lib" regex=".*\.jar" />
<lib dir="../../../dist/" regex="solr-langid-\d.*\.jar" />
```

2. Register the LangDetect processor to the UpdateRequestProcessorChain in solrconfig.xml:

```
<processor
class="org.apache.solr.update.processor.
LangDetectLanguageIdentifierUpdateProcessorFactory">
  <lst name="defaults">
    <str name="langid.fl">title,abstract,content</str>
    <str name="langid.langField">lang</str>
  </lst>
</processor>
```

3. Define the fields in schema.xml:

```
<field name="title" type="string" indexed="true" stored="true" />
<field name="abstract" type="string" indexed="true" stored="true" />
<field name="content" type="string" indexed="true" stored="true" />
<field name="lang" type="string" indexed="true" stored="true" />
```

Now, when you add this processor to the chain and register the chain to the update handler and index the documents, the lang field will be automatically populated based on the language detected in the title, abstract, and language fields of the document.

Generate Unique ID

If the documents being indexed don't have a unique ID and you want Solr to automatically assign one to each document, you need to configure the UUIDUpdateProcessorFactory in the update chain. Here are the steps:

1. Register the UUIDUpdateProcessorFactory to UpdateRequestProcessorChain in solrconfig.xml:

```
<processor class="solr.UUIDUpdateProcessorFactory">
  <str name="fieldName">id</str>
</processor>
```

2. Add the id field of type String or UUID to hold the unique IDs generated by the processor, in schema.xml:

```
<field name="id" type="string" indexed="true" stored="true" required="true"/>
```

3. Optionally, register the id field as a uniqueKey:

```
<uniqueKey>id</uniqueKey>
```

If the document being indexed doesn't contain an `id` value, a random ID will be generated and indexed to the field. If the document contains a value, then Solr won't generate it and will use the one provided with the document.

Deduplication

`UniqueKey` can ensure that no duplicate documents are indexed, but it identifies duplicates on the basis of values in a field. What if your requirement is much more complex? Let's say you have a system that contains information about features of a car; the make, model, and year create a unique entity, so you want to ensure that no two documents are indexed with the same make, model, and year information. You can use `SignatureUpdateProcessorFactory` to achieve this feature.

When you add a document, the `SignatureUpdateProcessor` generates a signature on the basis of a set of fields provided in the `fields` parameter, using the signature generation algorithm configured in `signatureClass` and writes it to `signatureField`. For exact duplicate detection, you can use `MD5Signature` or `Lookup3Signature` implementation and for fuzzy or near similar duplicate detection, you can use `TextProfileSignature`. The following are the steps for configuring deduplication:

1. Register the `SignatureUpdateProcessorFactory` to `UpdateRequestProcessorChain` in `solrconfig.xml`:

   ```
   <processor class="solr.processor.SignatureUpdateProcessorFactory">
     <bool name="enabled">true</bool>
     <str name="signatureField">signature</str>
     <bool name="overwriteDupes">false</bool>
     <str name="fields">make,model,year</str>
     <str name="signatureClass">solr.processor.Lookup3Signature</str>
   </processor>
   ```

2. Add a signature field in `schema.xml`:

   ```
   <field name="make" type="string" stored="true" indexed="true"
   multiValued="false"/>
   <field name="model" type="string" stored="true" indexed="true"
   multiValued="false"/>
   <field name="year" type="string" stored="true" indexed="true"
   multiValued="false"/>
   <field name="signature" type="string" stored="true" indexed="true"
   multiValued="false"/>
   ```

You can also add a signature to an existing field such as `id`, instead of adding it to a separate field signature.

Document Expiration

On many occasions, you'll want documents to be valid for only a limited time span. For example, for a flash sale on e-commerce web sites, you want a document to expire at a specific time or after a specified period. Solr provides `DocExpirationUpdateProcessorFactory` for automatically deleting the expired documents. The list of expired documents is identified on the basis of the expiration field configured. The automatic deletion is done by a background thread forked by the factory that wakes up every N seconds and performs a `deleteByQuery`.

This processor provides two functionalities. First, it computes the expiration date for a document and populates it to a field based on the time to live (TTL) value provided. The TTL indicates that the provided document has a limited life and is supposed to expire after N seconds. The processor allows you to provide TTL information in two ways:

> _ttl_ request parameter: The duration after which all the documents in the update request will expire.

> _ttl_ field: The value of this field provides the TTL for that document and overrides the _ttl_ request parameter.

To clarify any confusion, _ttl_ field is per document, and _ttl_ request parameter is global. Based on the TTL information provided, the processor computes the expiration date from NOW and stores it in the expiration field. The following steps configure the document expiration:

1. Register the DocExpirationUpdateProcessorFactory to UpdateRequestProcessorChain in solrconfig.xml:

```
<processor class="solr.processor.DocExpirationUpdateProcessorFactory">
  <str name="expirationFieldName">_expire_me_at_</str>
</processor>
```

This populates the _expire_me_at_ field of the document, with the expiry time based on the _ttl_ parameter. No automatic deletion will happen. You either need to delete the documents manually or you can hide the documents from Solr requests by adding a filter query such as fq=-_expire_me_at_:[* TO NOW].

Along with setting the expiration time, the second functionality this processor provides is automatic deletion of a document. If you want to delete the documents automatically, you can add autoDeletePeriodSeconds to the processor. This triggers the deletion thread every N seconds:

```
<processor class="solr.processor.DocExpirationUpdateProcessorFactory">
  <int name="autoDeletePeriodSeconds">300</int>
  <str name="expirationFieldName">_expire_at_</str>
</processor>
```

2. Add _expire_me_at_ field in schema.xml:

```
<field name="_expire_me_at_" type="string" stored="true" indexed="true"
multiValued="false"/>
```

3. Index the documents. When you index the documents, provide the TTL information for expiration to work:

```
$ curl -X POST -H 'Content-Type: application/xml' 'http://localhost:8983/solr/
hellosolr/update?commit=true
&_ttl_=+4HOURS' -d '<add>
<doc>
  <field name="id">1</field>
  <field name="title">This title will persist for 4 hours</field>
  <field name="abstract">This abstract will persist for 4 hours</field>
  <field name="content">This content will persist for 4 hours</field>
</doc>
```

```
<doc>
  <field name="id">2</field>
  <field name="title">This title will persist for 30 minutes</field>
  <field name="abstract">This abstract will persist for 30 minutes</field>
  <field name="content">This content will persist for 30 minutes</field>
  <field name="_ttl_">+30MINUTES</field>
</doc>
<add>'
```

Indexing Performance

Along with everything we have discussed, indexing performance is a crucial factor to look into. Enterprise searches need to deal with varying volumes of data, which can be broadly categorized as small, medium, or large. Along with the volume, another important factor is velocity. Some search engines require high-speed indexing, either to handle a large volume of data or to support near real-time search needs.

A deep dive into Solr indexing performance is beyond the scope of this book. This section provides a basic overview of indexing performance; Chapter 10 provides more detail.

Based on the data volume and indexing speed requirements, you need to make necessary design decisions and customizations, some of which are noted here:

Solr architecture: Based on the data volume, scalability needs, and fault-tolerance requirements, an appropriate architecture should be designed.

Indexing tool: Indexing tools have different capabilities; one provides simplicity, while another offers fast indexing. For example, DataImportHandler is single-threaded, and if you are indexing a lot of data, you might want to have a custom multithreaded implementation.

CPU and memory optimization: Many Solr features can be tuned for optimal CPU and memory utilization. The solrconfig.xml file also provides configurations to customize the utilization of resources.

Table 5-2 provides information on Solr architecture and the indexing tools that can be considered based on data volume.

***Table 5-2.** Data Volume Decisions*

Data Volume	Solr Architecture	Indexing Tool
Small	Stand-alone Replicated	SimplePostTool DataImportHandler
Medium	Sharded and replicated SolrCloud	SolrJ
Large	SolrCloud	SolrJ

The following are some measures you can take to optimize indexing performance:

- Perform batch writes and find the optimal batch size based on available resources.

- Store only the fields you really need to be stored.

- Index only the fields that really need to be searchable.

- Avoid costly preprocessing and text analysis, if possible.

- Avoid frequent hard commits.

Custom Components

Solr provides out-of-the-box implementations for most of the common problems and important use cases, for each of its components such as RequestHandler and UpdateRequestProcessor. In this chapter, you saw implementations of RequestHandler for indexing XML, importing from databases, and extracting from PDF files; and implementations of UpdateRequestProcessor for needs such as generating a unique ID and deduplication. But you might have a requirement for a feature not provided by Solr or you might want to write a custom implementation. For such scenarios, Solr allows you to develop custom components by extending the existing base classes and plugging them into Solr.

In this section, you will learn to extend UpdateRequestProcessor and plug in a custom logic.

Custom UpdateRequestProcessor

Until now, you have used UpdateRequestProcessors provided by Solr or as a contrib module. Solr also enables you to write your own UpdateRequestProcessor and chain it to the updateRequestProcessorChain. Here are the steps for writing a custom processor:

1. Extend the UpdateRequestProcessorFactory.

2. Override the getInstance() method to create an instance of CustomUpdateProcessor. If you want to do some initialization on core load, you can override the init() method.

3. Your CustomUpdateProcessor should extend the abstract class UpdateRequestProcessor.

4. Override the processAdd() method, to hook in your code to process the document being indexed. This is the method where all the action happens. Its argument AddUpdateCommand has the getSolrInputDocument() method, which contains a reference to the SolrInputDocument.

5. Get the values from the fields in SolrInputDocument, do your processing, update or delete the value of those fields, or add the result to a new field altogether.

6. super.processAdd() should always be the last statement of the method.

The following is an example custom update processor, which adds the popular field and sets its value to true, if the download count of a document is more than 1 million. This requires the following changes:

1. Write your custom code in Java:

Custom implementation of UpdateRequestProcessorFactory

```
package com.apress.solr.pa.chapter05.processor;

import java.io.IOException;

import org.apache.solr.common.SolrInputDocument;
import org.apache.solr.common.util.NamedList;
import org.apache.solr.request.SolrQueryRequest;
```

```
import org.apache.solr.response.SolrQueryResponse;
import org.apache.solr.update.AddUpdateCommand;
import org.apache.solr.update.processor.UpdateRequestProcessor;
import org.apache.solr.update.processor.UpdateRequestProcessorFactory;

public class CustomUpdateProcessorFactory extends UpdateRequestProcessorFactory
{

/**
 * Initialize your factory.
 * This method is not mandatory.
 */
public void init(NamedList args) {
        super.init(args);
}

@Override
public UpdateRequestProcessor getInstance(SolrQueryRequest req,
SolrQueryResponse rsp, UpdateRequestProcessor nxt)
  {
    return new CustomUpdateProcessor(nxt);
  }
}

class CustomUpdateProcessor extends UpdateRequestProcessor
{
  public CustomUpdateProcessor ( UpdateRequestProcessor nxt) {
    super( nxt );
  }

  @Override
  public void processAdd(AddUpdateCommand cmd) throws IOException {
    SolrInputDocument doc = cmd.getSolrInputDocument();

    Object obj = doc.getFieldValue( "downloadcount" );
    if( obj != null ) {
      int dc = Integer.parseInt( String.valueOf(obj) );
      if( dc > 1000000 ) {
        doc.setField("popular", true);
      }
    }

    // you must make this call
    super.processAdd(cmd);
  }
}
```

2. Add the executable JAR of the program to lib and register the processor in solrconfig.xml:

```
<lib dir="../lib" regex="solr-practical-approach-*.jar" />

<requestHandler name="/update" class="solr.UpdateRequestHandler">
  <lst name="defaults">
    <str name="update.chain">customprocessor</str>
  </lst>
</requestHandler>

<updateRequestProcessorChain name="customprocessor">
  <processor class="com.apress.solr.pa.chapter05.processor.
CustomUpdateProcessorFactory" />
  <processor class="solr.LogUpdateProcessorFactory" />
  <processor class="solr.RunUpdateProcessorFactory" />
</updateRequestProcessorChain>
```

3. Add the required field to schema.xml:

```
<field name="id" type="string" indexed="true" stored="true" required="true"/>
<field name="downloadcount" type="int" indexed="true" stored="true" />
<field name="popular" type="boolean" indexed="true" stored="true"
                                                  default="false" />
```

4. Index documents:

```
$ curl -X POST -H 'Content-Type: application/xml'
'http://localhost:8983/solr/apress/update?commit=true' -d '<add>
<doc>
   <field name="id">123</field>
   <field name="downloadcount">1200000</field>
</doc>
</add>'
```

When you index this document, the value true will automatically be indexed and stored in the popular field.

Frequently Occurring Problems

This section explores the common problems encountered while indexing documents.

Copying Multiple Fields to a Single-Valued Field

While indexing a document, ensure that you don't add multiple fields to a single-valued field. This will throw an exception. For example, if you try to index the following document, which contains multiple values for the text field and is defined as multiValued="false" in schema.xml, Solr will throw an exception. So you either need to set the text field to multiValued="true" or provide only one text element for each document.

schema.xml:

```
<field name="text" type="string" indexed="true" stored="true" multiValued="false"/>
```

XML document:

```
<add>
  <doc>
    <field name="id">1</field>
    <field name="text">Red Wine</field>
    <field name="text">White Wine</field>
  </doc>
</add>
```

Document Is Missing Mandatory uniqueKey Field

If you have defined UniqueKey in schema.xml, providing a value for that field is mandatory. If the document being indexed doesn't contain that field, Solr will throw the following exception:

```
Document is missing mandatory uniqueKey field: <field>
```

If your use case doesn't require a unique key, provide an additional attribute to the uniqueKey element in schema.xml:

```
<uniqueKey required="false">id</uniqueKey>
```

Data Not Indexed

If your indexing process doesn't index the data, the best place to check is the log files for errors and exceptions. If no information is present in the log file, and if you have modified the processor chain, the probable reason is that you have missed something while chaining the processors. Ensure that RunUpdateProcessorFactory is the last processor in the chain. If you have written your custom processor, check that it passes the reference to the next processor in the chain.

Indexing Is Slow

Indexing can be slow for many reasons. The following are factors that can improve indexing performance, enabling you to tune your setup accordingly:

> *Memory*: If the memory allocated to the JVM is low, garbage collection will be called more frequently and indexing will be slow.

> *Indexed fields*: The number of indexed field affects the index size, memory requirements, and merge time. Index only the fields that you want to be searchable.

> *Merge factor*: Merging segments is an expensive operation. The higher the merge factor, the faster the indexing.

> *Commit frequency*: The less frequently you commit, the faster indexing will be.

> *Batch size*: The more documents you index in each request, the faster indexing will be.

Remember, each of these factors has trade-offs. Consider the memory and search requirements of your system to come up with optimal settings for your indexing process.

OutOfMemoryError—Java Heap Space

Chapter 2 introduced OutOfMemoryError, but I want to discuss it again because the indexing task is memory intensive, and if not properly planned, you can get an exception. When you index documents, Solr fits them all into memory, so the document size matters. To avoid this error, you can increase the memory allocated to the JVM. Another solution is to index documents in smaller chunks. If you are using DataImportHandler, it provides the batchSize attribute to fetch data in batches and reduce memory usage.

Another important factor to consider is commit time. Solr keeps all the documents indexed since the last commit into heap memory and releases it on commit. To fix OutOfMemoryError, you can change the frequency of autoCommit to trigger at a shorter duration or on the addition of fewer documents, in solrconfig.xml, as shown here:

```
<autoCommit>
  <maxDocs>100000</maxDocs>
  <maxTime>60000</maxTime>
</autoCommit>

<autoSoftCommit>
  <maxDocs>5000</maxDocs>
  <maxTime>5000</maxTime>
</autoSoftCommit>
```

Summary

In this chapter, you learned how to index documents. You saw that Solr supports a variety of input formats including XML and JSON, and a variety of input sources including file systems and databases. To index data, you need some sort of tool to do the indexing. You learned about the tools bundled with Solr, the utilities provided by your operating system, and other libraries available for indexing documents.

We are not always lucky enough to have our data properly formatted and structured. Solr enables you to preprocess and enrich your documents before they get indexed. It provides a set of processors that can be used to transform the document being indexed. If the bundled or contributed processors don't fit your needs, you can write your own processor and add it to the chain. You learned to chain processes and to write a custom processor.

After your documents are indexed, they are ready for search queries. In the next chapter, you will learn what you have been waiting for: how to search documents in Solr.

CHAPTER 6

■ ■ ■

Searching Data

All the previous chapters have been a stepping stone to this chapter. By now, you know the basics of Solr, configuring the core, defining a schema, and indexing documents. After your documents are indexed successfully, you are ready to search for results.

Solr offers a wide range of search capabilities such as querying, faceting, hit-highlighting, spell-checking, suggestions, and autocompletion. This chapter presents the search process, followed by an overview of the primary components. Then it gets into the details of querying for results. This chapter covers the following topics:

- Prerequisites
- Search process
- Search components
- Types of queries
- Query parsers
- JSON Request API
- Custom SearchComponent
- Frequently asked questions

Search Basics

In the previous chapter, you looked at tools for indexing documents. The same tools can be used for searching results. You can also execute your query from a browser or any GET tool such as Wget.

For analysis and development, the Solr admin console is the best place to run your query, as it provides a rich GUI and comes in handy even if you don't remember the URL and request parameters. For a standard set of features, the console provides relevant text boxes; and relevant new boxes load automatically based on the feature you choose. If there is no text box for your request parameters, you can supply the key-value pair in the Raw Query Parameters text box. In this text box, each pair should be delimited by an ampersand (&), and the rules of standard HTTP request parameters apply.

The following is a sample user query: the request is sent to the /select endpoint of the hellosolr core with the q parameter, which contains the user query *solr search engine*:

```
$ curl http://localhost:8983/solr/hellosolr/select?q=solr search engine
```

For those who are new to Solr and who want to compare querying in Solr with querying in SQL databases, the mapping is as follows. Remember, the results returned by SQL and Solr can be different.

- *SQL query:*

```
select album,title,artist
        from hellosolr
        where album in ["solr","search","engine"]
        order by album DESC limit 20,10;
```

- *Solr query:*

```
$ curl http://localhost:8983/solr/hellosolr/select?q=solr search engine
&fl=album,title,artist&start=20&rows=10&sort=album desc
```

Prerequisites

Solr search capabilities and behavior depend a lot on the field properties, which are based on the field definitions in `schema.xml`. You can verify the field properties in `schema.xml` itself or in the Schema Browser in the Solr admin UI. To search fields and display matching documents, the following are some prerequisites:

- The searchable fields (the fields on which you query) should be indexed. This requires you to specify the `indexed="true"` attribute in the field definition in `schema.xml`. Here is a sample field definition with the `indexed` attribute marked in bold:

  ```
  <field name="name" type="text_general" indexed="true" stored="true"/>
  ```

- The fields to be retrieved as part of a Solr response (the fields in the `fl` parameter) should be stored. This requires you to specify the `stored="true"` attribute in the field definition in `schema.xml`. Here is a sample field definition with the `stored` attribute marked in bold:

  ```
  <field name="name" type="text_general" indexed="true" stored="true"/>
  ```

Chapter 4 provides more details on field definitions and how attributes affect search behavior.

Solr Search Process

This section presents the underlying querying process with respect to the `/select` endpoint, which is the most frequently used and the default endpoint in the Solr admin console. When you make a request to `/select`, it gets processed by `SearchHandler`, which is the primary request handler for querying documents. If you go through `solrconfig.xml`, you will find this handler defined and mapped to `/select`, as shown here:

```
<requestHandler name="/select" class="solr.SearchHandler">
  <!-- default values for query parameters can be specified, these
     will be overridden by parameters in the request -->
  <lst name="defaults">
    <str name="echoParams">explicit</str>
    <int name="rows">10</int>
  </lst>
</requestHandler>
```

The SearchHandler executes a chain of SearchComponents to process the search request. QueryComponent, the SearchComponent responsible for addressing search queries, executes the configured QueryParser, which parses the raw query to translate it into a format that Solr understands. The parsed query is used by SolrIndexSearcher for matching indexed documents. The matched documents are formatted by ResponseWriter on the basis of the wt request parameter, and then the user finally gets the response. Figure 6-1 depicts how the search query flows through various components to retrieve the matching documents.

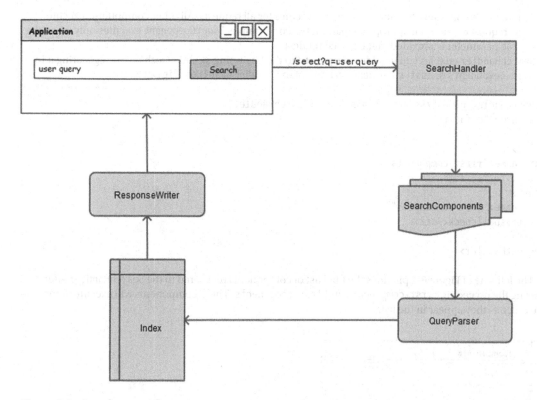

Figure 6-1. *Search request flow*

SearchHandler

SearchHandler is the controller responsible for handling search requests. The handler declares a chain of components and hands over the processing of requests to them. The components execute in the order they are registered in the chain. Each component in the chain represents a search feature such as querying or faceting.

Registered Components

The following are components that are by default registered in SearchHandler:

- QueryComponent
- FacetComponent

- MoreLikeThisComponent

- HighlightComponent

- StatsComponent

- DebugComponent

- ExpandComponent

Among these components, QueryComponent executes for all requests. All other components execute only if the request contains an appropriate parameter. For example, FacetComponent executes only when the facet=true parameter is provided in the search request.

SearchHandler enables you to add a component to the beginning or end of a chain, by registering it in the first-components or last-components section of the handler in solrconfig.xml:

```
<requestHandler name="/select" class="solr.SearchHandler">
  <lst name="defaults">
    ..
  </lst>
  <arr name="first-components">
    <str>terms</str>
  </arr>
  <arr name="last-components">
    <str>spellcheck</str>
  </arr>
</requestHandler>
```

The left side of Figure 6-2 provides the final list of components registered to the SearchHandler after declaring the preceding first-components and last-components. These components will execute in the same order as they appear in the list.

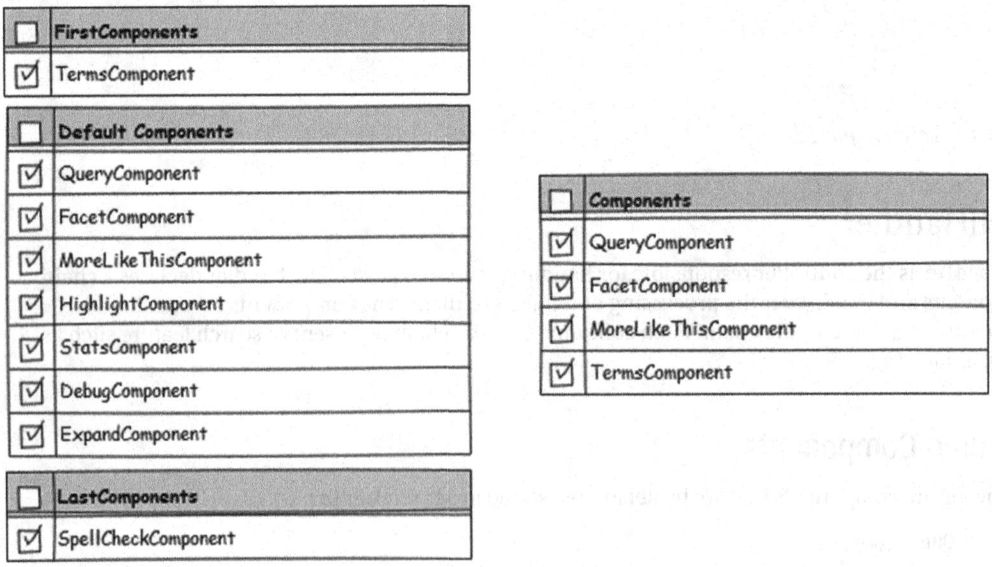

☐ FirstComponents
☑ TermsComponent

☐ Default Components
☑ QueryComponent
☑ FacetComponent
☑ MoreLikeThisComponent
☑ HighlightComponent
☑ StatsComponent
☑ DebugComponent
☑ ExpandComponent

☐ LastComponents
☑ SpellCheckComponent

☐ Components
☑ QueryComponent
☑ FacetComponent
☑ MoreLikeThisComponent
☑ TermsComponent

Figure 6-2. *Chain of SearchComponents*

You can override the default components and execute only the components you desire by registering them in the components section. For example, if you want to execute only the QueryComponent, FacetComponent, MoreLikeThisComponent, and TermsComponent, you can register them in the components section as shown next. The chain of components will look like the table on the right side of Figure 6-2.

```
<arr name="components">
  <str>query</str>
  <str>facet</str>
  <str>mlt</str>
  <str>terms</str>
</arr>
```

You are not allowed to register first-components and last-components along with the components section, and such an attempt will throw SolrException:

```
SolrException: First/Last components only valid if you do not declare 'components'
```

The component name that you register to components, first-components, or last-components must be defined in solrconfig.xml for Solr to map it to the corresponding executable Java class. For example, if you register terms as a component in SearchHandler, solrconfig.xml should have the following definition:

```
<searchComponent name="terms" class="solr.TermsComponent"/>
```

■ **Note**   If using the first-components or last-components section, the DebugComponent is designed to always occur last. If this is not desired, you must explicitly declare all the components in the components section.

Declare Parameters

SearchHandler enables you to control the values of request parameters by specifying the parameters within various lists, based on desired manipulation of the user provided request parameters. It allows you to declare parameters in three ways.

defaults

The defaults value specifies the list of parameters and their default values. This value will be overridden if the user request contains the same parameter. In the following example, rows is declared in the default list; if the user request doesn't contain this parameter, by default 10 documents will be returned in the response.

```
<lst name="defaults">
  <int name="rows">10</int>
</lst>
```

appends

The appends value specifies the list of parameters that should be appended to all search requests instead of being overridden, as in the case of the defaults section. For the following example, if the user request is q=bob marley, the appends section will add fq=genre:reggae to the request. It even appends if the same parameter is specified in the defaults section.

```
<lst name="appends">
  <int name="fq">genre:reggae</int>
</lst>
```

invariants

The invariants value specifies the list of parameters whose values are mandatorily applied and cannot be overridden by any other definition of the parameter, such as in the user query request or defaults section. This is a good place to configure features whose behavior you don't want to let the user control. The following is an example definition of request parameters in invariants section.

```
<lst name="invariants">
  <str name="fq">country:usa<str>
 </lst>
```

SearchComponent

SearchComponent is an abstract Java class, and each implementation of this class represents a search feature. The implementing class should be declared in solrconfig.xml and then registered in the handler. Here is the configuration of TermsComponent, a component to access indexed terms, in solrconfig.xml:

```
<searchComponent name="terms" class="solr.TermsComponent"/>

<requestHandler name="/terms" class="solr.SearchHandler" startup="lazy">
 <lst name="defaults">
  <bool name="terms">true</bool>
  <bool name="distrib">false</bool>
</lst>
<arr name="components">
  <str>terms</str>
</arr>
```

In this example, TermsComponent is registered in the components section, so no other component such as query or facet will be registered by default.

Table 6-1 provides key information about the primary components provided by Solr. In the table, the Name column signifies the default name of the components, and you can change it. The Default column lists the components that are by default configured in SearchHandler. To use a component that is not the default, you need to register it to an existing handler or configure a new handler and register it to that.

Table 6-1. *Solr Primary Components*

Component	Name	Default	Description
QueryComponent	query	True	Processes the query parameters to retrieve the relevant documents.
FacetComponent	facet	True	Generates facets, the aggregation that generally appears on the left of many pages.
MoreLikeThisComponent	mlt	True	Queries for documents similar to the resulting document.
HighlightComponent	highlight	True	Highlights the query terms in the response.
StatsComponent	stats	True	Gets statistical information about the values in the field.
DebugComponent	debug	True	Gets the debug information such as parsed query or document score explanation.
TermsComponent	terms	False	Finds the indexed term and its count. Useful for features like autocompletion.
TermVectorComponent	tvComponent	False	Gets additional information about matching documents.
SpellCheckComponent	spellcheck	False	Gets terms similar to the query term. Useful for features like spell-correction and did-you-mean.
QueryElevationComponent	elevation	False	Configures the top results for the query. Ideal for campaigns, and promotional and paid searches.
SuggestComponent	suggest	False	Suggests terms similar to the query term. Useful for building an autosuggest feature.

For each incoming request, a SearchComponent executes in two phases: prepare and process. The SearchHandler executes all the prepare methods in the order they appear in the chain and then executes all the process methods. The prepare method does the initialization for the request, and the process method does the actual processing. All the prepare methods are guaranteed to execute before any process method.

You will learn about some of these important components in detail in Chapters 7 and 9.

QueryParser

QueryParser parses the user query to convert it into a format understood by Solr. QueryComponent invokes an appropriate parser based on the defType request parameter. The same query can fetch different results for a different query parser, as each parser interprets the user query differently. Some of the query parsers supported by Solr are the standard, DisMax, and eDisMax query parsers. You will learn more about QueryParser later in this chapter.

QueryResponseWriter

By default, Solr returns responses to queries in XML format. To get a response in another supported format, the wt parameter can be specified in the request or configured in the handler. The other supported formats are JSON, CSV, XSLT, javabin, Velocity, Python, PHP, and Ruby.

A javabin response returns a Java object that can be consumed by Java clients. It's the preferred response format for requests using the SolrJ client. Similarly, Python, PHP, and Ruby formats can be directly consumed by clients available for those languages. Velocity is another interesting response format that's supported, which allows you to transform a response into web page by using the Apache Velocity templating engine.

Solr 5.3.0 supports a new *smile* format, a binary format that can be used by non-Java languages for efficient responses. Refer to `http://wiki.fasterxml.com/SmileFormat` to learn about this format.

Solr Query

You have already done some querying and know that you send a query request by using the q parameter. But there is more to it. In this section, you will look at query syntax, used to control the behavior of document matching and ranking. Then you will look at various parsers.

Your query sent with the q parameter is checked for syntax and parsed by the query parser. The query is tokenized during the analysis phase of the field, and the generated tokens are matched against the index and ranked on the basis of a scoring algorithm.

Figure 6-3 depicts how the user query is processed to search for relevant results. This figure provides the flow for search requests for retrieving relevant documents and doesn't cover components such as SearchHandler. Refer to Figure 6-1 for the broader view of the flow, which applies to any search feature such as faceting and suggestions, and not specifically to retrieving documents.

The example in Figure 6-3 depicts the search flow for the user query *kills the mockingbird*. Chapter 4 used this example in covering field analysis. I intentionally used this partially matching query to give you an understanding of matching in real scenarios. Also, let's assume that the handler is configured to use ExtendedDismaxQParser for query parsing, which allows you to perform a free text search similar to that in Google.

Here are the steps performed by Solr as depicted in Figure 6-3:

1. The user-provided query is passed to the query parser. The purpose of the query parser is to parse the user query and convert it into a format that Lucene understands.

2. The query parser sends the query to appropriate analyzers to break the input text into terms. In this example, the analyzer for the title and artist fields are invoked, which is based on the qf parameter provided in the request.

3. The query parser returns the Query object, which is provided to SolrIndexSearcher for retrieving the matching documents. The Query object contains the parsed query, which you can see if you execute the search request in debug mode (by providing the additional request parameter debug="true").

4. SolrIndexSearcher does lots of processing and invokes all the required low-level APIs such as for matching and ranking the documents. It also performs several other tasks such as caching.

5. SolrIndexSearcher returns the TopDocs object, which is used to prepare the response to send it back to the application.

All the tasks specified in Figure 6-3 (and explained in the preceding steps) are coordinated by the QueryComponent class, which is a SearchComponent responsible for executing the search requests.

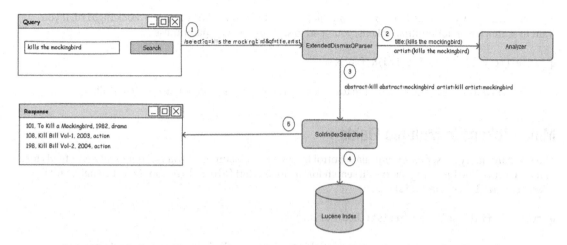

Figure 6-3. *Search request processing*

Default Query

In Solr, when we say *query*, by default we mean matching on the basis of terms. The terms are the smallest unit for matching. A term can be composed of a word, subsequent words, or a portion of a word. Suppose, you want to match parts of words, you can create smaller terms by using N-grams, which create tokens of N characters in the word. This section describes how you query.

Query a Default Field

When you specify only the query string along with the q parameter, you are querying the default field for results:

```
q=to kill a mockingbird
```

You can specify the default field by using the df parameter. In the following example, Solr will perform a query on the field album:

```
q=to kill a mockingbird&df=album
```

Query a Specified Field

The standard syntax for querying a specific field uses a field name followed by a colon and value, as shown here:

```
title:mockingbird
```

This will search for the term mockingbird in the title field.
Now, what if your query contains multiple tokens and you specify it as follows:

```
q=title:to kill a mockingbird&df=album
```

This will query the title field for to, and the album field for the tokens catch a mockingbird. If you want to search a field for multiple tokens, you need to surround it with parentheses:

```
q=title:(to kill a mockingbird)&df=album
```

This will query the title field for the tokens, and the album field will not be queried at all.

Match Tokens in Multiple Fields

The standard query parser offers granular control for querying documents. You can query different fields for different terms. The following query will search for the tokens buffalo soldier on the title field, and the tokens bob marley on the artist field:

```
q=title:(buffalo soldier) artist:(bob marley)
```

The default operator applied between the fields and tokens is OR. Solr supports a set of operators that allows you to apply Boolean logic to queries for specifying conditions for matching documents. The preceding query can also be expressed by explicitly specifying the operator:

```
q=title:(buffalo OR soldier) OR artist:(bob OR marley)
```

Hence, both of the preceding queries will retrieve all the documents that contain any of those terms.

Query Operators

The following are operators supported by query parsers:

> OR: Union is performed and a document will match if any of the clause is satisfied.

> AND: Association is performed and a document will match only if both the clauses are satisfied.

> NOT: Operator to exclude documents containing the clause.

> +/-: Operators to mandate the occurrence of terms. + ensures that documents containing the token must exist, and - ensures that documents containing the token must not exist.

Please note that AND/OR/NOT are case sensitive in the standard query parser. Hence the query bob and marley is not the same as bob AND marley. The first query will search for documents that contain any of the tokens bob, and, or marley. The second query will search for documents that contain both the tokens bob and marley.

Also, you can format your query in multiple ways. For example, q=(Bob AND marley) and q=(+bob +marley) form the same query.

Phrase Query

The preceding query matches all the documents in which the terms exist anywhere in the stream. If you want to find documents with consecutive terms, you need to perform a phrase search. A *phrase search* requires the query to be specified within double quotes. For example, q="bob marley" is a phrase query.

Proximity Query

A *proximity query* matches terms that appear in proximity to one another. You can view it as a liberal phrase query, which considers nearby terms. A proximity query requires the phrase query to be followed by the tilde (~) operator and a numeric distance for identifying the terms in proximity.

To help you understand all these concepts, consider the following example index that contains four documents and supports case insensitive matching.

Index
```
doc1: While Bob took the initial lead in race Marley finally won it.
doc2: Bob Marley was a legendary Jamaican reggae singer.
doc3: Jamaican singer Bob Marley has influenced many singers across the world.
doc4: Bob is a renowned rugby player.
```

Query
```
q=bob marley \\ Default operator OR. All 4 documents match
q=(bob AND marley) \\ AND operator. Both the terms must exist. First 3 documents match
q="bob marley" \\ Phrase query. doc2 and doc3 matches
q="jamaican singer" \\ Phrase query. Only doc3 matches
q="jamaican singer"~1 \\ Proximity query. Both doc2 and doc3 match
q="singer jamaican"~1 \\ Proximity query. Only doc3 matches
q="jamaican singer"~3 \\ Proximity query. Both doc2 and doc3 match
```

Specifying the numeric value 1 in the proximity query q="jamaican singer"~1 matches doc2 and doc3 because moving one term in doc2's Jamaican reggae singer sequence would form the phrase. But in the query q="singer jamaican"~1, only doc3 matches, as singer precedes jamaican and would require more movement to match doc2's phrase. As you see in the last example, the numeric value 3 in the query will make it match both doc2 and doc3.

Fuzzy Query

Along with matching terms exactly, if you want similar terms to match, you can use a *fuzzy query*. A fuzzy query is based on the Damerau-Levenshtein Distance or Edit Distance algorithm, which identifies the minimum number of edits required to convert one token to another. To use it, the standard query parser expects a tilde (~) symbol after the term, optionally followed by a numeric value. The numeric value can be in the range of 0 to 2. The default value 2 matches the highest number of edits, and value 0 means no edit and is the same as a term query. The score of a fuzzy query is based on the number of edits: 0 edits means the highest score (because it's least lenient), and 2 edits means the lowest score (because it's most lenient). Here is the syntax for a fuzzy query:

Syntax
```
q=<field>:<term>~
q=<field>:<term>~N // N specifies the edit distance
```

Example
```
q=title:mockingbird~2
q=title:mockingbird~     // effect is same as above
q=title:mockingbird~1.5 // invalid
```

Earlier, Solr allowed specifying N as a float value in the range of 0.0 to 1.0, which was converted to an appropriate edit distance. In release 4.0, a more straightforward approach of specifying an integer value of 0, 1 or 2 was introduced, where indicates N insertions, deletions, or substitutions. Solr doesn't allow a fractional edit distance and will respond with the following error if your query contains one:

```
"error": {
    "msg": "org.apache.solr.search.SyntaxError: Fractional edit distances are not allowed!",
    "code": 400
  }
```

A fuzzy query works as a good solution for searching text that is prone to spelling mistakes (such as for tweets, SMS, or mobile applications), where stemming and phonetic techniques are not enough.

The tilde in a fuzzy query is not to be confused with that in a proximity query. In a proximity query, the tilde is applied after the quotation mark (for example, q="jamaican singer"~1). A fuzzy query has no quotation mark, and the tilde is applied after the token (for example, q=bob~1 marley~1).

Wildcard Query

The Solr standard query parser supports wildcard searches for single-term queries. You can specify the wildcard character ?, which matches exactly one character, or *, which matches zero or more characters. They cannot be applied to numeric or date fields. The following is a sample wildcard query:

```
q=title:(bob* OR mar?ey) OR album:(*bird)
```

A classic example of a wildcard query is *:*, which matches all terms in all fields and retrieves all the documents in the corpus. Note that you cannot use a wildcard on field names to search for a term or terms following a pattern (you can search a term or terms following a pattern over a complete index). The following queries are invalid and will throw an exception:

```
q=*:mockingbird // undefined field *
q=ti*:mocking*  // SyntaxError: Cannot parse 'ti*:mocking*'
```

A wildcard query can be slow to execute, as it needs to iterate over all the terms matching the pattern. You should avoid queries starting with a wildcard, as they can be even slower. Wildcard queries return a constant score of 1.0 for all the matching documents.

Range Query

A *range query* supports matching field values between a lower and upper boundary. Range queries are widely used for numeric and date fields but can be used for text fields also. Range queries allow the boundary to be inclusive, exclusive, or a combination of both. They also support wildcards. Here are example range queries:

```
q=price:[1000 TO 5000] // 1000 <= price <= 5000
q=price:{1000 TO 5000} // 1000 < price > 5000
q=price:[1000 TO 5000} // 1000 <= price > 5000
q=price:[1000 TO *]    // 1000 <= price
```

The query parser's syntax requires square brackets, [ ], to denote inclusive values and curly braces, { }, to denote exclusive values. The connector TO should be specified in uppercase; otherwise, the parser will throw an exception. A range query provides a constant score of 1.0 to all the matching documents.

Function Query

In a real-world scenario, you don't always want documents to be ranked only on the basis of TF-IDF matching. Other factors can play a role, and you might want those factors to contribute to the overall document ranking. For example, a popularity count plays an important role in product ranking in an e-commerce website, a user rating plays a role in movie or product reviews, and spatial information plays a role in a local search.

The function query's parser enables you to define a function query, which generates a score on the basis of a numeric value (either a constant or a value indexed in a field or a calculation from another function).

A function query gets its name from using a function to derive the value. The function queries can be applied while computing a score, returning a field value, or sorting documents. This topic is covered in depth in Chapter 7, where you will see how function queries can help in deducing a practical relevancy score.

Filter Query

A *filter query* helps you filter out documents that are not relevant to the request, leaving you with a subset of documents on which the main query executes. The filter clauses are only matched against the index and not scored and the documents that don't match the filter conditions are rejected outright. The filter query should be specified in the request parameter fq. The filter clauses can be specified in the main query also, but the filter query proves advantageous in getting a fast response time. Solr maintains a separate cache for filter queries. When a new query comes with the same filter condition, a cache hit occurs that results in reduced query time. Parsers allow multiple filter queries, and a separate cache is created for each fq parameter. Hence, you can either have all filter clauses in the same fq parameter, or each filter clause in a different fq parameter. The choice of where to put the condition depends totally on your business case. This example specifies the same query clauses in different ways:

```
// no filter cache
q=singer(bob marley) title:(redemption song) language:english genre:rock

// one cache entry
q=singer(bob marley) title:(redemption song)&fq=language:english AND genre:rock

// two cache entry
q=singer(bob marley) title:(redemption song)&fq=language:english&fq=genre:rock
```

The fq parameters are associative. If multiple fq parameters are specified, the query parser will select the subset of documents that matches all the fq queries. If you want the clauses to be OR'ed, the filter query should be part of a single fq parameter.

For example, in a legal search engine, lawyers generally search for cases from a court of law in a specific country. In this scenario, the country name makes a good filter query, as shown here:

```
q=labour laws&fq=country:usa
```

Similarly, in a spatial search such as a local deals search, the city and deal categories can use the fq parameter, as follows:

```
q=product:restaurant&fq=city:california&fq=category:travel
```

But if most of the queries in the city Las Vegas are for travel deals, the request can be formed as follows:

```
q=product:hotel&fq=city:"las vegas" AND category:travel
```

Query Boosting

Not all terms are equally important in a query, so Solr enables you to boost query terms to specify their significance. A *query boost* is a factor that Solr considers when computing a score; a higher boost value returns a higher score. The factor by which you boost the term depends on your needs, the relative importance of terms, and the degree of desired contribution by the term. The best way to come up with an optimal value is through experimenting.

A boost is applied by specifying a carat (^) operator after the token, followed by the boost factor. The DisMax and eDisMax query parsers allow you to boost the query fields, resulting in boosting all the terms searched on that field. By default, all the fields and tokens get a boost of 1.0.

The following is an example query with a boost applied. This query specifies that *redemption* and *song* are the most significant terms, with a boost of 2.0, followed by the terms *bob* and *marley*, with a boost of 1.4; all other terms get the default boost of 1.0.

```
q=singer(bob marley)^1.4 title:(redemption song)^2.0 language:english genre:rock
```

You will learn how query boosting contributes to document scores in Chapter 8.

Global Query Parameters

Solr provides a set of query parameters. Some are generic and work for all kind of search requests, and others are specific to the query parser used for processing the request.

This is a comprehensive reference section for the query parameters that are applicable to all search requests. The request parameters that are specific to query parsers are covered in the "Query Parsers" section in this chapter.

q

This parameter defines the main query string for retrieving relevant documents. This is a mandatory parameter, and if not specified, no other parameter will have any effect.

fq

Filter queries are specified with this parameter. A request can have multiple fq parameters, each of which is associative. You learned about this parameter previously, in the "Filter Query" section.

rows

Specifies the number of documents to be retrieved in the result set. The default value is 10. Don't specify a very high value, as that can be inefficient. A better alternative is to paginate and fetch documents in chunks. You can specify rows=0, when you are interested only in other search features such as facets or suggestions.

start

Specifies the offset from which the documents will be returned. The default value is 0 (which returns results from the first matching document). You can use start and rows together to get paginated search results.

defType

Specifies the query parser to be used for parsing the query. Each parser differs in behavior and supports specialized parameters.

sort

Specifies the comma-separated list of fields on which the result should be sorted. The field name should be followed by the asc or desc keyword to sort the field in ascending or descending order, respectively. The fields to be sorted upon should be single valued (multiValued=false) and should generate only one token. Non-numeric fields are sorted lexicographically. To sort on score, you can specify score as the field name along with the asc/desc keyword. By default, the results are sorted on score. Here is an example:

```
sort=score desc,popularity desc
```

fl

Specifies the comma-separated list of fields to be displayed in the response. If any field in the list doesn't exist or is not stored, it will be ignored. To display a score in the result, you can specify the score as the field name. For example, fl=score,* will return the score of the documents along with all the stored fields.

wt

Specifies the format in which the response should be returned, such as JSON, XML, or CSV. The default response format is XML. The response is formatted by the response writer, which was covered at the beginning of this chapter.

debugQuery

This Boolean parameter works wonders to analyze how the query is parsed and how a document got its score. Debug operations are costly and should not be enabled on live production queries. This parameter supports only XML and JSON response format currently.

explainOther

explainOther is quite useful for analyzing documents that are not part of a debug explanation. debugQuery explains the score of documents that are part of the result set (if you specify rows=10, debugQuery will add an explanation for only those 10 documents). If you want an explanation for additional documents, you can specify a Lucene query in the explainOther parameter for identifying those additional documents. Remember, the explainOther query will select the additional document to explain, but the explanation will be with respect to the main query.

timeAllowed

Specifies the maximum time in milliseconds that a query is allowed to execute. If this threshold is reached, Solr will return a partial result.

omitHeader

A Solr response by default contains `responseHeader`, which provides information such as response status, query execution time, and request parameters. If you don't want this information in response, you can specify `omitHeader=true`.

cache

By default, caching is enabled. You can disable it by specifying `cache=false`.

Query Parsers

You have already learned a bit about query parsers and know that the `defType` parameter specifies the query parser name. In this section, you will look at the primary query parsers: standard, DisMax, and eDisMax.

Standard Query Parser

The *standard query parser* is the default parser in Solr. You don't need to specify the `defType` parameter for this. The standard query parser is suitable for a structured query and is a wonderful parser for forming complex queries, but it has some limitations. It expects you to tightly adhere to syntax, and if it encounters any unexpected characters, it will throw an exception. Special characters and symbols should be properly escaped, or Solr will throw a syntax error:

```
<lst name="error">
  <str name="msg">org.apache.solr.search.SyntaxError:
Cannot parse 'article:mock:bird': Encountered " ":" ":
"" at line 1, column 12.
Was expecting one of:
    <EOF>
    <AND> ...
    <OR> ...
    <NOT> ...
    "+" ...
    "-" ...
    <PREFIXTERM> ...
    <LPARAMS> ...
    ...
    <NUMBER> ...
    </str>
  <int name="code">400</int>
```

DisMax Query Parser

The standard query parser is the default Solr parser, but it provides little flexibility as it is structure-based and accepts Boolean queries such as `title:(buffalo OR soldier) OR singer:(bob OR marley)` that must be syntactically correct. If the syntax is incorrect, or the user query contains a symbol that has special meaning in the syntax, Solr will throw an exception.

Solr provides the *DisMax parser* to handle human-like natural queries and phrases. It allows organic searches across fields, such that it is not limited by values in a particular field. It also allows you to add weight to fields, which is a more practical way of querying any search domain. For example, for a typical e-commerce website, a brand would have a high associated search relevance.

Using the DisMax Query Parser

The DisMax parser makes a better candidate for a search engine like Google, and the standard parser is preferred for advanced searches, where the user explicitly specifies what to search on which field. For example, in a legal search, advocates might prefer specifying a litigation detail in one box, a petitioner detail in another, and the court name in yet another box.

Because DisMax is meant for natural user queries, it makes its best attempt to gracefully handle error scenarios and hardly throws any query parse exceptions.

Another difference is that the standard parser sums up the scores of all the subqueries, whereas DisMax considers the maximum of the scores returned by all the subqueries—hence the name DisMax, which means *disjunction maximum*. If you want DisMax scoring to behave like the standard parser, you can apply a tiebreaker, which can make it score like the standard parser.

If you are building your first search engine, DisMax is an easier alternative to start with than standard. Here is an example DisMax query:

```
$ curl http://localhost:8983/solr/hellosolr/select?
q=to kill a mockingbird&qf=movie^2 artist^1.2 description
&rows=10&fl=score,*&defType=dismax
```

Query Parameters

Along with the common query parameters previously mentioned, DisMax supports additional parameters that are specific to it. These parameters can be used to control the matching and ranking of documents, without making any changes to the main query. The Query tab in the Solr admin console provides a check box for the DisMax parser; after you click it, parameters specific to the parser will automatically become visible. Here are additional parameters supported by DisMax:

q

Specifies the user query or phrase. The values provided to this parameter are natural queries and are not structured as in the standard query.

qf

This parameter specifies the list of fields on which the query provided in the q parameter should be applied. All the query terms are matched in all the specified fields, and you cannot selectively specify different terms to match different fields. If a query contains a string but your qf parameter specifies an int or date field, don't worry; that will be handled gracefully, and only the integers in the query will be matched to an int field.

All the fields in the qf parameter should be separated by whitespace and can optionally have boosts, as shown next. If your list specifies a field that is not defined in schema.xml, it will be ignored.

```
qf=album^2 title^2 description
```

q.alt

DisMax has a fallback mechanism for a query. If the q parameter is missing, it will parse the query specified in the q.alt parameter by using the standard query parser.

mm

In the standard query parser, you explicitly apply the Boolean operator on terms and subqueries. The mm parameter, which means *minimum should match*, provides a more practical approach to the problem by allowing you to control the number of clauses that should match. Its value can be either an integer, a percentage, or a complex expression. Here are the details:

> *Integer*: This specifies the minimum number of clauses that must match. You can also specify a negative value, which means the maximum number of nonmatching optional clauses that are acceptable. For example, if a query contains four clauses, mm=1 means that at least one clause must match, and mm=-1 means that at least three clauses must match. A higher value makes the search stricter, and a lower value makes it more lenient.

> *Percentage*: An integer applies hard values and is fixed. A percentage specifies the minimum number of clauses to match with respect to the total number of optional clauses. For example, if a query contains four clauses, mm=25% means that at least one clause should match, and mm=-25% means that at least three clauses (75%) should match. Specifying mm=100% means that all the clauses must match, and the behavior will be the same as applying the AND operator on all query clauses. Specifying mm=0% means that there is no minimum expectation, and the behavior will be the same as applying the OR operator on all query clauses. If the number computed from the percentage contains a decimal digit, it gets rounded to the nearest lower integer.

> *Expression*: You can apply one or more conditional expressions separated by a space in the format n<integer|percent. An expression specifies that if the number of optional clauses is more than n, the specified condition applies; otherwise, all the clauses are mandatory. If multiple conditions are specified, each one is valid only for the value of n greater than the one specified in the condition before it. For example, the expression 2<25% 4<50% specifies that if the query has up to two optional clauses, they all are mandatory; if it has three or four optional clauses, at least 25% of them should match; and if it has more than four clauses, at least 50% should match.

qs

A query phrase slop allows you to control the degree of proximity in a phrase search. In a standard query parser, you perform a proximity search by specifying a tilde (~) followed by a proximity factor. The DisMax parser provides an additional parameter, qs, to control the proximity factor and keep the main query simple. The following is an example that applies the same proximity when using standard and DisMax parsers:

```
q="bob marley"~3&defType=standard
q="bob marley"&qs=3&defType=dismax
```

pf

The DisMax parser enables you to boost matched documents. You specify a list of fields along with the boost in the pf parameter, and the matching phrases in those fields are boosted accordingly. It's important to remember that this parameter plays a role in ranking the matched phrase higher and doesn't affect the number of documents matched. The pf parameter can reorder the result, but the total result count will always remain unchanged.

```
pf=album^2 title^2
```

ps

This parameter allows you to apply a proximity factor to the phrase field and has no meaning without the pf parameter. As pf contributes only to matched document ranking and plays no role in deciding the match count, the same rule applies to ps.

tie

The standard parser sums up the scores of subqueries, but DisMax takes the maximum of the scores of subqueries—and hence the name *(dis)max*. Once you apply the tie, DisMax starts summing up the scores, and the computation behaves similarly to the standard parser. A float value in the range of 0.0 to 1.0 is allowed. tie=0.0 will take the maximum score among the subqueries, and tie=1.0 will sum up the score of all the subqueries. DisMax uses the following algorithm to compute the score:

```
score = max(subquery1,..,subqueryn) + (tie * sum(other subqueries)
```

If two documents get the same score, you can use this parameter to let subqueries influence the final score and break the tie between them.

bq

The boost query parameter enables you to add a query clause to boost the score of matching documents. Multiple bq parameters can be provided, and the score of clauses in each parameter gets added to the score of the main query. For example, you can use bq to boost titles with a high rating:

```
q=bob marley&bq=rating:[8 TO *]
```

bf

Boost functions can be used to boost documents by applying function queries. The boost function is provided in the bf request parameter. As with bq, you can specify this parameter multiple times, and the score is additive. The following is an example of a boost function that uses the sqrt() function query to compute the boosting factor by taking the square root of the rating. Chapter 7 covers the function query in more detail.

```
q=bob marley&bf=sqrt(rating)
```

Sample DisMax Query

Here is an example for an almost full-blown DisMax query:

```
$ curl http://localhost:8983/solr/hellosolr/select?
q=to kill a mockingbird&qf=album^2 title^2 description
&rows=10&fl=album,title&defType=dismax&qs=3&mm-25%
&pf=album^3 title^3&ps=2&tie=0.3
&bf=sqrt(rating)&bq=rating:[8 TO *]
```

eDisMax Query Parser

As its name indicates, the Extended DisMax query parser is an extension of the DisMax query parser. It supports the features provided by DisMax, adds smartness to some of them, and provides additional features. You can enable this query parser by setting defType=edismax.

The eDisMax query parser supports Lucene query parser syntax, which DisMax doesn't support. DisMax doesn't allow you to search specific fields for specific tokens. You specify the sets of fields to search in the qf parameter, and your query gets applied to all those fields. However, because eDisMax supports Lucene queries, you can execute a specific token on a specific field also. Here is an example query:

Query
```
$ curl http://localhost:8983/solr/hellosolr/select?
q=buffalo soldier artist:(bob marley)&debugQuery=true
&defType=dismax&qf=album title
```

DebugQuery
```
<str name="parsedquery">
(+(DisjunctionMaxQuery((title:buffalo | album:buffalo))
DisjunctionMaxQuery((title:soldier | album:soldier))
DisjunctionMaxQuery(((title:artist title:bob) | (album:artist album:bob)))
DisjunctionMaxQuery((title:marley | album:marley))) ())/no_coord
</str>
```

In this debug query, you can see that DisMax considers the artist field as a query token and searches for it on all the fields specified in the qf parameter. We expect that the parser will search for bob marley in the field artist. Because eDisMax supports Lucene queries, it will meet your expectation.

Query
```
$ curl http://localhost:8983/solr/hellosolr/select?
q=buffalo soldier artist:(bob and marley)
&debugQuery=true&defType=edismax&qf=album title
```

DebugQuery
```
<str name="parsedquery">
(+(DisjunctionMaxQuery((title:buffalo | album:buffalo)) DisjunctionMaxQuery((title:soldier |
album:soldier)) (+artist:bob +artist:marley)))/no_coord
</str>
```

Also, you can notice that eDisMax parsed and as the Boolean operator and mandated the tokens bob and marley by applying the + operator before them. eDisMax supports Boolean operators such as AND, OR, NOT, + and -. The Lucene query parser doesn't consider lowercase tokens and/or as Boolean operators, but eDisMax treats them as valid Boolean operators (equivalent to AND/OR).

The request parameters of DisMax are supported by eDisMax. The following are the additional request parameters that eDisMax provides:

lowercaseOperators

In the preceding example, you saw that eDisMax considers the lowercase and as the Boolean operator AND. If you want to disable this feature and let eDisMax treat and and or as any other token, you can set lowercaseOperators=false. By default, this Boolean parameter is set to true.

boost

The functionality of the boost parameter is similar to that of bf, but its score is multiplied to the score of the main query, whereas the bf score is added. eDisMax allows multiple boost parameters and uses BoostedQuery to multiply the score of each of them to the score of the main query.

Query
```
boost=log(popularity)&boost=sum(popularity)
```

DebugQuery
```
<str name="parsedquery">
BoostedQuery(boost...,
product(log(int(popularity)),sum(int(popularity)))))
</str>
```

pf2/pf3

The pf parameter boosts the score of documents that match the exact phrase. pf2 and pf3 create shingles of size 2 and 3, respectively, and matches against the documents to boost them. For the query top songs of bob marley, the phrases created will be as follows:

```
pf=['top songs of bob marley']
pf2=['top songs','songs of','of bob','bob marley']
pf3=['top songs of','songs of bob','of bob marley']
```

As with pf, multiple pf2/pf3 parameters can be specified in the request.

ps2/ps3

As with the pf parameter, slop can be applied on pf2 and pf3 by using ps2 and ps3, respectively. If this parameter is not specified, the value of the ps parameter becomes its default value.

stopwords

eDisMax allows you to bypass the StopFilterFactory configured in the analysis chain of fields by setting the Boolean parameter stopwords=false.

uf

This parameter specifies the user fields (which fields the user is allowed to query). The value can be a specific field name or a wildcard pattern for the fields. Any alias name can also be used as a field name.

alias

Just as SQL databases allow you to provide an alias name to the columns, eDisMax supports an alias name for the fields. The alias name can map to a single field or a set of fields defined in schema.xml. The parameter can be configured as follows:

```
f.song.qf=title
```

This also proves helpful when you want to club the fields related to a concept together, as shown in this example:

```
f.artist.qf=singer,musician,actor,actress
```

JSON Request API

Throughout this chapter, you have used request parameters for querying results, but this approach has the following limitations:

- It is unstructured, so specifying parameters that apply to a specific field is inconvenient. You will see field-level parameters in features such as faceting and terms component, where you generally want to search different fields differently. Chapter 7 presents examples of these queries.

- Creating requests with a large number of parameters is inconvenient, and you may end up adding the same parameter multiple times because of a lack of readability.

- It is untyped and treats everything as a string.

- A wrong parameter name gets silently ignored, and there is no way to validate it.

To address all these limitations of query parameters, Solr 5.1 introduced the JSON Request API. This API allows you to specify requests in JSON format, which can be sent in either the request body or as part of the json request parameter. Solr also allows you to combine the JSON and request parameters in a query such that some of the parameters can be in the JSON body while others can be in the request parameters separated by an ampersand (&).

Table 6-2 provides a sample query for each JSON request provision supported by the API. The first request in the table is based on the standard request parameter to help you compare both types of requests. Also, the examples use the /query endpoint instead of /select as it is by default configured in solrconfig.xml to return a JSON response. Note that all the requests in the table return the same JSON response.

Table 6-2. *Approaches for Search Queries*

Request Type	Sample Query	Description

Request parameter	`$ curl http://localhost:8983/`
	`solr/hellosolr/query?q=bob`
	`marley&rows=20`
		Standard approach that we have been using throughout this book.

GET request body	`$ curl http://localhost:8983/`
	`solr/hellosolr/query -d`
	`'{`
	`"query":"bob marley",`
	`"limit":20`
	`}'`
		Query in JSON format is specified in the request body by using the `GET` method. If you are using any other client, you may need to specify `Content-Type: application/json` in the request.

POST request body	`$ curl -H "Content-Type:`
	`application/json" -X POST`
	`http://localhost:8983/solr/`
	`hellosolr/query -d`
	`'{`
	`"query":"bob marley",`
	`"limit":20`
	`}'`
		Query in JSON format is specified in the request body by using the `POST` method. This approach is useful if you are using a REST client such as Postman.

JSON in request parameter	`$ curl http://localhost:8983/`
	`solr/hellosolr/query?json='{`
	`"query":"bob marley",`
	`"limit":20`
	`}'`
		Query is specified in the `json` request parameter.

Combination of both	`$ curl http://localhost:8983/`
	`solr/hellosolr/query?json='{`
	`"query":"bob marley"`
	`}'&rows=20`
		Query uses a combination of both JSON API and request parameter.

Request parameter in JSON	`$ curl http://localhost:8983/`
	`solr/hellosolr/query -d`
	`'{`
	`params: {`
	`q:"bob marley",`
	`rows:20`
	`}`
	`}'`
		Query with JSON body that specifies standard request parameter within the params block. The params block allows you to specify any standard request parameter in the JSON body.

Parameter substitution	`$ curl http://localhost:8983/`
	`solr/hellosolr/query?QUERY=bob`
	`marley&RESULTCOUNT=20 -d`
	`'{`
	`"query":"${QUERY}",`
	`"limit":${RESULTCOUNT}`
	`}'`
		JSON body uses parameter substitution for populating the parameter values. JSON request body is fully compatible with parameter substitution, which you will learn about in Chapter 7.

The JSON request API has yet to mature to incorporate all the request parameters. As of now, it supports only a subset of parameters supported by Solr. Also, the names of the JSON body parameters are different from the standard request parameters. For example, if you specify the defType parameter in the JSON body, which is a valid request parameter, Solr will report the following exception:

```
error":{
    "msg":"Unknown top-level key in JSON request : defType",
    "code":400
}
```

Table 6-3 lists JSON body parameters and the standard request parameters that they correspond to. Solr throws the same exception mentioned previously if you provide an invalid JSON parameter.

Table 6-3. JSON API Parameter Name Mapping

Standard Request Parameter	JSON API Parameter
q	Query
fq	Filter
fl	Fields
start	Offset
rows	Limit
sort	Sort

Customizing Solr

In this chapter, you learned about search handlers, search components, and query parsers, and their implementations provided by Solr. These implementations work great for standard use cases, and Solr tries to make them highly configurable to accommodate a wide variety of requirements. However, you may still have a case that is specific to your needs, or you may be developing something that would make a good contribution to Solr. In these scenarios, you may want to write a custom component and hook it to Solr.

Solr provides an extensive option for hooking your plug-in, an example of which you have already seen in Chapter 5. You can find the list of pluggable classes in Solr in the official documentation at https://cwiki.apache.org/confluence/display/solr/Solr+Plugins. The integration process is fairly straightforward and doesn't require you to modify the Solr source code. You can consider your plug-in as similar to those provided by the Solr contrib module.

Following are the high-level steps for adding any custom plug-in to Solr:

1. Create a Java project and define your class, which extends an API provided by Solr based on where you want to hook your implementation in Solr. You need to add the required Solr dependencies to your project to access the API classes.

2. Add your custom functionality by overriding the API methods. This requires you to understand the input parameters of the API, to read the required values from them, and to add your functionality for processing. You may also need to consider other factors such as how your custom functionality would affect the other components downstream in the chain, if applicable.

3. Package your project as a JAR file and add it to lib directory, which is available in Solr's classpath.

4. Define the feature in either solrconfig.xml, schema.xml, or another file where it fits.

5. Wire your named definition to the appropriate component. As Solr assembles the customizable components through XML configuration to build a feature, you either need to replace the existing name with what you defined in step 4 or add your name to the chain, if applicable.

In the next section, you will learn to hook a custom SearchComponent in Solr with an example.

Custom SearchComponent

Assume that you want to perform a spell-check on the basis of common spelling errors uploaded in a file. The Solr-provided SpellCheckComponent, described in Table 6-1, will not be of help in that case. In such a scenario, you may want to write your own implementation for a spell-checker. You can hook this custom functionality to Solr by extending the SearchComponent API and plugging it into Solr.

The following are the steps to be followed for plugging in a custom SearchComponent.

Extend SearchComponent

Create a Java class and extend the SearchComponent abstract class. You need to add the required dependencies to your project.

```
public class CustomSearchComponent extends SearchComponent {
}
```

You can add solr-core-5.3.1 from the $SOLR_DIST/dist directory to your project classpath or Maven dependency, whichever is applicable, as follows:

```
<dependency>
    <groupId>org.apache.solr</groupId>
    <artifactId>solr-core</artifactId>
    <version>5.3.1</version>
</dependency>
```

Override the Abstract Methods

Override the prepare(), process(), and getDescription() methods. In the getDescription() method, provide a short description of the component. The prepare() methods execute before the process() method of any of the registered components. If the purpose of your component is to modify the processing of any other component, the prepare() method is a good place to modify the request parameter that is used by the process method of the component whose behavior you want to change. The process() method is the place where you can write all the custom logic.

```
@Override
public String getDescription() {
  return null;
}
```

```
@Override
public void prepare(ResponseBuilder rb) throws IOException {
}

@Override
public void process(ResponseBuilder rb) throws IOException {
}
```

Get the Request and Response Objects

Get the request and response objects from `ResponseBuilder` to fetch the information required for custom processing:

```
@Override
public void process(ResponseBuilder rb) throws IOException {
    SolrQueryRequest req = rb.req;
    SolrQueryResponse rsp = rb.rsp;
    // your custom logic goes here

}
```

Add the JAR to the Library

Add the executable JAR to the Solr library.

Register to the Handler

To execute the custom component, it should be defined in `solrconfig.xml` and registered to the desired handler.

Sample Component

The following is a simple `SearchComponent` implementation that mandates a JSON response. If the wt parameter is not specified in the request, it sets it to JSON. If it's specified as something else, it resets it to JSON and responds in JSON along with the appropriate message. The message is returned in a separate section. If you are implementing a new feature, you can similarly return the result in a separate section.

The following example also modifies the request parameter. The `SolrParams` retrieved from the request object is read-only, so you need to create an instance of `ModifiableSolrParams`, copy all the existing parameters, and do all the modifications and set it in the request, replacing the existing value.

All the logic in the following example is written in the `prepare()` method, as you want it to execute before the actual processing of the request is done.

Java Source Code

Here is the Java source code:

```java
package com.apress.solr.pa.chapter06.component;

import java.io.IOException;

import org.apache.solr.common.params.CommonParams;
import org.apache.solr.common.params.ModifiableSolrParams;
import org.apache.solr.common.params.SolrParams;
import org.apache.solr.common.util.NamedList;
import org.apache.solr.common.util.SimpleOrderedMap;
import org.apache.solr.handler.component.ResponseBuilder;
import org.apache.solr.handler.component.SearchComponent;
import org.apache.solr.request.SolrQueryRequest;
import org.apache.solr.response.SolrQueryResponse;

public class JsonMandatorComponent extends SearchComponent {

    public static final String COMPONENT_NAME = "jsonmandator";
    @Override
    public String getDescription() {
        return "jsonmandator: mandates JSON response.";
    }

    @Override
    public void prepare(ResponseBuilder rb) throws IOException {
        SolrQueryRequest req = rb.req;
        SolrQueryResponse rsp = rb.rsp;

        SolrParams params = req.getParams();
        ModifiableSolrParams mParams
            = new ModifiableSolrParams(params);

        String wt = mParams.get(CommonParams.WT);

        if(null != wt && !"json".equals(wt)) {
            NamedList nl = new SimpleOrderedMap<>();
            nl.add("error",
            "Only JSON response supported. Ignoring wt parameter!");

            rsp.add(COMPONENT_NAME, nl);
        }

        mParams.set(CommonParams.WT, "json");
        req.setParams(mParams);
    }
```

```
    @Override
    public void process(ResponseBuilder rb) throws IOException {

    }

}
```

solrconfig.xml

Following are the changes to be done in solrconfig.xml:

```
<lib dir="directory" regex="solr-practical-approach-1.0.0.jar" />

<searchComponent name="jsonmandator"
class="com.apress.solr.pa.chapter06.component.JsonMandatorComponent" />

<requestHandler name="/select" class="solr.SearchHandler">
  <!-- default values for query parameters can be specified, these
      will be overridden by parameters in the request
  -->
  <lst name="defaults">
    <str name="echoParams">explicit</str>
    <int name="rows">10</int>
  </lst>

   <arr name="first-components">
    <str>jsonmandator</str>
   </arr>

 </requestHandler>
```

Query

Create a query by specifying the response format as XML, which is not supported for search requests, in the wt parameter:

```
$ curl http://localhost:8983/solr/hellosolr/select?q=product:shirt&wt=xml&indent=true
```

Response

The custom components force a JSON response and add a section with an appropriate error message. Figure 6-4 shows the response returned by Solr for the preceding query.

```
{
    "responseHeader": {
        "status": 0,
        "QTime": 0,
        "params": {
            "q": "product:shirt",
            "wt": "xml"
        }
    },
    "jsonmandator": {
        "error": "Only JSON response supported. Ignoring wt parameter!"
    },
    "response": {
        "numFound": 5,
        "start": 0,
        "docs": [
            {
                "id": "2",
                "sku": "A111",
                "product": "Blue Shirt",
                "category": "Shirt",
                "brand": "wranger",
                "size": "M",
                "price": 1500,
                "_version_": 1501966804800503800
            },
```

Figure 6-4. *Search request manipulation by the custom SearchComponent*

Frequently Asked Questions

This section presents some of the common questions asked while searching results.

I have used KeywordTokenizerFactory in fieldType definition but why is my query string getting tokenized on whitespace?

The unexpected tokenization can be due to the query parser, and there should be no problem in query-time field analysis. The query parser tokenizes on whitespace to identify the query clauses and operators, so by the time the query reaches the filter, it's already tokenized. You can handle this problem by escaping the whitespaces in the query string. The following is a sample escaped query which exhibits your expected behavior.

```
q=bob\ marley&debugQuery=true&defType=edismax&qf=album title
```

How can I find all the documents that contain no value?

You can find all the documents that contain a blank or null value for a field by using a negation operator. Here is an example:

```
-field:* or -field:['' TO *]
```

How can I apply negative boost on terms?

The default boost in Solr is 1.0, and any value higher than this is a positive boost. Solr doesn't support negative boosting, and you cannot specify a boost such as `music:jazz^-5.0`.

If you apply a low boost on the terms such as `music:rock^100 music:metal^100 music:jazz^0.02`, the documents containing *jazz* will still rank above the documents containing only *rock* and *metal*, because you are still giving some boost to *jazz*. The solution is to give a very high boost to documents that don't contain *jazz*. The query should be boosted as follows:

```
q=music:rock^100 music:metal^100 (*:* -music:jazz)^1000
```

Which are the special characters in query string. How should they be handled?

Special characters are the characters that have special meaning in Solr. For example, a plus sign (+) before a clause signifies that it's mandatory. What if your query also contains a + symbol? The query parser cannot make out that it's a valid term. To make the parser understand that the symbol is a valid term and not a special instruction, it should be escaped. You can escape such characters by using a slash (\) before them. Following is the current list of valid special characters:

```
+ - && || ! ( ) { } [ ] ^ " ~ * ? : \ /
```

If you are using a Lucene query parser, you need to escape these special characters before making a request. Otherwise, Solr might throw an exception. But the DisMax query parser handles these exceptions gracefully, and you need to escape only if your query contains quotes or +/- operators. Here is an example that escapes a special character:

```
a \+ b
```

Summary

This chapter covered the most important aspect of Solr: searching for results. You saw how Solr processes a query, the components involved, and the request flow. You learned about the various types of queries and their significance, as well as query parsers and their request parameters. You saw how the DisMax and eDisMax parsers can be used to build a Google-like search engine, and how the Lucene parser can be used to get finer control. You learned to extend the `SearchComponent` to customize the search process. As in previous chapters, you learned about some practical problems and their solutions.

The next chapter covers the search process in more detail and presents other important aspects of searching.

CHAPTER 7

■ ■ ■

Searching Data: Part 2

This chapter is an extension of the previous chapter. In the previous chapter, you learned about searching data. You saw various components that play an important role in the search process, the various types of queries and parsers supported by Solr, and the request parameters that can be provided to control the search behavior.

This chapter covers other important aspects of searching documents. Beyond the core capabilities, a search engine needs to offer other features that address practical use cases and user needs. Also, each domain has its own unique challenge. A web search engine should group results from the same web site. An e-commerce web site typically offers faceted navigation so that the user can easily browse through the catalog based on features of the products. Solr provides out-of-the-box solutions for such common problems.

Most important, textual similarity between documents is not always the best criteria for computing relevancy. A music discovery web site generally considers a popular and trending song as more relevant than other songs with a similar score. Solr provides the function query to compute scores on such numerical values. Solr allows you to combine all these factors—including text similarity, popularity, and rating—to deduce practical relevance ranking and tame real-world search problems.

This chapter describes Solr's search features along with practical use cases and prerequisites, so that you can easily analyze whether a certain feature can solve your business problem and understand the challenges in implementing it in your project. As examples are the best way to learn, each section concludes with an example.

This chapter covers the following topics:

- Local parameters
- Result grouping
- Statistics
- Faceted search
- Reranking query
- Join query and block join
- Function query
- ExternalFileField

Local Parameters

Local parameters, also called LocalParams, allow you to provide additional attributes in request parameters and customize their behavior. LocalParams are supported only by certain parameters, and their effects are local to that parameter. For example, you can change the QParser used by the q parameter, without changing it for other parameters such as fq. Remember, Solr allows only one LocalParam for each request parameter.

Syntax

To use a LocalParam, it should be added at the beginning of a parameter value. LocalParams should start with { ! and end with } and all local parameters should be specified between them as a key-value pair separated by whitespace. The following is the syntax for using a LocalParam in a request parameter:

```
<query-parameter>={!<key1>=<value1> <key2>=<value2> .. <keyN>=<valueN>}<query>
```

Specifying the Query Parser

The name of the query parser to be used in the local parameter section can be specified in the type parameter. Solr also offers a short-form representation for it, by allowing you to specify only the value, and Solr assigns it the implicit name type. The following is the syntax:

```
{!type=<query-parser> <key1>=<value1> .. <keyN>=<valueN>}<query> // explicit
{!<query-parser> <key1>=<value1> .. <keyN>=<valueN>}<query> // implicit
```

Specifying the Query Inside the LocalParams Section

Instead of specifying the query after the closing brace }, you can also specify it in the LocalParam by using the v key.

```
<query-paramter>={!<query-parser> <key1>=<value1> .. <keyN>=<valueN> v=<query>}
```

Using Parameter Dereferencing

Using parameter dereferencing, you can simplify the query further. You specify the query in the same request parameter, either following a closing curly brace or as a value of the key v, but parameter dereferencing allows you to read the query from another parameter. This approach provides a convenience to the client application, which can just provide the value for the additional parameter referenced by LocalParams and configure the LocalParams in solrconfig.xml. The syntax for parameter dereferencing is provided here:

```
<query-paramter>={!<query-parser> <key>=<value> v=$<param>}&param=query
```

Example

In this section, you will see a few examples of LocalParams and their syntax.

The default operator for all the requests is OR, but you can change it to AND for the q parameter, using LocalParams as follows. When you use this syntax, the operator for the fq parameter still remains the same (OR):

```
$ curl http://localhost:8983/solr/music/select?
q={!q.op=AND}singer:(bob marley)&fq=genre:(reggae beat)
```

Say you want to find results for the keyword bob marley, ensuring that both the tokens must match and the parser used is Lucene. The following example shows various approaches to the same problem:

```
q={!type=lucene q.op=AND}bob marley // type parameter specifies the parser
q={!lucene q.op=AND}bob marley // shortened form for specifying the parser
q={!lucene q.op=AND v='bob marley'} // v key for specifying query
q={!lucene q.op=AND v=$qq}&qq=bob marley // query dereferencing
```

Result Grouping

Result grouping is a feature that groups results based on a common value. In Solr, documents can be grouped on the values of a field or the results of a function query. For a query, result grouping returns the top *N* groups and top *N* documents in each group. This feature is also called *field collapsing*, as conceptually you collapse the results on the basis of a common value.

Suppose you are building a web search engine, and for a query all the top results are from the same web site. This would lead to a bad user experience, and you would be penalizing all other web sites for no reason. Field collapsing is useful for eliminating the duplicates and collapsing the results of each web site into a few entries. Even Google does this!

Result grouping is also frequently used by e-commerce web sites to address queries that find matches in different categories—for example, shirt can be of type formal, casual, or party wear. Result grouping allows you to return top results from each category.

Prerequisites

The following are the prerequisites for using result grouping:

- The field being grouped should be indexed and should support a function query if you are grouping on function queries.

- The field must be single-valued.

- The field shouldn't be tokenized.

■ **Note**   As of now, result grouping on a function query doesn't work in a distributed search.

Request Parameters

Solr provides additional request parameters for enabling result grouping and controlling its behavior. The supported parameters are specified in Table 7-1.

Table 7-1. *Result Grouping Request Parameters*

Parameter	Description
group	By default, result grouping is disabled. It can be enabled by specifying group=true.
group.field	Specifies the Solr field that shares the common property and on which the result should be grouped. The parameter can be specified multiple times.
group.query	All documents matching the query are returned as a single group. The parameter can be specified multiple times.
group.func	Specifies the function query, on the unique output of which the result will be grouped. It can be specified multiple times. This feature isn't supported in distributed search.
start	Specifies the initial offset of the groups.
rows	Specifies the number of groups to return. By default, it returns 10 groups.
group.offset	Specifies the initial offset of the documents in each group.
group.limit	By default, only the top document of the group is returned. This parameter specifies the number of documents to return per group.
sort	By default, the groups are sorted on score desc. You can change the group sorting order by using this parameter.
group.sort	This parameter sorts the documents within each group. By default, this is also sorted on score desc.
group.format	Result grouping supports two response formats: grouped and simple. By default, the results are grouped. The simple format provides a flattened result for easy parsing. In this feature, rows and start perform the task of group.limit and group.offset.
group.ngroups	This parameter, if set to true, returns the count of matching groups. If for a query there are two matching groups, additional information will be added to the response as shown here: `<int name="ngroups">2</int>` In a distributed search, this parameter gives the correct count only if all the documents in the group exist in the same shard.
group.facet	This Boolean parameter defaults to false. If enabled, grouped faceting is performed on the field specified in the facet.field parameter, on the basis of the first specified group. In a distributed environment, it gives a correct count only if all the documents in the group exist in the same shard.
group.truncate	This Boolean parameter defaults to false. If enabled, the facet count is on the basis of the top document in each group.
group.cache.percent	If the value is greater than 0, the result grouping enables a cache for the query during the second phase. The default value of 0 disables grouping the cache. As per the official Solr reference guide, caching improves performance with Boolean queries, wildcard queries, and fuzzy queries. For other types of queries, it can have a negative impact on performance.

(continued)

Table 7-1. (*continued*)

Parameter	Description
group.main	If true, the result of the first field grouping command is used as the main result list in the response, using group.format=simple. It's mandatory to provide at least one grouping provision (the group.field or group.query or group.func parameter should be provided). If all these parameters are missing, Solr will report the error: ```\n<lst name="error">\n <str name="msg">\n Specify at least one field, function or query to group by.\n </str>\n <int name="code">400</int>\n</lst>\n```

Example

This section presents an example of each result grouping type: field grouping, query grouping, and function query grouping. The example assumes that you have a core named ecommerce that contains the respective fields satisfying all grouping prerequisites.

Group the results of each brand that manufactures a shirt, using field grouping

```
$ curl http://localhost:8983/solr/ecommerce/select?q=product:shirt&wt=xml&group=true&group.
field=brand
```

```
<lst name="grouped">
  <lst name="brand">
    <int name="matches">5</int>
    <arr name="groups">
      <lst>
        <str name="groupValue">wrangler</str>
        <result name="doclist" numFound="2" start="0">
        <doc>
          <str name="id">2</str>
          <str name="sku">A111</str>
          <str name="product">Blue Shirt</str>
          <str name="category">Shirt</str>
          <str name="brand">wrangler</str>
          <str name="size">M</str>
          <int name="price">1500</int>
        </doc>
        </result>
      </lst>
      <lst>
        <str name="groupValue">adidas</str>
        <result name="doclist" numFound="3" start="0">
          <doc>
            <str name="id">1</str>
```

```
            <str name="sku">A110</str>
            <str name="product">Blue T-Shirt</str>
            <str name="category">T-shirt</str>
            <str name="brand">adidas</str>
            <str name="size">M</str>
            <int name="price">1000</int>
          </doc>
        </result>
      </lst>
    </arr>
  </lst>
</lst>
```

Group documents in two price ranges using a group.query for the product "shirt"

```
$ curl http://localhost:8983/solr/ecommerce/select?
q=product:shirt&wt=xml&group=true&group.query=price:[1 TO 1000]
&group.query=price:[1001 TO *]
```

```
<lst name="grouped">
  <lst name="price:[1 TO 1000]">
    <int name="matches">5</int>
    <result name="doclist" numFound="2" start="0">
      <doc>
        <str name="id">1</str>
        <str name="sku">A110</str>
        <str name="product">Blue T-Shirt</str>
        <str name="category">T-shirt</str>
        <str name="brand">adidas</str>
        <str name="size">M</str>
        <int name="price">1000</int>
      </doc>
    </result>
  </lst>
  <lst name="price:[1001 TO *]">
    <int name="matches">5</int>
    <result name="doclist" numFound="3" start="0">
      <doc>
        <str name="id">2</str>
        <str name="sku">A111</str>
        <str name="product">Blue Shirt</str>
        <str name="category">Shirt</str>
        <str name="brand">wrangler</str>
        <str name="size">M</str>
        <int name="price">1500</int>
      </doc>
    </result>
  </lst>
</lst>
```

Group documents on price range in multiples of 1,000, using a group function query

```
$ curl http://localhost:8983/solr/ecommerce/select?q=product:shirt&wt=xml&group=true&group.
func=ceil(div(price,1000))
```

```xml
<lst name="grouped">
  <lst name="ceil(div(price,1000))">
    <int name="matches">5</int>
    <arr name="groups">
      <lst>
        <double name="groupValue">2.0</double>
        <result name="doclist" numFound="3" start="0">
          <doc>
            <str name="id">2</str>
            <str name="sku">A111</str>
            <str name="product">Blue Shirt</str>
            <str name="category">Shirt</str>
            <str name="brand">wrangler</str>
            <str name="size">M</str>
            <int name="price">1500</int>
          </doc>
        </result>
      </lst>
      <lst>
        <double name="groupValue">1.0</double>
        <result name="doclist" numFound="2" start="0">
          <doc>
            <str name="id">1</str>
            <str name="sku">A110</str>
            <str name="product">Blue T-Shirt</str>
            <str name="category">T-shirt</str>
            <str name="brand">adidas</str>
            <str name="size">M</str>
            <int name="price">1000</int>
          </doc>
        </result>
      </lst>
    </arr>
  </lst>
</lst>
```

Statistics

Solr's StatsComponent allows you to generate statistics on numeric, date, or string fields. Not all statistics are supported on the string and date fields.

Request Parameters

Before we discuss the methods, let's have a look at the request parameters supported by the statistics components. The parameters are specified in Table 7-2.

Table 7-2. Statistics Request Parameters

Parameter	Description
stats	You can enable StatsComponent by setting this Boolean parameter to true.
stats.field	Specifies the field name on which statistics should be generated. This parameter can be specified multiple times to generate statistics on multiple fields.
stats.facet	Specifies the facet on each unique value for which statistics will be generated. A better alternative to this parameter is using a stats.field with pivot faceting. You will learn about pivot faceting later in this chapter.
stats.calcdistinct	When this Boolean parameter is set to true, all the distinct values in the field will be returned along with their counts. If the number of distinct values is high, this operation can be costly. By default, it is set to false. This request parameter is deprecated, and it's advised to use countDistinct and distinctValues LocalParams.

Supported Methods

StatsComponent supports a variety of statistical methods. All the methods, except percentiles, countDistinct, distinctValues and cardinality, are computed by default. You can enable the method by specifying it along with its value as a LocalParam. If you explicitly enable any of the statistics, other default statistics will be disabled. The percentiles method accepts numeric values such as 99.9, whereas all other methods are Boolean. Table 7-3 lists the primary statistics.

Table 7-3. Statistical Methods and Types Supported

LocalParam	Description	Supported Types
min	Finds the minimum value in the input set	All
max	Finds the maximum value in the input set	All
sum	Computes the sum of all the values in the input set	Date/Number
count	Counts the number of values in the input set	All
missing	Counts the number of documents for which the value is missing	All
mean	Computes the average of all the values in the input set	Data/Number
stddev	Computes the standard deviation for the values in the input set	Data/Number
sumOfSquares	Computes the output by squaring each value and then summing it up	Data/Number
percentiles	Computes the percentile based on the cutoff specified	Number
countDistinct	Returns the count of distinct values in the field or function in the document set. This computation can be expensive.	All
distinctValues	Returns all the distinct values in the field or function in the document set. This computation can be expensive.	All

(*continued*)

Table 7-3. (*continued*)

LocalParam	Description	Supported Types
cardinality	The countDistinct statistical method doesn't scale well, as it needs to fit everything into memory. The cardinality method uses HyperLogLog, a probabilistic approach for counting distinct values, which estimates the count instead of returning the exact value. Refer to http://algo.inria.fr/flajolet/Publications/FlFuGaMe07.pdf for details of the HyperLogLog algorithm. A floating point number between 0.0 and 1.0 can be provided as input value to specify the aggressiveness of the algorithm, where 0.0 indicates less aggressive and 1.0 indicates more aggressive. High aggressiveness provides a more accurate count but leads to higher memory consumption. Alternatively, a Boolean value true can be specified to indicate a floating point value of 0.3.	All

LocalParams

Along with the preceding statistics, StatsComponent also supports the LocalParams in Table 7-4.

Table 7-4. *StatsComponent LocalParams*

Parameter	Description
ex	Local parameter to exclude the filter
key	Parameter to change the display name of a field
tag	Parameter for tagging the statistics, so that it can be used with pivot faceting

Example

This section presents examples for generating various types of statistics in Solr.

Generate statistics on the "price" field

```
$ curl http://localhost:8983/solr/ecommerce/select?
q=*:*&wt=xml&rows=0&indent=true&stats=true&stats.field=price

<lst name="stats">
  <lst name="stats_fields">
    <lst name="price">
      <double name="min">1000.0</double>
      <double name="max">5000.0</double>
      <long name="count">6</long>
      <long name="missing">0</long>
      <double name="sum">11500.0</double>
      <double name="sumOfSquares">3.393E7</double>
      <double name="mean">1916.6666666666667</double>
      <double name="stddev">1541.968438933387</double>
```

```
        <lst name="facets"/>
      </lst>
    </lst>
  </lst>
```

Generate facet on the field "size" and for each value of it, get the statistics. The statistics will be generated as a subsection in stats on the field "price".

```
$ curl http://localhost:8983/solr/ecommerce/select?q=*:*&wt=xml&rows=0
&indent=true&stats=true&stats.field=price&stats.facet=size

<lst name="facets">
  <lst name="size">
    <lst name="L">
      <double name="min">1000.0</double>
      <double name="max">5000.0</double>
      <long name="count">2</long>
      <long name="missing">0</long>
      <double name="sum">6000.0</double>
      <double name="sumOfSquares">2.6E7</double>
      <double name="mean">3000.0</double>
      <double name="stddev">2828.42712474619</double>
      <lst name="facets"/>
    </lst>
    <lst name="M">
      <double name="min">1000.0</double>
      <double name="max">1800.0</double>
      <long name="count">4</long>
      <long name="missing">0</long>
      <double name="sum">5500.0</double>
      <double name="sumOfSquares">7930000.0</double>
      <double name="mean">1375.0</double>
      <double name="stddev">350.0</double>
      <lst name="facets"/>
    </lst>
  </lst>
</lst>
```

Change the display name for the price field to "mrp"

```
$ curl http://localhost:8983/solr/ecommerce/select?q=*:*&wt=xml&rows=0&indent=true&stats=true
&stats.field={!key=mrp}price

<lst name="stats">
  <lst name="stats_fields">
    <lst name="mrp">
      ...
    </lst>
  </lst>
</lst>
```

Get the mininum value for the "price" field using min method

```
$ curl http://localhost:8983/solr/ecommerce/select?q=*:*&wt=xml&rows=0&indent=true
&stats=true&stats.field={!min=true}price
```

```
<lst name="stats">
  <lst name="stats_fields">
    <lst name="price">
      <double name="min">1000.0</double>
    </lst>
  </lst>
</lst>
```

Faceting

Solr's faceting feature is nothing less than a Swiss Army knife, one feature that does many things—especially since Solr 5.1, when the component was revamped, and in version 5.2, when more features were added. *Faceting* is a feature that classifies a search result into several categories, allowing the user to filter out unwanted results or drill down to a more specific result. This feature enables a better user experience, enabling users to easily navigate to a particular document.

Faceting is a kind of must-have feature in e-commerce web sites, especially ones with large product catalogs. The user makes a search request, and the response shows categories either on the left or right of the page—which is the facet. The items in each category are either clickable or come with a check box to filter the results. For a user query such as *blue formal shirt*, a web site may return hundreds or thousands of results. Faceting lets users easily navigate to products of their choice by filtering the results on preferred brand, favorite color, or fitting size, for example. Figure 7-1 shows an example of a faceted search at Amazon.com; the facets are shown in a rectangular box.

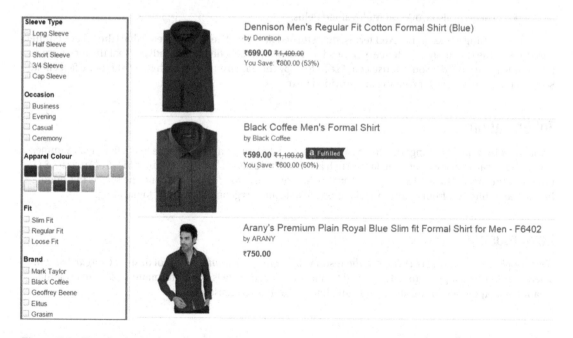

Figure 7-1. *Faceting in an e-commerce web site*

Faceting is easy to use in Solr. For example, *field faceting*, a faceting type based on field data, gets the indexed terms from a field and displays the facet values along with search results. Since the values are retrieved from the index, Solr always returns the unique values for that field. When a user selects a faceted value, it can be used to create a new query with an additional filter condition, such as fq=<facet-field>:'<user selected facet value>' and to get a fresh result, which will be a subset of the original result. Similarly, if a user deselects a facet value, it can be used to make a fresh search request without that clause in the filter query to broaden the search result. This approach allows the user to navigate through the product easily.

Faceting is widely used in the following scenarios:

- Result classification

- Guided navigation

- Autocompletion

- Decision tree

- Analytics and aggregation

- Trend identification

Prior to release 5.1, Solr provided only a count on the facets. But now it supports aggregation, which runs a faceted function to generate statistics on categorized results. Using a faceted function, you can retrieve statistical information such as average, sum, and unique value. Solr 5.1 also supports the new JSON API for making requests, which facilitates providing field-specific parameters and nested commands.

Prerequisites

Here are the prerequisites for using faceting in Solr:

- The field must be indexed or should have docValues.

- Faceting also works on multivalued fields.

Since faceting works on indexed terms, the returned facets will be the indexed value (the tokens emitted after index-time text analysis). Hence, you need to analyze the facet field differently, so that the terms are as per your response needs. You can use copyField to copy the data from the searchable field to the facet field. Some standard practices for faceting are provided next.

Tokenization

If you tokenize a field, faceting will return each token, and that might make no sense to the user. For example, a tokenized brand field will generate facets such as "facet_fields":{"brand":["Giorgio",6,"Armani",8]}, but the user expects "facet_fields":{"brand":["Giorgio Armani",5]}, so that once he selects this brand, he can see results only from this brand. Therefore, tokenization is generally avoided for faceting.

Lowercasing

If you apply LowerCaseFilterFactory, the result will be *giorgio armani* instead of desired *Giorgio Armani*. Therefore, lowercasing is generally avoided for faceting. If your data is poorly formatted, you can do some cleanup and apply standardization to ensure that formatting is consistent.

Syntax

Solr provides two provisions for faceted searches: traditional request parameters, and the JSON API.

Traditional Request Parameters

You can enable faceting by specifying additional request parameters, the way you do for other features. The syntax is provided here:

```
facet.<parameter>=<value>
```

Some of the request parameters can be specified on a per field basis. They follow the syntax `f.<fieldname>.facet.<parameter>`. For example, if the faceting parameter `facet.count` is to be applied specifically on the field brand, the request parameter will be `f.brand.facet.count`.

JSON API

The nested structure of JSON provides ease of use in constructing requests, especially for field-specific request parameters. Solr provides the new JSON-based API. The JSON is specified as part of the `json.facet` request parameter:

```
json.facet={
  <facet_name>:{
    <facet_type>:{
      <param1>:<value1>,
      <param2>:<value2>,
      ..
      <paramN>:<valueN>
    }
  }
}
```

Example

This section provides examples of both faceting approaches.

Traditional request parameter-based approach

```
$ curl http://localhost:8983/solr/ecommerce/select?q=*:*&facet=true
&facet.field={!key=brand}ut_brand&facet.limit=10&facet.mincount=5
```

New JSON API-based approach

```
$ curl 'http://localhost:8983/solr/ecommerce/select?q=*:*&json.facet={
  brand: {
    type : "term"
    field : "ut_brand",
    limit : 10,
    mincount : 5
  }
}'
```

Faceting Types

This section describes the types of faceting supported by Solr. Each faceting type supports a set of request parameters, a few of which are generic and apply to all faceting types, and a few that are specific to a faceting type. The JSON API identifies the faceting type based on the key type, the value of which corresponds to the type of faceting.

General Parameter

This section specifies the faceting parameter that applies to all types of faceting requests.

facet

Faceting is one of the default components registered in SearchHandler, but its execution is disabled. It can be enabled by providing the parameter facet=true. Along with this parameter, another supporting parameter, which contains information about the type of faceting or how to facet, should be provided.

Field Faceting

Field faceting, also called *term faceting*, allows you to build a facet on the indexed value in a field. You specify the field name on which to facet, and Solr returns all the unique terms in it. Remember, you may want to keep the field on which you build the facet as untokenized.

Specific Parameters

The following are the request parameters specific to field faceting.

facet.field

This specifies the field for faceting. It can be specified multiple times to generate facets on multiple fields.

facet.prefix

This returns the facets that match the specified prefix and is useful for building features such as autosuggestion. This parameter can be applied on a per field basis. In Chapter 9, you will learn to build an autosuggestion feature by using facets.

facet.contains

This returns the facets that contain the specified text. This parameter can be applied on a per field basis.

facet.contains.ignoreCase

Set this Boolean parameter to true to ignore case while performing the facet.contains matching.

facet.sort

This parameter supports two values: index and count. By default, the results are sorted on index (lexicographically on the indexed terms), but if the facet.limit parameter is set to a value greater than 0, the results will be sorted on count. This parameter can also be specified on a per field basis.

facet.offset

This specifies the offset for the faceted result. This parameter can be specified on a per field basis. This parameter, along with `facet.limit`, can be used to enable pagination.

facet.limit

This specifies the maximum number of faceted results to return for each field. A negative value specifies unlimited results. By default, 100 results are returned. This parameter can be specified on a per field basis.

facet.mincount

By default, faceting returns all the unique terms in a field. With this parameter, you can filter out the terms with frequency less than a minimum count. It allows faceting to return only those terms that have some minimum prominence. The default value is 0. This parameter can be specified on a per field basis.

facet.missing

On setting `facet.missing=true`, faceting returns the count for those documents that don't have a facet value (the documents that match the user query, but the value for that faceted field is missing). By default, this parameter is set to `false`. This parameter can be specified on a per field basis.

facet.method

The `facet.method` parameter allows you to choose the algorithm for faceting. This parameter can be specified on a per field basis. The following are the supported methods:

> enum: This method gets all the terms in a field and performs an intersection of all documents matching it with all documents matching the query. Each unique term in the field creates a filter cache, so this approach should be used when the number of unique terms is limited. When using this method, ensure that the size of `filterCache` is large enough.

> fc: The name `fc` stands for `FieldCache`. This method iterates over all the matching documents, counting the terms in the faceted field. This method works faster for indexes where the number of distinct terms in the field is high but the number of terms in the document is low. Also, it consumes less memory than other methods and is the default method. This method creates an uninverted representation of field values for matching, so the first request will be slow.

> fcs: This method works only for single-valued string fields and supports faster faceting for a frequently changing index, as `fc` does uninversion whenever the index changes.

facet.enum.cache.minDF

This parameter is applicable only for the enum faceting method and allows you to tweak caching. By default, the enum method uses `filterCache` for all the terms. If you set this parameter to value N, then terms with document frequency less than N will not be cached. A higher value will add fewer documents to `filterCache`, so the memory required will be less but you will have a performance trade-off.

facet.threads

This specifies the maximum number of threads to be spawned for faceting. By default, it uses the thread of the main request. If the value is negative, threads up to Integer.MAX_VALUE will be created. If the value is 0, the request will be served by the main thread.

facet.overrequest.count

In a distributed environment, the facet count returned is not accurate. To improve the accuracy, you request more facets from each shard than are specified by facet.limit. The overrequest is based on the following formula:

```
facet.overrequest.count + (facet.limit * facet.overrequest.ratio)
```

The default value for facet.overrequest.count is 10.

facet.overrequest.ratio

As you saw in the previous parameter, facet.overrequest.ratio also helps to control the number of facets fetched from each shard by multiplying to the facet.limit. The default value for this parameter is 1.5.

If you don't specify any of these parameters, Solr by default fetches 25 facets for each field, based on the computation 10 + (10 * 1.5), where the first 10 is the default value for facet.overrequest.count, the second 10 is the default value for facet.limit, and 1.5 is the default value for facet.overrequest.ratio.

Query Faceting

Query faceting allows you to provide a Lucene query for faceting. You can specify this parameter multiple times to generate multiple facets.

Specific Parameters

The following is the request parameter for query faceting.

facet.query

This specifies the Lucene query for generating the facet. If you want to use another query parser, it can be specified using LocalParams. The following is an example of a facet query:

```
facet=true&facet.query=singer:"bob marley"&facet.query=genre:pop // lucene query
facet=true&facet.query={!dismax}bob marley // faceting with dismax qparser
```

Range Faceting

Suppose you want to build a facet based on the date or price of a product. It would not be a good idea to display all the unique dates or prices. Instead, you should display year ranges, such as 2001–2010, or prices such as $201–$300. A way to build this with a field facet is by indexing the range in a separate field. However, to change the range in the future, you would need to reindex all the documents. Well, that doesn't seem to be a great idea. You could achieve this with a faceted query, but you would need to specify multiple queries.

Solr provides a built-in solution to the problem through *range faceting*. This can be applied on any field that supports a range query.

Specific Parameters

The following are the request parameters specific to range faceting.

facet.range

This specifies the field on which the range query should be applied. It can be provided multiple times to perform a range query on multiple fields.

facet.range.start

This specifies the lower boundary for the range. Index values lower than the range will be ignored. It can be specified on a per field basis.

facet.range.end

This specifies the upper boundary for the range. Index values above the range will be ignored. It can be specified on a per field basis.

facet.range.gap

This specifies the size of the range. For a date field, the range should adhere to `DataMathParser` syntax. This parameter can be specified on a per field basis.

facet.range.hardend

Suppose you set the start at 1 and the end at 500, and set a gap of 200. The facets generated will be 1–200, and 201–400, but for the third range there is an ambiguity of whether the range should be 401–500 or 401–600.

The Boolean parameter `facet.range.hardend` allows you to specify whether the end should be strictly followed. If you set this parameter to `true`, the last range will be 401–500; if you set it to `false`, the last range will be 401–600. The default value for this parameter is `false`, and it is allowed on a per field basis.

facet.range.include

This parameter allows you to handle lower and upper boundary values. The following are the options available:

> `lower`: Include the lower boundary.
>
> `upper`: Include the upper boundary.
>
> `edge`: Include the edge boundary (include the lower boundary for the first range and upper boundary for the last range).
>
> `outer`: When the `facet.range.other` parameter is specified, its before and after ranges will include the boundary values.
>
> `all`: Applies all of the preceding options.

This parameter can be specified multiple times to set multiple options. By default, faceting includes the lower boundary and excludes the upper boundary. If you set both `lower` and `upper` or `outer` or `all`, the values will overlap, so set it accordingly. This parameter can be applied on a per field basis.

facet.range.other

This parameter allows you to get additional counts. Here are the available options:

> below: Facet on all values below the lowest range (facet.range.start).

> above: Facet on all values beyond the highest range.

> between: Facet on all records between the lower and upper boundary.

> all: Apply all of the preceding options.

> none: Do not apply any of these options.

This parameter can be specified multiple times to set multiple options, but the none option overrides all. It can be applied on a per field basis.

facet.mincount

This parameter specifies the count below which the range facet should be ignored. You saw this parameter in field faceting also.

Example

This section presents an example of range faceting. In this example, you are applying range faceting on a price field to get the count of products in the price ranges of 201–400; 401–600; 601–800; 801–1,000; and 1,001–1,200. You set hardend=false, so the highest facet is of 1,001–1,200 instead of 1,001–1,100. Create a facet for all values below the minimum range and all values above the maximum range. Include only the terms that have a minimum count of 5.

```
$ curl http://localhost:8983/solr/ecommerce/select?q=*:*
&facet.range=price&facet.range.start=201&facet.range.end=1100
&facet.range.gap=200&facet.mincount=5&facet=true
&facet.range.hardend=false&f.price.facet.range.include=lower
&f.price.facet.range.other=below&f.price.facet.range.other=above
```

Interval Faceting

This form of faceting is an alternate way of performing facet queries with range queries but with a different implementation. *Interval faceting* works on docValues and so requires docValues to be enabled on fields you facet and offers different performance depending on the content. You need to run some tests to identify whether interval faceting or a facet query with range queries provides better performance for you. Interval faceting provides better performance when getting multiple ranges on the same field, but a faceted query is good for a system with effective caching.

Specific Parameters

The following are the request parameters specific to interval faceting

.facet.interval

This parameter specifies the field name on which interval faceting should be applied. This parameter can be applied on a per field basis.

facet.interval.set

In this parameter, you specify the syntax for building interval facets. You can specify it multiple times for multiple intervals, and it can be applied on a per field basis. Here is the syntax for setting the interval:

```
[<start-value>,<end-value>]
```

The square brackets can be replaced with parentheses. A square bracket means the values are inclusive, and the parentheses means the values are exclusive. An opening square bracket can end with a closing parenthesis, and vice versa. The bracket you choose will depend on your condition. The following are a few examples:

(1,100): Greater than 1 and less than 100

[1,100): Greater than or equal to 1, and less than 100

[1,100]: Greater than or equal to 1, and less than or equal to 100

(1,100]: Greater than 1, and less than or equal to 100

For an unbounded interval, the special character * can be used as a value.

Example

This section presents examples of interval faceting.

Example of interval faceting

```
$ curl http://localhost:8983/solr/ecommerce/select?q=*:*
&facet=true&facet.interval=mrp&f.mrp.facet.interval.set=[1,500]
&f.mrp.facet.interval.set=[501,1000]&f.mrp.facet.interval.set=[1001,*]
```

Interval faceting also supports key replacement. The same query can be written as follows:

```
$ curl http://localhost:8983/solr/ecommerce/select?q=*:*&facet=true
&facet.interval={!key=price}mrp&f.mrp.facet.interval.set={!key=less than 500}[1,500]
&f.mrp.facet.interval.set={!key=500 to 1000}[501,1000]
&f.mrp.facet.interval.set={!key=more than 1000}[1001,*]
```

Pivot Faceting: Decision Tree

Pivot faceting helps you build multilevel facets (a facet within facet). All the facets previously mentioned provide only top-level facets. Now, to build another facet on that facet, you need to send another request to Solr. But the pivot facet saves the day. You can build a decision tree without sending additional requests to Solr with additional filter queries. Hence, pivot faceting reduces the number of round-trips.

Specific Parameters

The following are the request parameters specific to pivot faceting.

facet.pivot

This parameter specifies the comma-separated list of fields to pivot. This parameter can be specified multiple times, and each parameter will add a separate facet_pivot section to the response.

```
facet.pivot=brand,size
```

facet.pivot.mincount

This parameter specifies the lower threshold. Terms with a count less than mincount will be ignored.

Pivot faceting also supports the following request parameters of field faceting (please refer to the field faceting section for details):

- facet.limit
- facet.offset
- facet.sort
- facet.overrequest.count
- facet.overrequest.ratio

Example

This section presents an example of pivot faceting.

In a single request, build a facet on a brand, and for each brand build a facet on size

```
$ curl http://localhost:8983/solr/ecommerce/select?q=*:*&facet=true&facet.pivot=brand,size
```

```
<lst name="facet_pivot">
  <arr name="brand,size">
    <lst>
      <str name="field">brand</str>
      <str name="value">adidas</str>
      <int name="count">3</int>
      <arr name="pivot">
        <lst>
          <str name="field">size</str>
          <str name="value">M</str>
          <int name="count">2</int>
        </lst>
        <lst>
          <str name="field">size</str>
          <str name="value">L</str>
          <int name="count">1</int>
        </lst>
      </arr>
    </lst>
    ...
  </arr>
</lst>
```

Reranking Query

Solr 4.9 introduced the *reranking query*, which allows you to provide an additional query to rerank the top N results returned by the main query. This feature is useful if you want to run a query that is too costly to run on all the documents, or you want to reorder the top N results based on a custom requirement. It's possible that documents beyond the N result could be of interest and that the reranking query might miss it. But that's a trade-off for performance.

The reranking attributes can be specified using local parameters in the additional request parameter rq. Solr provides ReRankQParserPlugin, a query parser for parsing the reranking queries. This parser is identified by the name rerank.

The reranking query provides debug and custom explain information, when you set debug=true. You can use this to analyze the reranked score of the document. The reranking query also plays well with other features of Solr, and you can use them together.

Request Parameters

The following are the request parameters supported by ReRankQParserPlugin.

reRankQuery

This mandatory parameter specifies the query that is parsed by the ReRankQParser to rerank the top documents.

reRankDocs

The parameter specifies the minimum number of top documents from the main query to consider for reranking. The default value is 200.

reRankWeight

This parameter specifies the factor by which the score of the rerank query is multiplied. The resultant score is added to the score of the main query. The default value is 2.0.

Example

This section presents an example of a reranking query.

This example uses ReRankQParser to rerank the top 200 documents returned by the main query provided in the q parameter. The reranking query is provided in the reRankQuery parameter by dereferencing, using the rrq parameter for convenience. The example queries all rock songs and reranks rock music of type reggae and beat:

```
$ curl http://localhost:8983/solr/music/select?q=genre:rock
&rq={!rerank reRankQuery=$rrq reRankDocs=200 reRankWeight=3.0}
&rrq=genre:(regge beat)
```

Join Query

Generally, you denormalize your data before indexing it to Solr, but denormalization is not always an option. Suppose you have a frequently changing value, and for each change, you need to find all the occurrences of that value and update the documents containing it. For such scenarios, Solr provides the *join query*, which you can use to join two indexes.

Solr implements this feature by using `JoinQParser`, which parses the user query provided as a LocalParam and returns `JoinQuery`. Here is the `JoinQuery` syntax:

```
{!join fromIndex=<core-name> from=<from-field> to=<to-field>}
```

Limitations

A join query in Solr is different from SQL joins, and it has these limitations:

- You can join on `from` documents but cannot return values from `from` documents along with the results in the `to` documents.

- The score of `from` documents cannot be used for computing the score of `to` documents.

- Both `from` and `to` fields should be compatible and should go through similar analysis in order for documents to match.

- Both `from` and `to` indexes should exist on the same node.

Example

This section presents an example of a join query.

Find a list of all titles sung by the singer Bob Marley, where the song metadata is in the music core and the singer information is in the singer core

```
$ curl http://localhost:8983/solr/music/select?
q={!join fromIndex=singer from=id to=singerid}
singer:"Bob Marley"&fl=title
```

Block Join

A join query performs a join at query time to match related fields in different indexes. Using a *block join*, you can index nested documents and query them by using `BlockJoinQuery`. A block join can offer better query-time performance, as the relationship is stored in a block as parent-child, and document matching doesn't need to be performed at query time.

Prerequisites

The following are prerequisites for a block join:

- Define the additional field `_root_` in `schema.xml`.

- Index the additional field, which differentiates the parent document from the child document.

- During indexing, child documents should be nested inside the parent document.

- When updating nested documents, you need to reindex the whole block at once. You cannot reindex only the child or parent document.

Solr provides two parsers to support the block join: BlockJoinParentQParser and BlockJoinChildQParser. BlockJoinChildQParser matches the query against the parent documents and returns the child documents in that block. Here is the syntax:

```
{!child of=<field:value>}<parent-condition>
```

The LocalParam of contains the field name and value that differentiate the parent document from the children. The condition following the closing brace can be a Lucene query against the parent document for finding the matching child document. The returned result set will be the nested documents in the matched block.

BlockJoinParentQParser matches the query against the child documents and returns the parent document of that block. Here is the syntax:

```
{!parent which=<field:value>}<children-condition>
```

The LocalParam which contains the field name and value, which differentiate the parent document from the children. The condition following the closing brace can be a Lucene query against the child documents for finding the matching parent document. The returned result set will be the nested documents in the matched block.

Example

This section presents an example of indexing block documents and performing a search by using a block-join child query and a block-join parent query.

Index an album as a parent document and all its tracks as children documents. Add the Boolean field isParent to differentiate the parent document from the child. The following is an XML document.

```xml
<add>
  <doc>
    <field name="id">1</field>
    <field name="album">Imagine</field>
    <field name="singer">John Lennon</field>
    <field name="isParent">true</field>
    <doc>
      <field name="id">2</field>
      <field name="title">Imagine</field>
      <field name="length">3.01</field>
    </doc>
    <doc>
      <field name="id">3</field>
      <field name="title">Crippled Inside</field>
      <field name="length">3.47</field>
    </doc>
  </doc>
</add>
```

```
<doc>
  <field name="id">4</field>
  <field name="album">Confrontation</field>
  <field name="singer">Bob Marley</field>
  <field name="isParent">true</field>
  <doc>
    <field name="id">5</field>
    <field name="title">Buffalo Soldier</field>
    <field name="length">3.01</field>
  </doc>
</doc>
</add>
```

Solr also supports indexing nested documents in native JSON format or using SolrJ. For indexing in JSON format, you need to specify key _childDocuments_ to differentiate the child documents. A sample structure of nested JSON is provided here.

```
[
  {
    "id":"1",
    ...
    "_childDocuments_": [
      {
        ...
      }
    ]
  }
]
```

Search for an album named "imagine" by using a block-join child query

```
$ curl http://localhost:8983/solr/music/select?q={!child of=isParent:true}album:imagine
```

Search for a singer named "bob marley" by using a block-join parent query

```
$ curl http://localhost:8983/solr/music/select?
q={!parent which=isParent=true}singer:("bob marley")
```

Function Query

When a search query is submitted to Solr for retrieving documents, it executes a ranking formula for computing the score of each document matching the query terms. The resultant documents are ordered on the basis of relevancy.

Lucene uses a combination of the Boolean model (BM) and a modified form of the vector space model (VSM) for scoring the documents. You learned the basics of these information retrieval models in Chapter 3. The score is primarily based on term frequency (which signifies that documents containing the query terms more often are ranked higher) and inverse document frequency (which signifies that rarer terms are ranked higher). Chapter 8 covers more details on Solr scoring.

Now, assume that you have defined the required searchable fields, given them appropriate boosts, and created a proper text-analysis chain, Solr will match the user query with document terms by using its scoring formula. This scoring algorithm might be doing a great job determining the relevance of documents, but it has a limitation: the score is computed on the basis of textual similarity. The ranking achieved from this score might not consider factors of practical importance and user needs, especially in real-world cases that require other factors to be considered. The following are examples from different domains, where other factors play an important role:

- A music search engine generally considers popularity and user ratings in deciding the relevancy of songs. The idea is that for two textually similar documents, the one with higher popularity and ratings should be ranked higher.

- In a news site, the freshness of news is crucial, so recency and creation time become important factors.

- A restaurant discovery application ranks nearby restaurants higher for users querying to order a pizza. In any geographical search system, the location and coordinates are more important factors than textual similarity.

A *function query* allows you to compute the score of documents on the basis of external factors such as a numeric value or a mathematical expression, which can complement the existing Solr score to come up with the final score for a document.

Function queries use functions for computing the score, which can be of any of the types listed in Table 7-5.

Table 7-5. *Function Types*

Type	Description	Example
Constant value	Assigns a constant score.	`_val_:2.0`
String literal	Uses a string literal value for computing the score. A string literal is not supported by all functions.	`literal("A literal value")`
Solr field	A Solr field can be specified. The field must exist in `schema.xml` and follow the prerequisites mentioned in the next section.	`sqrt(popularity)`
Function	Solr allows you to use one function inside another.	`sqrt(sum(x,100))`
Parameter substitution	Solr allows you to use parameter substitution as a function.	`q=_val_:sqrt($val1)&val1=100`

Function queries are supported by the DisMax, eDisMax, and standard query parsers.

Prerequisites

If you are using a Solr field in a function query, it has the following prerequisites:

- The field must be indexed and single-valued.

- It must emit only one term from text analysis.

Usage

Function queries are not limited to complementing the score for relevance ranking of documents. These queries can also be used for sorting the results or computing the value to be returned in the response. Function queries can be used in Solr in the following ways:

- FunctionQParserPlugin: Solr provides FunctionQParserPlugin, a dedicated QParserPlugin for creating a function query from the input value. It can be invoked by using LocalParams or by specifying the parser in the defType parameter, as shown in this example:

  ```
  q={!func}sqrt(clicks) // LocalParams
  q=sqrt(clicks)&defType=func // defType
  ```

- FunctionRangeQParserPlugin: This is similar to FunctionQParserPlugin but creates a range query over a function. The Javadoc at https://lucene.apache.org/solr/5_3_1/solr-core/org/apache/solr/search/FunctionRangeQParserPlugin.html provides a list of supported parameters. It can be used in a filter query via LocalParams, as shown here:

  ```
  fq={!frange l=0 u=2.0}sum(user_rating,expert_rating)
  ```

- q *parameter*: The function query can be embedded in a regular search query by using the _val_ hook. All the rules of _val_ apply to it.

  ```
  q=singer:(bob marley) _val_:"sqrt(clicks)"
  ```

- bf *parameter*: The bf parameter in DisMax and Extended DisMax allows you to specify a list of function queries separated by whitespace. You can optionally assign a boost to the queries. The following is an example of a function query applied using the bf parameter.

  ```
  q=singer:(bob marley)&bf="sqrt(clicks)^0.5 recip(rord(price),1,1000,1000)^0.3"
  ```

- boost *parameter*: Similar to bf, function queries can be applied on a boost parameter or boost query parser, as shown here.

  ```
  q=singer:(bob marley)&boost="sqrt(clicks)^0.5 recip(rord(price),1,1000,1000)^0.3"
  q={!boost b=sqrt(popularity)}singer:(bob marley)
  ```

- sort *parameter*: Solr allows you to sort the results by using a function query. The following is an example of result sorting in descending order, based on the computed sum of user_rating and expert_rating field:

  ```
  q=singer:(bob marley)&sort=sum(user_rating,expert_rating) desc
  ```

- fl *parameter*: Function queries can be used in the fl parameter to create a pseudo field and return the output of the function query in response. The following example returns the rating of titles computed by taking the average of user_rating and expert_rating:

  ```
  q=singer:(bob marley)&fl=title,album, div(sum(user_rating,expert_rating),2),score
  ```

Function Categories

In the previous section, you saw a few examples of functions such as sqrt(), sum(), and rord(). The functions supported by Solr can be broadly categorized into the following groups:

- *Mathematical function*: These functions support mathematical computations such as sum(), div(), log(), sin(), and cos(). Refer to java.util.Math Javadocs for details of these mathematical functions.

- *Date function*: For use cases such as news and blogs, the documents need to be boosted on recency. Solr provides the ms() function to return the millisecond difference since the epoch of midnight, January 1, 1970 UTC. In the next section, you will see an example of boosting recent documents.

- *Boolean function*: The Boolean functions can be used for taking appropriate action if a condition is met. The following example modifies the previous FunctionQParserPlugin example to assign a default user_rating of 5, if the value is missing in that field:

  ```
  fq={!frange l=0 u=2.0}sum(def(user_rating,5),expert_rating)
  ```

- *Relevancy function*: Solr provides a set of relevancy functions to retrieve information about the indexed terms, such as document frequency and term frequency.

  ```
  q=idf(color,'red')
  ```

- *Distance function*: Solr provides functions for computing a distance between two points by using, for example, Euclidian distance or Manhattan distance. It also allows you to compute the distance between two strings by using formulas such as the Levenshtein distance or Jaro-Winkler. The following example computes the distance between the terms *red* and *raid* by using the Jaro-Winkler edit-distance formula.

  ```
  strdist("red","raid",jw)
  ```

- *Geospatial search*: Solr supports location data and geospatial searches and provides function queries such as geodist(). The preceding functions for computing distance between points are also widely used in spatial searches. Refer to the Solr documentation at https://cwiki.apache.org/confluence/display/solr/Spatial+Search for more details on spatial search.

- *Other functions*: Solr supports some additional functions such as ord(), which returns the ordinal of the indexed field value within the indexed list of terms for that field.

■ **Note**   Refer to the Solr official documentation at https://cwiki.apache.org/confluence/display/solr/Function+Queries for a complete list of supported methods and their uses.

Example

You have already seen a couple of examples in our discussions about the function query. Let's see a few more examples illustrating some common needs for tuning the relevance ranking of documents by using function query.

Function query to specify that the recently released titles are more relevant

```
$ curl http://localhost:8983/solr/music/select?
q=bob marley&boost=recip(ms(NOW,releasedate),3.16e-11,1,1)
&defType=edismax
```

Function query to specify that titles that have been played more than a certain number of times are more relevant

```
$ curl
http://localhost:8983/solr/music/select?
q=bob marley&boost=div(log(sum(clicks,1),10))&defType=edismax
```

Caution

A function query is a wonderful tool for addressing real-world ranking needs, but it demands to be used cautiously. The following are some of the important factors to be taken care of while using it:

- The function query should be fair, and its impact should be optimally set. If the output of a function query or the boost value is very high, it can lead to documents with poor textual similarity also ranking very high. In a worst-case scenario, it can be possible that whatever query you give, a document with a very high function score always appears as the most relevant document.

- A function query runs for each matching document. Therefore, costly computation should be avoided, as it can affect the performance drastically. Solr recommends functions with fast random access.

- While writing a mathematical expression, the default values should be handled appropriately. For example, product(x,y) can result in a score of 0 if either of the input values is 0.

■ **Note** If there is no value for a field in the index, 0 is substituted for use in the function query.

Custom Function Query

In the previous section, you learned about functions provided by Solr to use in function queries. At times the Solr-provided functions might not fit your business needs, and you may want to plug in your own named function to Solr.

Lucene defines classes for function queries in the package org.apache.lucene.queries.function.*. To write your custom function, you need to extend the following two Lucene classes:

ValueSourceParser: A factory that parses user queries to generate ValueSource instances.

ValueSource: An abstract class for creating a function query. The custom function will be defined in the class extending it.

In this section, you will learn to write a custom function.

Assume that you are working for a highly fashionable e-commerce company, where a majority of units sold are of the top trending products. You have analyzed that each trend starts small in your company, grows slowly, reaches a peak, and then begins to fall and slowly go off the chart. The trend moves like a bell curve. For this specific need, you decide to develop a function using a Gaussian formula, which provides a score that follows the bell curve. Here are the steps you need to follow:

1. Extend the ValueSourceParser abstract class.

    ```
    public class GaussianValueSourceParser extends ValueSourceParser {
    }
    ```

2. Implement the parse() abstract method and return an instance of the custom ValueSource implementation, which you will create in the next step. Also, get the ValueSource from FunctionQParser and pass it to the custom ValueSource. You will need it in your custom algorithm. You can optionally pass additional parameters, as shown in this example.

    ```
    @Override
    public ValueSource parse(FunctionQParser fp) throws SyntaxError {
      ValueSource vs = fp.parseValueSource();

      return new GaussianValueSource(vs, stdDeviation, mean);
    }
    ```

3. If you want to read parameters from the factory definition in solrconfig.xml, you can optionally extend the init() method. You read the standard deviation and mean values and provide them to the constructor of the custom ValueSource.

    ```
    public void init(NamedList namedList) {
      this.stdDeviation = (Float) namedList.get(STD_DEVIATION_PARAM);
      this.mean = (Float) namedList.get(MEAN_PARAM);
    }
    ```

4. Create a custom class by extending the ValueSource abstract class. Define the constructor for setting the instance variables.

    ```
    protected final ValueSource source;
    protected float stdDeviation = 1.0f;
    protected float mean = 1.0f;
    protected float variance = 1.0f;

    public GaussianValueSource(ValueSource source, float stdDeviation, float mean) {
      this.source = source;
      this.stdDeviation = stdDeviation;
      this.variance = stdDeviation * stdDeviation;
      this.mean = mean;
    }
    ```

5. Override the getValues() method of ValueSource. The method should return an implementation of FloatDocValues, an abstract class to support float values. In this method, also get the FunctionValues, using the getValues() method of the ValueSource instance provided by the factory.

    ```
    @Override
    public FunctionValues getValues(Map context, LeafReaderContext readerContext)
            throws IOException {
      final FunctionValues aVals =  source.getValues(context, readerContext);

      return new FloatDocValues(this) {
      ..
        };
    }
    ```

6. Override the floatVal() method of the FloatDocValues class and get the value from the floatVal() method of the FunctionValues class that you instantiated in the previous step. This value is based on the function query type, such as the value of a Solr field.

    ```
    @Override
    public float floatVal(int doc) {
      float val1 = aVals.floatVal(doc);
      ..
    }
    ```

7. Write your custom logic that acts as the value and return the float score. The Gaussian formula is shown here; you can replace it with any other formula.

    ```
    float score = (float) Math.pow(Math.exp(-(((val1 - mean)
      * (val1 - mean)) / ((2 * variance)))), 1 /
                (stdDeviation * Math.sqrt(2 * Math.PI)));
    return score;
    ```

8. Override the abstract methods toString() in the FloatDocValues implementation.

    ```
    @Override
    public String toString(int doc) {
      return "Gaussian function query (" + aVals.toString(doc) + ')';
    }
    ```

9. Override the abstract method hashCode() in the ValueSource implementation.

    ```
    @Override
    public int hashCode() {
      return source.hashCode() + "Gaussian function query".hashCode();
    }
    ```

10. Build the program and add the path of Java binary JAR to the lib definition in
    `solrconfig.xml`.

    ```
    <lib dir="./lib" />
    ```

11. Register the custom ValueSourceParser in `solrconfig.xml`.

    ```
    <valueSourceParser name="gaussian"
    class="com.apress.solr.pa.chapter07.functionquery.
    GaussianValueSourceParser" >
      <float name="stdDeviation">1.0</float>
      <float name="mean">8</float>
    </valueSourceParser>
    ```

12. Use the new named function in your search, gaussian in this case.

    ```
    $ curl http://localhost:8983/solr/ecommerce/select?q=blazer&defType=edismax
    &fl=score,product,trendcount&boost=gaussian(trendcount)
    ```

Java Source Code

The following is the complete Java source code for the Gaussian ValueSource discussed in this section.

GaussianValueSourceParser.java

```java
package com.apress.solr.pa.chapter07.functionquery;

import org.apache.lucene.queries.function.ValueSource;
import org.apache.solr.common.util.NamedList;
import org.apache.solr.common.util.Utils;
import org.apache.solr.search.FunctionQParser;
import org.apache.solr.search.SyntaxError;
import org.apache.solr.search.ValueSourceParser;
public class GaussianValueSourceParser extends ValueSourceParser {
        private static final String STD_DEVIATION_PARAM = "stdDeviation";
         private static final String MEAN_PARAM = "mean";

         private float stdDeviation;
         private float mean;

      public void init(NamedList namedList) {
              this.stdDeviation = (Float) namedList.get(STD_DEVIATION_PARAM);
              this.mean = (Float) namedList.get(MEAN_PARAM);
      }

      @Override
      public ValueSource parse(FunctionQParser fp) throws SyntaxError {
              ValueSource vs = fp.parseValueSource();
              return new GaussianValueSource(vs, stdDeviation, mean);
      }
}
```

GaussianValueSource.java

```java
package com.apress.solr.pa.chapter7.functionquery;

import java.io.IOException;
import java.util.Map;

import org.apache.lucene.index.LeafReaderContext;
import org.apache.lucene.queries.function.FunctionValues;
import org.apache.lucene.queries.function.ValueSource;
import org.apache.lucene.queries.function.docvalues.FloatDocValues;
import org.apache.lucene.queries.function.valuesource.FloatFieldSource;

public class GaussianValueSource extends ValueSource {
        protected final ValueSource source;
        protected float stdDeviation = 1.0f;
        protected float mean = 1.0f;
        protected float variance = 1.0f;

        public GaussianValueSource(ValueSource source, float stdDeviation, float mean) {
                this.source = source;
                this.stdDeviation = stdDeviation;
                this.variance = stdDeviation * stdDeviation;
                this.mean = mean;
        }

        @Override
        public String description() {
                return "Gaussian function query (" + source.description() + ")";
        }

        @Override
        public boolean equals(Object arg0) {
                return false;
        }

        @Override
        public FunctionValues getValues(Map context, LeafReaderContext readerContext)
                        throws IOException {
                final FunctionValues aVals =  source.getValues(context, readerContext);

                return new FloatDocValues(this) {
                        @Override
                        public float floatVal(int doc) {
                                float val1 = aVals.floatVal(doc);
                                float score = (float) Math.pow(Math.exp(-(((val1 - mean) *
                                (val1 - mean)) / ((2 * variance)))), 1 / (stdDeviation *
                                Math.sqrt(2 * Math.PI)));
                                return score;
                        }

                        @Override
```

```
              public String toString(int doc) {
                return "Gaussian function query (" + aVals.toString(doc) + ')';
                }
          };
      }

      @Override
      public int hashCode() {
              return source.hashCode() + "Gaussian function query".hashCode();
      }

}
```

Referencing an External File

A function query uses information such as user ratings, download count, or trending count to compute the function score. If you look at these values, they change more frequently than values in other fields. For example, a video-sharing web site like YouTube requires updating the trending count every few hours, as it's common these days for a video to get a million hits in a day.

Indexing this frequently changing information requires updating other fields also, which change less frequently. To address such use cases, Solr provides ExternalFileField, a special implementation of FieldType, which allows you to specify the field values in an external file. The external file contains the mapping from the key field in the document to the external value. Solr allows you to modify the file at a desired frequency without reindexing the other fields.

The caveat is that the external fields are not searchable. They can be used only for function queries or returning a response.

Usage

Following are the steps to configure ExternalFileField in your search engine:

1. Define the FieldType for ExternalFileField in schema.xml and specify the appropriate parameters. The following are the special parameters provided by ExternalFileField:

    keyField: Specifies the Solr field that should be used for mapping the value.

    defVal: Defines the default value, if entry for the key is missing in the external file.

    valType: Specifies the type of value in the file. The valid values for this attribute are float, pfloat, and tfloat.

A sample fieldType definition is provided here:

```
<fieldType name="trendingCount" stored="false" indexed="false"
keyField="trackId" defVal="0" class="solr.ExternalFileField"
valType="pfloat"/>
```

2. Create the external file with the name external_<fieldname> in Solr's index
    directory, which is $SOLR_HOME/<core>/data by default. The file should contain
    a key-value pair delimited by =. The external file for the trendingCount field
    mentioned previously should look like this:

```
$ cat external_trendingCount
doc1=1.0
doc2=0.8
doc3=2
```

The external file name can also end with an extension, such as external_trendingCount.txt. If
Solr discovers multiple files with a .* pattern, it will sort the files on name and refer the last one.

3. Solr allows you to define an event listener, which activates whenever a
    new searcher is opened or an existing searcher is reloaded. Register the
    ExternalFileField to the desired listener. The following is an example for
    registering to the listener:

```
<listener event="newSearcher"
class="org.apache.solr.schema.ExternalFileFieldReloader"/>
<listener event="firstSearcher"
class="org.apache.solr.schema.ExternalFileFieldReloader"/>
```

After following these steps, ExternalFileField is ready to be configured in any field definition, which
can be used in a function query like any other field that you've seen.

Summary

The previous chapter focused on the core component of Solr: querying. In this chapter, you learned to get
granular control over querying by using LocalParams and the reranking query, to join indexes by using a join
query, and to index hierarchical data by using a block join. Then you learned about other features such as
result grouping, faceting, and statistics.

You saw how nontextual information such as popularity, recency, and trends are crucial for deciding
the relevance ranking of documents, and how to use that information in Solr. You also learned to write a
custom named function for use in a function query.

In the next chapter, you will learn about Solr scoring. At the end of that chapter, you will understand
how a document ranks at a particular position in the result set and why a document appears before or after
another document.

CHAPTER 8

■ ■ ■

Solr Scoring

While evaluating the search response, you've probably wondered why a particular document ranks above another and how these documents get their score. In this chapter, you will learn about Solr scoring.

This chapter starts with the default ranking implementation and the factors that control the score, and gradually proceed into more details so that you can override the existing scoring factors or write a custom scorer. Even though scoring is an advanced topic and this chapter covers some mathematical formulas, you don't need to be a mathematical wizard to understand it.

I could have added a brief introduction to scoring in Chapter 3, but I wanted to dive into more detail, get beyond the basic concepts, and discuss Solr scoring at the implementation level, which requires a dedicated chapter.

■ **Note** In Chapter 3, you learned about information retrieval concepts; if you skipped that chapter, I advise you to read it now, before continuing with this chapter, though it's not mandatory.

This chapter covers the following topics:

- How Solr ranks a document
- Default ranking model and factors
- Alternate models supported
- Diagnosing a document score
- Custom scoring

Introduction to Solr Scoring

Relevance ranking is the core of any search engine, and so it is for Solr. To rank documents for a user query, Solr computes the score of each matching document based on the model's algorithm and ranks them on their relative score. It orders the document with the highest score to the top of the result set.

Initially, Lucene supported only the TF-IDF-based vector space model for ranking documents, but later release 4.0 introduced additional models to allow more-flexible ranking. Each of these models extends the abstract Similarity class of Lucene to implement the algorithm. The existing TF-IDF-based model, implemented in the DefaultSimilarity class, continues to be the default model for ranking. You will learn about these models in this chapter.

A majority of Solr setups use `DefaultSimilarity`, which works well for most requirements. I recommend that you not worry about changing the model and continue using the default similarity, unless you really understand why you need an alternate model or custom implementation.

In 90% of cases, you will be able to manipulate and control the ranking of documents by applying different tuning methods either while indexing or querying, and without touching the `Similarity` class. These methods contribute to the score of the document in one way or another, and tuning it appropriately should bring the desired result. To put it together, here are the ways in which the ranking of documents can be controlled:

- Query syntax, operators, and other combinations such as phrase, slop, and fuzzy matching

- Query parser and its configuration

- Text analysis

- Document and field boosts while indexing

- Term boost while querying

- Function queries

If these customizations get the desired result, you should avoid changing the ranking model and should manipulate it only if there is really a need. I recommend that you clearly understand the changes you are making to the ranking and test them thoroughly.

Even if you have no plans of changing the ranking model, it's still important to learn about them so that you understand how the preceding factors contribute to the final score and you can gauge the effect of any tuning on your document ranking.

You might have a business case where you feel that tuning these parameters is of no help, and your scoring requirements are different from the default implementation provided by Solr. In such a scenario, you can do the following:

- Use the alternate `Similarity` implementation provided by Lucene and tune it as per your requirement.

- Extend the default similarity to manipulate its scoring factor.

- Write your custom implementation. This will require you to have an expert-level understanding of your ranking needs and the algorithm you are planning to use. You need to be cautious, as this may get you into a loop of iterations without any considerable improvement in the ranking.

Before you get any further, the following are some important facts about Solr scoring that will help you avoid any assumptions:

Lucene: The scoring implementation in Solr is provided by Lucene. The `org.apache.lucene.search.similarities` package contains all the `Similarity` classes that implement the various ranking models. For wiring your custom implementation, you can package your classes in a separate JAR and add it to the Solr classpath without worrying about changing the Solr or Lucene package.

Sorted by relevance: By default, the search response is sorted by score in descending order, and the top document is identified as the best match.

Maximum score: No upper boundary has been specified for the score of documents. The maximum value is based on several scoring factors, including boosts, which combined together can lead to a very high score. The `maxScore` parameter in a search response returns the maximum score for that query. Figure 8-1 shows an example that marks the `maxScore` for a query.

```
"response": {
  "numFound": 14089,
  "start": 0,
  "maxScore": 3.771758,
  "docs": [
    {
```

Figure 8-1. *Maximum score for a user query*

No negative score: The scores are always floating-point numbers greater than 0.0, and no document can have a negative score.

Scores are relative: For a given query, the scores of documents are relative to each other and comparable. Multiple documents can have the same score as all scoring factors individually, or their scores summed up can generate the same value. If a normalized score is desired, you can divide the score of each document by the maximum score for the query.

Per field computation: The scores are computed per field. The individual scores of each field are summarized to compute the final score for the document.

Pluggable: Solr allows you to extend the available Similarity implementation as well as plug in your own scoring algorithm.

■ **Note** The terms *relevance ranking*, *Solr scoring*, and *similarity* and are used interchangeably. In contrast, the term *ranking model* refers to the algorithm used to implement the similarity.

Default Scoring

The default scoring approach of Lucene is what makes it so popular. It is fast, optimally tuned, easy to understand and use, and practical for most use cases. It's kind of a *one size fits (almost) all* approach.

Default Lucene scoring is based on a combination of the Boolean model (BM) and vector space model (VSM). For a given query, not all documents in the corpus are ranked, but only a subset of documents that satisfy the Boolean condition (specified using the Boolean operator). These narrowed-down documents also reduce the processing time by saving the VSM from unnecessarily ranking the irrelevant documents. To put it simply, documents approved by the BM are ranked by the VSM. The numFound parameter in the search response specifies the number of documents approved by the BM. Figure 8-2 marks the numFound parameter, to show the number of matching documents.

```
"response": {
    "numFound": 14089,
    "start": 0,
    "maxScore": 3.771758,
    "docs": [
```

Figure 8-2. Number of matching documents

Implementation

The default scoring in Lucene is implemented by the DefaultSimilarity class, which extends the TFIDFSimilarity class. The DefaultSimilarity class derives an advanced form of TF-IDF-based scoring for practical score computation. In the next section, you will learn about TF, IDF, and other factors of default scoring.

No additional definition is required in solrconfig.xml or schema.xml, and Solr abstracts all the implementation details from the user. If you want to explicitly specify this similarity, though it makes no sense, you can do so in schema.xml as follows:

```
<schema>
  ..
  <similarity class="solr.DefaultSimilarity" />
</schema>
```

Scoring Factors

This section covers the factors that affect the document score. Once you understand these factors, you will learn about the formulas that normalize those factors and combines them to come up with a summarized score. An understanding of factors is sufficient for tuning the score by using provisions such as boosting, and understanding the formula is relatively less important for that.

■ **Note**   The term weight is computed on a per field basis. To compute the term score for a field, the scoring factors use the statistics of that particular field. The final weight of that term is computed by summarizing the scores of all the fields to which it applies.

Following are the primary factors that determine the score of a document:

Term frequency (TF): This is the number of times a term appears in a document's field. A document's score is directly proportional to its term frequency: the higher the count of a term in a document, the higher its score. The model assumes that if a term appears in the document more times, it is more relevant to the user.

Inverse document frequency (IDF): This factor computes a score on the basis of the number of documents in which the term appears. It takes the inverse of the count: the higher the count, the lower the weight. The idea is to give more importance to rarer words. Note that the document count is taken for that particular field, and the presence of the term in some other field is not considered.

In the previous chapters, you used a stop words list to filter out terms that are not important. The `stopFilterFactory` discards the terms present in the list outright and any query for that term will result in no match. But some terms are less important than other terms, and can in no way be filtered out. The IDF factor of scoring handles such highly frequent terms by weighting them low. For example, in the medical domain, terms such as *patient, result, treatment, protein*, and *disease* are frequent and of low importance, whereas terms such as *tumor, Parkinson's*, and *cyst* are comparatively rarer and of high importance. The IDF as a factor is crucial in full-text search to weight such terms appropriately.

> *Field length (*`lengthNorm`*)*: This factor considers the number of tokens in the field for determining the significance of a document. The shorter the field (the fewer the number of tokens indexed), the more significant the document. The idea behind length norm is to ensure that the presence of a term in a short field such as `title` should be given more importance than the presence of that term in a long field such as `abstract`.

> *Coordination factor (*`coord`*)*: This factor scores on the basis of terms overlapping between the query and the document. It signifies that a document that contains most of the query terms is more important and should be rewarded.

> *Boost*: Documents and fields can be boosted at index time, and terms can be boosted at query time. By giving a higher boost, you specify that a particular term or set of terms is more important and should be scored higher. This is the factor with which you can directly and easily tune the score of a specific document.

■ **Note**   `QueryNorm` is an additional factor but is not specified here because it doesn't affect the score between two documents. Instead, it normalizes the score between two queries. You will learn about `QueryNorm` while discussing the Lucene scoring formula.

Scoring Formula

The default similarity factors, discussed in the previous section, don't use the count as is to compute the document score. The raw value is normalized to get the most usable and balanced value that gives an optimal weight for computing the practical score for the document. Depending on the need and information availability, Solr normalizes the factors either at query time or index time, and its value is based either on the statistics of a field, a document, or the whole collection.

In the VSM, queries and documents are represented as weighted vectors in a multidimensional space, where each term is a dimension and the TF-IDF value constitutes the weight. VSM uses cosine similarity to compute the score of a document. If you find this mathematical concept too difficult to digest, you can skip this sentence for now. If it interests you or you want to brush up on the underlying concept, refer to Chapter 3 for details of the VSM.

As noted previously, Lucene uses an advanced form of TF-IDF to compute a practical score. This advanced form accommodates the provisions for boosting, length normalization, and coordination factors, along with term frequency and inverse document frequency. The formula for computing a score by using an advanced form of TF-IDF in Lucene is shown here:

$$score(q,d) = coord(q,d) \cdot queryNorm(q) \cdot \sum_{t\ in\ q} \left(tf(t\ in\ d) \cdot idf(t) \cdot t.getBoost(\ ) \cdot norm(t,d) \right)$$

This scoring formula contains six functions. Each function is responsible for computing the normalized value for a specific scoring factor. The output of these functions are combined, as mentioned in the equation, to generate the final score of the document.

Each function and its relationship with the Lucene scoring factor is described next. For simplicity of understanding, the functions have been defined assuming that the index has only one searchable field.

tf(t in d)

TF, as noted previously, is the abbreviation for *term frequency*. This function counts the number of occurrences of each query term in the document. The score of a document is directly proportional to its frequency. The higher the term's frequency, the higher the score. Lucene normalizes the TF weight by computing a square root of the frequency:

$$tf(t \ in \ d) = frequency^{1/2}$$

idf(t)

As you know, *IDF* is the abbreviation for *inverse document frequency*. This function computes the score by taking the inverse of the number of documents in which the term appears. Lucene normalizes the value by taking the logarithm of the inverted value:

$$idf(t) = 1 + log\left(\frac{numDocs}{docFreq + 1}\right)$$

The numeric constant 1 is added to docFreq and the logarithmic value, to avoid undefined values like numDocs/0 and log(0), respectively.

coord(q,d)

coord represents the *coordination factor*. This function computes the score based on the number of query terms that overlap in the document. The coordination factor is computed by using this formula:

$$coord(q,d) = \frac{overlap}{maxOverlap}$$

queryNorm(q)

We skipped this function while discussing document-ranking factors. The purpose of queryNorm is to normalize the scores between queries—in contrast to other factors, which normalize the score between documents. This function makes the score between two queries comparable. The same queryNorm value is applied on all the documents for a query, so it doesn't directly affect the score of a document. The queryNorm for a query term is computed as follows:

$$queryNorm(q) = \frac{1}{sumOfSquaredWeights^{1/2}}$$

where the sumOfSquaredWeights is computed by using the following formula:

$$sumOfSquaredWeights = q.getBoost(\ )^2 . \sum_{t\ in\ q}\left(idf(t). \ t.getBoost(\ )\right)^2$$

t.getBoost()

This function gets the term boost applied at query time, such as the query adidas^3 shoes. It's important to note that this function factors only the query-time boost and doesn't consider the field or document boost applied while indexing. The term boost directly affects the score of a document. If the query term doesn't contain any boost, the default value of 1.0 is implicitly applied.

norm(t,d)

This function is a product of two factors, namely lengthNorm and the index-time boost. The lengthNorm considers the length of the field for determining the significance of a document. The shorter the field (the fewer the number of tokens indexed), the more significant the document. An index-time boost is a boost applied on either the document or the field while indexing documents. The formula for computing the norm is shown here:

$$norm(t,d) = lengthNorm \ . \ \prod f.boost(\ )$$

The Similarity class computes the norm while indexing documents. If you apply an alternate model (a Similarity implementation), the documents should be reindexed.

The normalization factor (or norm) is computed at the time of indexing the document. An interesting thing about norm is that the computed norm value, which is float, is encoded into a single byte for being stored. At query time, the norm byte value is read from the index and decoded back to float. The purpose of encoding/decoding is to support efficient memory utilization and reduce the index size, but it comes at the expense of some precision loss.

If norms are omitted on a field, by setting omitNorms="true" in the field definition, the norm value for that field will be ignored.

While indexing, if any document has multiple fields with the same name, all its boosts are multiplied together to calculate the aggregate boost for that field.

■ **Note**   Refer to `https://lucene.apache.org/core/5_3_1/core/org/apache/lucene/search/` `similarities/DefaultSimilarity.html` for details of default similarity.

Limitations

The TF-IDF-based VSM is a simple yet powerful model that works great for most cases, especially full-text searches, but it has some limitations.

At a high level, this model is based on two primary concepts:

- Identifying the most interesting terms in a query and their weight

- Finding the most relevant documents based on weighted terms

A TF-IDF-based model considers rare terms as more interesting, but that's not always the case. For example, in a search engine for music metadata, terms such as *love* and *heart* are common, because many song titles contain these words, but they are in no way less important. If you have a similar scenario, you might want to turn off IDF as a scoring factor, maybe on that field. Later in this chapter, you'll see some sample code for overriding a default factor.

Another limitation of the underlying VSM is that it assumes the terms to be independent (there is no relation between the terms), but practically the terms are related. For example, for words such as *credit card* or *paper bag*, the relationship is lost in VSM.

Explain Query

The Solr search parameter `debugQuery=true` provides an explanation of the score computation for each document in the result set. The additional element `explain` in the search response contains an entry for each document (mapped to its `uniqueId`) and provides a description of the score returned by the functions and its aggregation to get the score for each of the query terms. Different fields can return different scores for the same query term, which is again summarized to compute the final score for the term. This term score is again summarized with the score of other query terms, if any, to return the final score of the document.

To better understand the query explanation, you will index a small set of documents and try to understand the score computation for a sample query:

1. Create a small set of sample documents. The following is a sample in CSV format:

    ```
    id,title,cat,units,popularity
    1,Apple iPhone,phone,100,9
    2,Apple iMac,desktop,9,8
    3,Apple MacBook Pro laptop,laptop,30,10
    4,Lenovo laptop,laptop,40,7
    5,Asus Laptop,laptop,60,8
    6,HP Laptop,laptop,50,7
    ```

2. Index the documents.

```
$ curl http://localhost:8983/solr/hellosolr/update/csv?commit=true
 --data-binary @explain-sample.csv
 -H 'Content-Type:text/plain; charset=utf-8'
```

3. Query with the additional parameter debugQuery=true.

```
$ curl http://localhost:8983/solr/hellosolr/select?
q=apple+laptop&fl=*,score&wt=xml&indent=true&debugQuery=true
&defType=edismax&qf=title+cat&lowercaseOperators=true
```

Figure 8-3 contains a snapshot of the query explanation returned by Solr. The following are some key points to note:

- The Similarity class used for the score computation of each term is specified in square brackets. An example is underlined in Figure 8-3.

- The score returned by each function is specified along with the input value that resulted in the score.

- The individual score of each function is aggregated to get the final score for the term on all fields that contain the token. In Figure 8-3, the term *laptop* matches in two fields, title and cat, and their score is computed separately, annotated as *d* and *e*.

- For a term, all its field scores are summarized to get a final score. The summarized field score depends on the query parser. eDisMax takes the maximum score, marked as *c* in Figure 8-3.

- The summarized score of each token is finally summed up to come up with the final score for the document. In Figure 8-3, the annotation *a* marks the final score, which is a sum of term scores *b* and *c*.

- The same queryNorm is applied on all the terms.

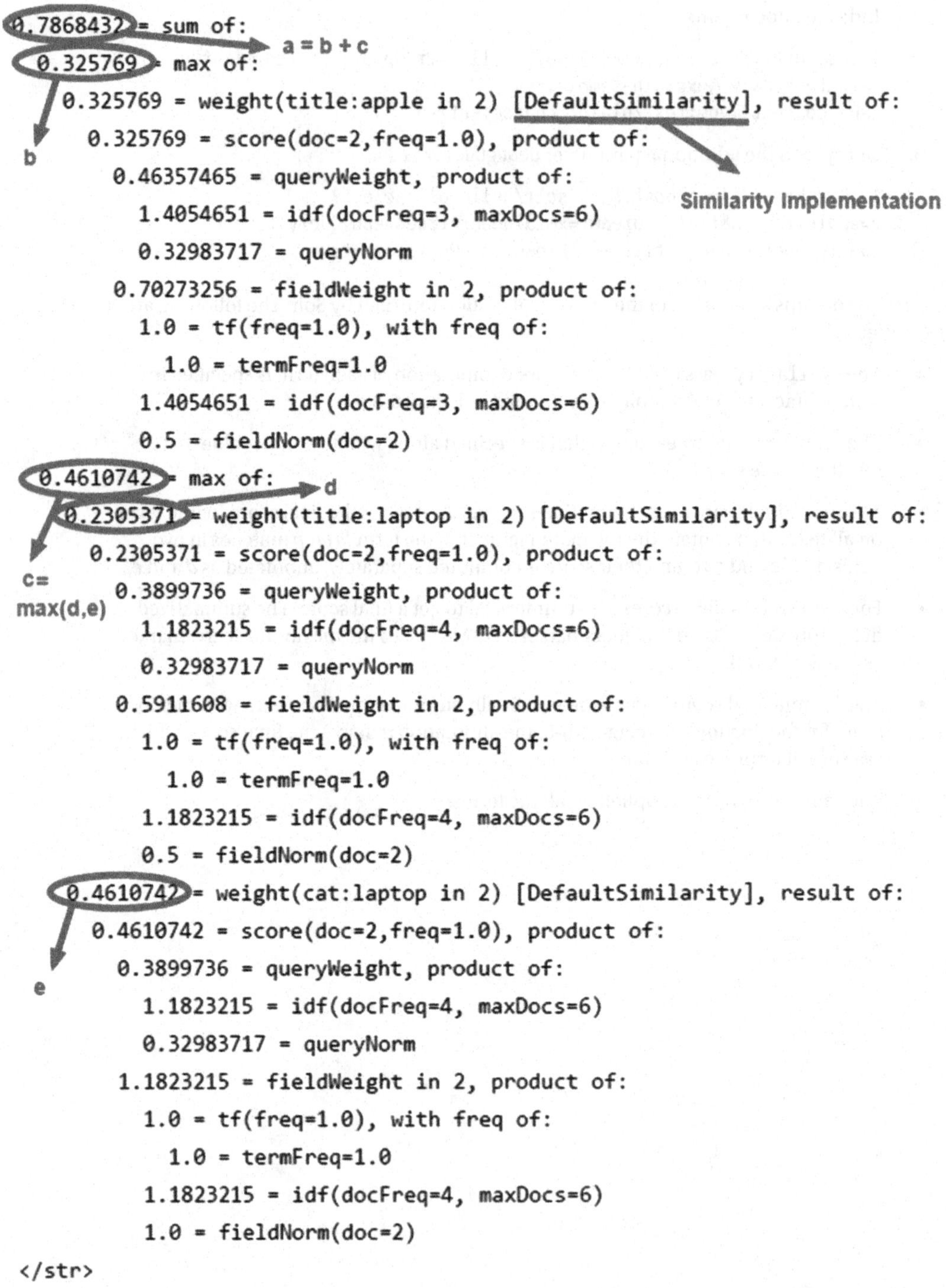

```
0.7868432 = sum of:
                          a = b + c
  0.325769 = max of:
    0.325769 = weight(title:apple in 2) [DefaultSimilarity], result of:
      0.325769 = score(doc=2,freq=1.0), product of:
 b      0.46357465 = queryWeight, product of:           Similarity Implementation
          1.4054651 = idf(docFreq=3, maxDocs=6)
          0.32983717 = queryNorm
        0.70273256 = fieldWeight in 2, product of:
          1.0 = tf(freq=1.0), with freq of:
            1.0 = termFreq=1.0
          1.4054651 = idf(docFreq=3, maxDocs=6)
          0.5 = fieldNorm(doc=2)
  0.4610742 = max of:       d
    0.2305371 = weight(title:laptop in 2) [DefaultSimilarity], result of:
      0.2305371 = score(doc=2,freq=1.0), product of:
 c=     0.3899736 = queryWeight, product of:
 max(d,e)  1.1823215 = idf(docFreq=4, maxDocs=6)
          0.32983717 = queryNorm
        0.5911608 = fieldWeight in 2, product of:
          1.0 = tf(freq=1.0), with freq of:
            1.0 = termFreq=1.0
          1.1823215 = idf(docFreq=4, maxDocs=6)
          0.5 = fieldNorm(doc=2)
    0.4610742 = weight(cat:laptop in 2) [DefaultSimilarity], result of:
      0.4610742 = score(doc=2,freq=1.0), product of:
        0.3899736 = queryWeight, product of:
 e        1.1823215 = idf(docFreq=4, maxDocs=6)
          0.32983717 = queryNorm
        1.1823215 = fieldWeight in 2, product of:
          1.0 = tf(freq=1.0), with freq of:
            1.0 = termFreq=1.0
          1.1823215 = idf(docFreq=4, maxDocs=6)
          1.0 = fieldNorm(doc=2)
</str>
```

Figure 8-3. *Explain query*

Alternative Scoring Models

In addition to the default VSM-based scoring, Lucene 4.0 introduced new scoring models. These models bring in additional flexibility to the ranking possibilities offered by Solr.

A majority of Solr- and Lucene-based applications still rely on default scoring. If you can get the desired result by tuning the TF-IDF weight or giving an appropriate boost, or if the idea of a mathematical computation scares you, you can continue using the default algorithm. These alternate models require some amount of mathematical understanding.

The `org.apache.lucene.search.similarities.*` package contains all the classes for computing the relevance ranking of documents. The abstract class `Similarity` is the base class, and like `DefaultSimilarity`, the implementation for these models also extends it.

If you are planning to evaluate any of these alternate models, first understand the underlying algorithm. Lots of research papers are available over the Web that provide a detailed description of the algorithms. Choose the model that fits closest to your requirements and then evaluate it to see whether it meets those needs. You can either create separate indexes using the models and compare the results or run A/B testing.

The default similarity doesn't require any additional parameters, but these alternate models allow you to control the behavior of the algorithm by using additional parameters.

■ **Note** Documents should be reindexed to utilize the full potential of the alternate scoring model as norms are computed at index time.

This section covers the two primary ranking alternatives supported by Lucene.

BM25Similarity

BM25Similarity is the most widely used ranking algorithm among the alternative implementations provided by Lucene. This similarity is based on the Okapi BM25 algorithm, where *BM* stands for *best matching* and is a probabilistic retrieval model. It can produce better results than TF-IDF-based ranking for indexes containing small documents.

This model is similar to the VSM, in the sense that it takes a bag-of-words approach and considers term frequency and inverse document frequency to compute and summarize the score. But it has some prominent differences. Two of the most important differences between these algorithms are as follows:.

> *Saturation*: In the VSM, the normalized term frequency of a document grows linearly with the growing term count and has no upper limit. In the BM25-based model, the normalized value grows nonlinearly, and after a point does not grow with the growing term count. This point is the saturation point for term frequency in BM25. Figure 8-4 shows a graph comparing term frequency for DefaultSimilarity (which is VSM based) and BM25Similarity (which is BM25 based).

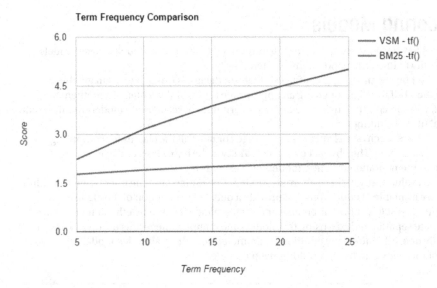

Figure 8-4. Term frequency in DefaultSimilarity vs. BM25Similarity

In BM25Similarity, if the term frequency goes beyond a threshold, the increasing count will have no additional effect on the score of the document, and the score of VSM will be more than that of BM25.

Field length (lengthNorm): BM25 considers the fact that longer documents have more terms, and so the possibility of higher term frequency is also more. As a term can have a high frequency due to the long length and might not be more relevant to the user query, this similarity applies an additional parameter, b, that normalizes the term frequency due to this possibility. Table 8-1 provides more details of this parameter.

Table 8-1. BM25SimilarityFactory Configuration Parameters

Parameter	Type	Description
k1	Float	This optional parameter controls the saturation level of the term frequency. The default value is 1.2. A higher value delays the saturation, while a lower value leads to early saturation.
b	Float	This optional parameter controls the degree of effect of the document length in normalizing the term frequency. The default value is 0.75. A higher value increases the effect of normalization, while a lower value reduces its effect.
discountOverlaps	Boolean	This optional parameter determines whether the overlapping tokens (the tokens with 0 position increments), should be ignored while computing the norm based on the document length. The default value is true, which ignores the overlapping tokens.

Here are the steps for computing a score by using BM25Similarity:

1. Register the BM25SimilarityFactory in schema.xml by using the similarity element. Globally, only one similarity class should be defined. If no similarity definition is available in schema.xml, by default DefaultSimilarity is used.

```
<schema>
  ..
  <similarity class="solr.BM25SimilarityFactory" />
</schema>
```

2. Specify the configuration parameters. Table 8-1 describes the parameters supported by BM25SimilarityFactory. Here is a sample configuration:

```
<similarity class="solr.BM25SimilarityFactory">
  <float name="k1">1.2</float>
  <float name="b">0.75</float>
</similarity>
```

There is no standard rule that specifies the ideal value for the parameters k1 and b. The optimal combination of k1 and b is to be computed by experimenting on the dataset.

3. Reindex the documents.

DFRSimilarity

DFRSimilarity implements the divergence from randomness model, which is a probabilistic model of information retrieval. This model computes term weights by measuring the divergence between actual term distribution and one obtained by a random process.

It was observed by the earlier form of this model that the distribution of informative terms are different from the distribution of noninformative terms. The informative terms appear more densely in a few documents, called *elite* documents, whereas noninformative words are randomly distributed among all the documents.

This framework is composed of three models, which should be configured while registering the factory in schema.xml. These three models are described in the next subsections.

Basic Model

This model selects the basic randomness model. The framework supports seven basic models, each using a different scoring algorithm. Table 8-2 provides details of supported models. This step can be followed by two normalization steps, which adds to the flexibility of the algorithm.

Table 8-2. *Basic Models Supported by Divergence from Randomness*

BasicModel	Value	Description
BasicModelBE	Be	Implements the limiting form of the Bose-Einstein model. It can lead to performance issues in some cases. BasicModelG is a better alternative.
BasicModelG	G	Implements the geometric approximation of the Bose-Einstein model.
BasicModelP	P	Implements the Poisson approximation of the binomial model.
BasicModelD	D	Implements the divergence approximation of the binomial model.
BasicModelIn	I(n)	Considers the inverse document frequency for computing the randomness.
BasicModelIne	I(ne)	Computes the randomness by using a combination of Poisson and inverse document frequency.
BasicModelIF	I(F)	Considers the approximation of inverse document frequency for computing the randomness.

After-Effect Model

This model is also called the *first normalization model*. It smooths the weight obtained from the basic model. Table 8-3 provides details of supported after-effect models.

Table 8-3. *AfterEffect Supported by Divergence from Randomness*

AfterEffect	Value	Description
AfterEffectL	L	Uses Laplace's law of succession.
AfterEffectB	B	Model of the information gain based on the ratio of two Bernoulli processes.
NoAfterEffect	none	This parameter disables the first normalization.

Normalization

This model is also called the *second normalization model*. It normalizes the field length that is used by the algorithm to normalize the term frequency. Table 8-4 provides details of supported normalization models.

Table 8-4. *Second Normalization Supported by Divergence from Randomness*

Normalization	Value	Description
NormalizationH1	H1	Assumes a uniform distribution of the term frequency.
NormalizationH2	H2	In this model, the term frequency is inversely related to the field length.
NormalizationH3	H3	Implements the term frequency normalization provided by Dirichlet priors.
NormalizationZ	Z	Implements the term frequency normalization provided by Pareto-Zipf normalization.
NoNormalization	none	Disables the second normalization.

Usage

Following are the steps to use DFRSimilarity for computing the score of documents:

1. Register the DFRSimilarityFactory in schema.xml by using the similarity element. The basicModel, afterEffect, and normalization parameters are mandatory, and the value of the desired class should be provided for each of these parameters. Tables 8-2, 8-3, and 8-4 provide options for basicModel, afterEffect, and normalization, respectively. The following is a sample schema.xml configuration:

   ```
   <schema>
     ..
     <similarity class="solr.DFRSimilarityFactory">
       <str name="basicModel">P</str>
       <str name="afterEffect">L</str>
       <str name="normalization">H2</str>
       <float name="c">7</float>
       <bool name="discountOverlaps">true</bool>
     </similarity>
   </schema>
   ```

   DFRSimilarityFactory supports the optional parameter c to allow normalization, which controls the behavior of the implementations NormalizationH1 and NormalizationH2.

2. Reindex the documents.

■ **Note**   Refer to http://terrier.org/docs/v3.5/dfr_description.html for full details of the divergence from randomness model.

Other Similarity Measures

Along with the previously discussed algorithms, Lucene supports a few more. Each can be configured by registering its factory in a similarity element, as you did for the preceding examples. Following are the other similarities supported by Lucene:

IBSimilarity: This provides a framework for information-based probabilistic models. This framework has lots of similarities to divergence from randomness. While registering the similarity, it requires three parameters: distribution, lambda, and normalization. Refer to the Javadoc at http://lucene.apache.org/core/5_3_1/core/org/apache/lucene/search/similarities/IBSimilarity.html for more details.

SweetSpotSimilarity: This is an extension of the DefaultSimilarity to provide additional tuning options for specifying the sweet spot of optimal term frequency and lengthNorm values based on your data. Refer to the Javadoc at http://lucene.apache.org/core/5_3_1/misc/org/apache/lucene/misc/SweetSpotSimilarity.html for more details.

LMDirichletSimilarity: This is based on the model of Bayesian smoothing using Dirichlet priors. It supports the additional smoothing parameter mu. Refer to the Javadoc at `https://lucene.apache.org/core/5_3_1/core/org/apache/lucene/search/similarities/LMDirichletSimilarity.html` for more details.

LMJelinekMercerSimilarity: This is a language model based on the Jelinek-Mercer smoothing method. It supports the additional smoothing parameter lambda. Refer to the Javadoc at `https://lucene.apache.org/core/5_3_1/core/org/apache/lucene/search/similarities/LMJelinekMercerSimilarity.html` for more details.

Per Field Similarity

You have learned about several similarity alternatives available in Lucene and how to implement them globally (whichever implementation you choose is applied to all fields). Lucene, and in turn Solr, allows you to use a different `Similarity` implementation for different fields.

From the behavior perspective, a global similarity will apply to all the fields unless a field-specific similarity is defined that overrides the default similarity for that field. Following are the steps to configure per field similarity:

1. Define `solr.SchemaSimilarityFactory` as the global similarity class that delegates similarity if there is a field-specific similarity definition. Here is an example:

    ```
    <schema>
      ..
      <similarity class="solr.SchemaSimilarityFactory">
    </schema>
    ```

    `SchemaSimilarityFactory` specifies the `DefaultSimilarityFactory` as an implicit global similarity, and any field-specific definition will apply the overriding similarity on that field.

2. The `schema.xml` can have only one global similarity factory. If any other `Similarity` implementation is defined, that should be commented out.

    ```
    <!--similarity class="solr.BM25SimilarityFactory"-->
    ```

3. To override the global similarity for specific field, specify the applicable similarity factory in the `fieldType` definition of that field. The following is a sample definition of `DFRSimilarity` on `text_general` `fieldType`.

    ```
    <fieldType name="text_general" class="solr.TextField" positionIncrementGap="100">
      <analyzer type="index">
        <tokenizer class="solr.StandardTokenizerFactory"/>
        <filter class="solr.StopFilterFactory" ignoreCase="true"
          words="stopwords.txt"/>
        <filter class="solr.LowerCaseFilterFactory"/>
      </analyzer>
      <analyzer type="query">
        <tokenizer class="solr.StandardTokenizerFactory"/>
        <filter class="solr.StopFilterFactory" ignoreCase="true"
          words="stopwords.txt"/>
        <filter class="solr.SynonymFilterFactory"
    ```

```
        synonyms="synonyms.txt" ignoreCase="true" expand="true"/>
      <filter class="solr.LowerCaseFilterFactory"/>
    </analyzer>
    <similarity class="solr.DFRSimilarityFactory">
      <str name="basicModel">I(F)</str>
      <str name="afterEffect">B</str>
      <str name="normalization">H2</str>
    </similarity>
  </fieldType>
```

■ **Note**   As of now, `coord` and `queryNorm` are not implemented as part of `SchemaSimilarityFactory`, so you will get different scores for TF-IDF.

Custom Similarity

Solr allows you to customize the `Similarity` implementation. If you want to tune the behavior of existing similarities, you can extend the `Similarity` implementation and override a method to plug in your desired computation.

Suppose you are developing a search engine for music metadata and you discover that terms such as *love* and *heart* are common but still as interesting as any other terms that are rare. If you are using default similarity, the IDF factor considers the rare terms as more important and weights them higher. But that's not the case in this scenario, and you would like to disable the IDF weight. You can use these steps to customize this default behavior:

1.   Extend the existing `Similarity` implementation provided by Lucene.

```java
import org.apache.lucene.search.similarities.DefaultSimilarity;

public class NoIDFSimilarity extends DefaultSimilarity {

  @Override
  public float idf(long docFreq, long numDocs) {
    return 1.0f;
  }
}
```

In this class, you have overridden the `idf()` method to always return a value of 1.0, which disables the role of IDF in computing the score of a document. If you want to provide your custom computation formula, you can put your code in the method and return the computed value. In `DefaultSimilarity`, the method computes the IDF score as follows:

```java
public float idf(long docFreq, long numDocs) {
  return (float)(Math.log(numDocs/(double)(docFreq+1)) + 1.0);
}
```

2.   Add the Java executable JAR of the project containing the class to the classpath.

```xml
<lib dir="../../../custom-lib" regex="solr-practical-approach-\d.*\.jar" />
```

3. Register the custom similarity in schema.xml either globally or on the desired fieldType. The following example configures the custom similarity on a specific field.

```
<fieldType name="text_general" class="solr.TextField" positionIncrementGap="100">
  <analyzer
    <tokenizer class="solr.StandardTokenizerFactory"/>
  </analyzer>
  <similarity class="com.apress.solr.pa.chapter08.similarity.NoIDFSimilarity"/>
</fieldType>
<similarity class="solr.SchemaSimilarityFactory">
```

Generally, you want to apply the custom implementation at the field level, as the default similarity works well for most cases and your implementation would address the requirement of a specific field.

4. For the preceding example, it's not necessary to rebuild the index. But it's advisable that you reindex the documents after changing the Similarity implementation.

5. Query for the result. Figure 8-5 contains a snapshot of the ranking explanation. You can see that NoIDFSimilarity (underlined) is used as the Similarity implementation for computing the score. You also can see that all IDF computation returns a constant score of 1.0. This constant value disables the default IDF implementation applied while computing the term weight.

```
<str name="3">
1.0606601 = sum of:
  0.35355338 = max of:
    0.35355338 = weight(title:apple in 2) [NoIDFSimilarity], result of:
      0.35355338 = score(doc=2,freq=1.0), product of:
        0.70710677 = queryWeight, product of:
          1.0 = idf(docFreq=3, maxDocs=6)
          0.70710677 = queryNorm
        0.5 = fieldWeight in 2, product of:
          1.0 = tf(freq=1.0), with freq of:
            1.0 = termFreq=1.0
          1.0 = idf(docFreq=3, maxDocs=6)
          0.5 = fieldNorm(doc=2)
  0.70710677 = max of:
    0.35355338 = weight(title:laptop in 2) [NoIDFSimilarity], result of:
      0.35355338 = score(doc=2,freq=1.0), product of:
        0.70710677 = queryWeight, product of:
          1.0 = idf(docFreq=4, maxDocs=6)
```

Figure 8-5. Explanation for custom similarity

The preceding example has a limitation: you can tune the existing factors for computing the similarity but cannot introduce a new factor altogether. Instead of extending the existing `Similarity` implementation, if you want to plug in a totally new similarity algorithm that is either based on a research paper or you have developed something of your own, you need to do a bit more work. First, you need to extend `SimilarityFactory` and implement the `getSimilarity()` method to return your custom similarity, which extends the abstract `Similarity` class.

Summary

In this chapter, you saw how Lucene powers the relevance ranking for Solr, the various relevance models supported by Lucene, and the details of the primary models. You saw that the default scoring of Lucene is simple yet powerful and is what makes Lucene more popular. You learned about the factors in the primary models that affect the score of documents. You also learned about the document score explanation, so that you can understand why a document ranks above another or comes up at the top of a result set. You also saw sample code that overrides the default similarity, to customize the behavior of scoring factors.

CHAPTER 9

■ ■ ■

Additional Features

The purpose of developing a search engine is to help users find the most relevant information in the most convenient way. In Chapters 6 and 7, you learned about various approaches for retrieving documents and implementations provided by Solr to achieve that.

In this chapter, you will learn about other important features of Solr that will bring in convenience and add to the user experience. You also will see other features that can be used to control document ranking and recommend other documents of interest to the user.

This chapter covers the following topics:

- Sponsored search
- Spell-checking
- Autosuggestion
- Document similarity

Sponsored Search

For a given query, you may want a set of handpicked documents to be elevated to the top of the search result. You generally need such a feature either to allow a sponsored search or to support editorial boosting. Google AdWords is a typical example of a sponsored search. In addition, at times a relevant document might rank low or an irrelevant document might rank high in the response, and you'll need a quick solution to fix these problems, especially when they are discovered in production.

Solr provides QueryElevationComponent as a quick and easy solution to address these needs. For a specified query, it supports the following behaviors, irrespective of the score of the document:

- Bringing a desired set of documents to the top of the search result
- Excluding a set of documents from the search result

■ **Note** QueryElevationComponent requires the uniqueKey field to be defined in schema.xml. It works in a distributed environment also.

Usage

Here are the steps for using the query elevation component:

1. Define the elevation file. This file contains the rules for elevating and excluding documents.

The filename must map to the name provided in the config-file parameter in QueryElevationComponent. The following is a sample query elevation file.

elevate.xml

```
<elevate>
 <query text="dslr camera">
  <doc id="101" />
  <doc id="103" />
 </query>

 <query text="laptop">
   <doc id="106" />
   <doc id="108" exclude="true" />
 </query>
</elevate>
```

The text attribute of the query element specifies the query to be editorially boosted. The doc element represents the documents to be manipulated. Its id attribute marks the document that should be elevated, and if the additional attribute exclude="true" is specified, the document is marked for exclusion. The provided id should map to the uniqueKey of a document.

The elevation file must exist either in the $SOLR_HOME/<core>/conf/ or $SOLR_HOME/<core>/data directory. If it exists in conf, modifications to the file will reflect on core reload; and if it exists in data, modifications will reflect for each IndexReader.

■ **Note** The component first looks for elevate.xml in the conf directory (or ZooKeeper, if applicable) and then in data. If you have the file in both directories, conf will get the priority.

---

2. Configure the QueryElevationComponent in solrconfig.xml. Table 9-1 describes the arguments supported to control the behavior of the component. The following is an example configuration.

```
<searchComponent name="elevator" class="solr.QueryElevationComponent" >
   <str name="config-file">elevate.xml</str>
   <str name="queryFieldType">string</str>
</searchComponent>
```

Table 9-1. *QueryElevationComponent Parameters*

Parameter	Description
config-file	Specifies the name of the file that contains the query elevation rules.
queryFieldType	Specifies the fieldType that should be used to analyze the user query. The analyzed terms are matched against the query defined in the elevation file. The specified fieldType must exist in schema.xml. If you want no analysis to be performed, specify string as the queryFieldType.
forceElevation	Query elevation introduces or eliminates documents from the result set as configured but respects sorting. If you apply any sorting other than score desc, the elevated documents will change their order based on the sort condition. Setting this parameter to true overrides this behavior.
editorialMarkerFieldName	This parameter helps to differentiate the elevated documents from organically ranked documents. The elevated documents get an additional field with this name. The default name is editorial.
	The marker is enabled when the assigned name is added to the fl request parameter. An example of using this marker has been provided further.
markExcludes	By default, the excluded documents are removed from the search result. Setting this parameter to true marks such documents as excluded instead of removing them altogether.
excludeMarkerFieldName	This parameter assigns a fieldname to the excluded documents. It works only with the markExcludes parameter. The default name assigned is excluded.

3. Register the component to the last-components list of the desired handler.

```
<requestHandler name="/select" class="solr.SearchHandler">
  <lst name="defaults">
    <str name="echoParams">explicit</str>
  </lst>
  <arr name="last-components">
    <str>elevator</str>
  </arr>
</requestHandler>
```

4. Provide additional request parameters for the component. Table 9-2 lists the additional parameters supported.

Table 9-2. *QueryElevationComponent Request Parameters*

Parameter	Description
enableElevation	This parameter enables the QueryElevationComponent.
exclusive	This Boolean parameter, if enabled, returns only elevated results. Organic results will be ignored.
elevateIds	This parameter specifies the comma-separated list of document IDs to be elevated.
excludeIds	This parameter specifies the comma-separated list of document IDs to be excluded.

5.   Query for results. The following are some sample queries.

Search request with QueryElevationComponent enabled

```
$ curl "http://localhost:8983/solr/hellosolr/select?q=laptop&enableElevation=true"
```

Search request that marks the elevated and excluded field

```
$ curl "http://localhost:8983/solr/hellosolr/select?q=laptop
&markExcludes=true&fl=*,[elevated],[excluded]"
```

Search request to mark the elevated field, if editorialMarkerFieldName is specified as paid

```
$ curl "http://localhost:8983/solr/hellosolr/select?q=laptop
&enableElevation=true&fl=*,[paid],score"
```

Search request that specifies the elevation and exclusion IDs

```
$ curl "http://localhost:8983/solr/hellosolr/select?q=cable
&df=product&excludeIds=IW-02&elevateIds=3007WFP,9885A004"
```

Spell-Checking

User queries are prone to error, so almost all popular search engines support a spell-checking feature. For a misspelled query, this feature suggests the corrected form of text. You will generally see the suggestion appear just below the search box. For example, go to Amazon.com and search for *laptap* (a misspelled form of *laptop*) and the response will contain additional information such as *Did you mean: laptop*.

Search engines take two approaches to spell-checking. They either execute the original query and provide a spelling suggestion or they execute a spell-corrected query with the option to run the original query instead. Web search engines such as Google, Bing, and Yahoo! take the optimistic approach of spell correction. They retrieve the result for the corrected form of the query and provide the user with an option to execute the original query.

Figure 9-1 depicts a typical spell-checking example (from Google), where the misspelled query *wikipadia* is spell-corrected to *wikipedia*, and a result is provided for it.

Figure 9-1. *Example of spell-checking in Google*

Solr provides out-of-the-box support for spell-checking. It allows you to provide suggestions based on terms maintained in a Solr field, an external Lucene index, or an external text file. Solr provides SpellCheckComponent, which extends SearchComponent to implement this feature and can be configured to any SearchHandler to get it to work.

If you just want to provide a spelling suggestion to the user, asking, for example, "Did you mean?", configure the SpellCheckComponent to the query handler, such as /select, and display the response from this component at an appropriate position for user's action. If your intention is to provide an autocorrected result to the user, configure the SpellCheckComponent in a separate handler, such as /spell, and query with collation enabled. You will learn about collation later in this section. The spell-corrected response returned by this handler should be used by the client to make a fresh request to the query handler, such as /select. This process of autocorrection requires two Solr requests.

SpellCheckComponent provides a set of alternative options for spell-checking, which can be specified in the classname parameter. Multiple spell-checkers can be configured to execute at once.

You should perform minimal analysis on the field used for spell-checking. Analysis that transforms the tokens to a totally different form, such as stemming or synonym expansion, should be avoided. For a Solr field–based spell-checker, it would be a good idea to have a separate field for spell-checking, to which the content of all fields that require spell suggestion can be copied.

SpellCheckComponent supports distributed environment.

Generic Parameters

Table 9-3 refers to the generic parameters, which can be used in any of the spell-checker implementations.

Table 9-3. *SpellCheckComponent Generic Parameters*

Parameter	Description
name	Assigns a name to the spell-checker definition. This parameter is useful when configuring multiple spell-checkers to the component.
classname	Specifies the spell-checker implementation to use. The value can be specified as solr.<implementation-class>, such as solr.FileBasedSpellCheck. The default implementation is IndexBasedSpellCheck.

Implementations

This section explains the spell-checker implementations available in Solr. Each provides a set of specific parameters that can be used along with the generic parameters in Table 9-3.

IndexBasedSpellChecker

IndexBasedSpellChecker uses a separate index for maintaining the spell-checker dictionary. This index is an additional index, also called a *sidecar index*, which is created and maintained separately from the main index. While configuring the spell-checker, you specify the source field to use for creating the sidecar index.

This is the default spell-checker implementation registered in SpellCheckComponent.

Table 9-4 specifies the additional parameters for configuring IndexBasedSpellChecker.

Table 9-4. *IndexBasedSpellChecker Parameters*

Parameter	Description
field	Specifies the Solr field, defined in schema.xml, to use for building the dictionary.
sourceLocation	Instead of loading the terms from the Solr field, this spell-checker also allows you to load it from an arbitrary Lucene index. This parameter specifies the directory of the Lucene index.
spellcheckIndexDir	Specifies the directory where the sidecar index will be created.
buildOnCommit	Setting this Boolean parameter to true builds the dictionary on each commit. By default, this parameter is set to false.

DirectSolrSpellChecker

Instead of building an additional index specifically for spell-checking, this implementation uses the main Solr index. Because of the use of the main index, the spell-checker always has the latest terms available and also saves you from rebuilding the index regularly.

Table 9-5 specifies the additional parameters for configuring DirectSolrSpellChecker.

Table 9-5. *DirectSolrSpellChecker Parameters*

Parameter	Description
field	Specifies the Solr field, defined in schema.xml, to be used for spell- checking.
accuracy	Specifies the accuracy level for suggestion. The default value is 0.5.
maxEdits	Specifies the maximum number of modifications allowed in the term.
minPrefix	Specifies the minimum number of initial characters after which edits are allowed. A higher value will lead to better performance. Also, you will notice that the first few characters are generally not misspelled. The default value is 1.
maxInspections	Specifies the maximum number of matches to inspect before returning the suggestion. The default value is 5.
minQueryLength	Specifies the minimum number of characters in the query for generating suggestions. No suggestion will be generated if the query is shorter than this length.
maxQueryFrequency	Specifies the maximum number of documents the query terms should appear in. If the count is more than the threshold specified, that term will be ignored. The value can be absolute (for example, 5) or a percentage (such as 0.01 or 1%). The default value is 0.01.
thresholdTokenFrequency	Specifies the minimum number of documents the query terms should appear in. If the count is less than the threshold specified, that term will be ignored. Similar to maxQueryFrequency, either absolute value or percentage can be specified. The default value is 0.0.

FileBasedSpellChecker

FileBasedSpellChecker uses an external text file as a source for spellings and builds a Lucene index out of it. This implementation is helpful when you don't want the spell-checker to be based on terms in the indexed documents, but extracted from another source such as log analysis of frequent queries or external thesauri.

The source file should be a simple text file having one word defined per line. Here is a sample file.

medical-spellings.txt

```
advanced
aided
assigned
assessed
assisted
..
```

Table 9-6 specifies the additional parameters for configuring FileBasedSpellChecker.

Table 9-6. *FileBasedSpellChecker Parameters*

Parameter	Description
sourceLocation	Specifies the path of the text file that contains the terms.
characterEncoding	Specifies the encoding of terms in the file.
spellcheckIndexDir	Specifies the directory where the index will be created.

WordBreakSolrSpellChecker

This implementation focuses on performing spell-check to detect spelling mistakes due to missing or unwanted whitespace. It is highly probable that the user can split a word into two words or join two words into one. A typical example is *spell checker* and *spellchecker*. WordBreakSolrSpellCheckeris developed to address this particular problem. It combines and breaks terms to offer suggestions.

Table 9-7 specifies the additional parameters for configuring WordBreakSolrSpellChecker.

Table 9-7. *WordBreakSolrSpellChecker Parameters*

Parameter	Description
field	Specifies the Solr field, defined in schema.xml, to use for building the dictionary.
combineWords	Specifies whether the adjacent terms should be combined. The default value is true.
breakWords	Specifies whether the spell-checker should try to break the term into multiple terms. The default value is true.
maxChanges	Specifies the maximum number of collation attempts the spell-checker should make.

How It Works

The SpellCheckComponent class in Solr implements SearchComponent, which utilizes the SpellChecker implementation provided by Lucene. The steps followed by the SpellCheckComponent for processing the requests are as follows:

1. The client makes a request to a SearchHandler that has SpellCheckComponent registered to it.

2. The SpellCheckComponent, like any other SearchComponent, executes in two phases, namely prepare and process.

3. If the received request is to build or reload the dictionary, it is done in the prepare phase. DirectSolrSpellChecker and WordBreakSolrSpellChecker don't require a build or reload.

4. In the process phase, Solr tokenizes the query with the applicable query analyzer and calls the appropriate SpellChecker with the provided request parameters.

5. The spell-checker implementation generates suggestions from the loaded dictionary or field as applicable.

6. If collation is required, Solr calls the SpellCheckCollator to collate the spellings.

7. The generated responses are returned to the client.

■ **Note** If you are interested in details of internal processing or are planning customization, you can refer to these steps; otherwise, Solr doesn't require you to know them.

Usage

Following are the steps to integrate and use spell-checker:

1. Define the SpellCheckComponent in solrconfig.xml, specify the implementation classname, and add the parameters from the table of corresponding classnames.

Register a single spell-checker

```
<searchComponent name="spellcheck" class="solr.SpellCheckComponent">
  <lst name="spellchecker">
    <str name="classname">solr.IndexBasedSpellChecker</str>
    <str name="spellcheckIndexDir">./spellchecker</str>
    <str name="field">spellings</str>
    <str name="buildOnCommit">true</str>
  </lst>
</searchComponent>
```

Register multiple spell-checkers

```
<searchComponent name="spellcheck" class="solr.SpellCheckComponent">
  <lst name="spellchecker">
    <str name="name">primary</str>
    <str name="classname">solr.IndexBasedSpellChecker</str>
    ..
  </lst>
  <lst name="spellchecker">
    <str name="name">secondary</str>
    <str name="classname">solr.FileBasedSpellChecker</str>
    ..
  </lst>
</searchComponent>
```

2. Register the component to the desired SearchHandler. You can register it either to your primary handler that serves the search request or a separate handler dedicated for spell-checking. The following is an example configuration that registers multiple spell-checkers to the /select handler.

```
<requestHandler name="/select" class="solr.SearchHandler">
  <lst name="defaults">
    <str name="spellcheck.dictionary">primary</str>
    <str name="spellcheck.dictionary">secondary</str>
  </lst>
  <arr name="last-components">
    <str>spellcheck</str>
  </arr>
</requestHandler>
```

Table 9-8 lists the request parameters supported by SpellCheckComponent.

Table 9-8. *SpellCheckerComponent Request Parameters*

Parameter	Description
spellcheck	By default, spell-checking is disabled. Set spellcheck="true" to turn on the feature.
spellcheck.q	Specifies the query for spell-checking. If this parameter is not specified, the component takes the value from the q parameter.
spellcheck.count	Specifies the maximum number of suggestions to return. The default value is 1.
spellcheck.dictionary	Specifies the dictionary to be used for the request.
spellcheck.build	This parameter clears the existing dictionary and creates a fresh copy with latest content from the source. This operation can be costly and should be triggered occasionally.
spellcheck.reload	Setting this parameter to true reloads the spell-checker and the underlying dictionary.

(*continued*)

Table 9-8. (*continued*)

Parameter	Description
spellcheck.accuracy	Specifies the desired accuracy level as a float value. Suggestions with scores less than this value will not be provided.
spellcheck.alternativeTermCount	Specifies the number of suggestions to return for each query term. This can be helpful in building context-sensitive spell correction.
spellcheck.collate	If there are multiple suggestions or you want to provide the results of a spell-corrected query to the user, setting this parameter to true is a good choice. This feature takes the best suggestion for each token in the query and combines them to form a new query, which you can execute to get the suggested result.
spellcheck.maxCollations	By default, Solr returns one collation. You can set this parameter to get more collations.
spellcheck.maxCollationTries	The feature of collation ensures that the collated query finds a match in the index. This feature specifies the number of tests to attempt on the index. While testing, the original query is substituted with collation and tried for a match. The default value of 0 can skip the test and hence lead to no match. A higher value ensures better collation but would be costly.
spellcheck.maxCollationEvaluations	Specifies the maximum number of combinations to evaluate and rank, for forming the collation to test on the index. The default value has been optimally set to 10,000 combinations.
spellcheck.collateExtendedResult	Setting this parameter to true extends the response to contain details of the collation.
spellcheck.collateMaxCollectDocs	While testing for a collation, if the hit count is not desired, this parameter helps in achieving performance improvement. For value 0, the exact hit-count is extracted by running a test on all the documents. For a value greater than 0, an estimation is provided based on those documents.
spellcheck.collateParam.*	You can use this prefix to override the default query parameter or provide an additional query parameter to the collation test query. All the fq parameters can be overridden by specifying the overridden value in spellcheck.collateParam.fq.
spellcheck.extendedResults	This Boolean parameter specifies whether to use the extended response format containing more detailed information. The extended response format is different from the standard suggestion; for each suggestion it provides the document frequency, and for each term it provides a suggestion block containing additional information such as term frequency The default value is false.
spellcheck.onlyMorePopular	If this parameter is set to true, suggestions are returned only if the suggested token has higher document frequency than the original term. By default, this parameter is set to false.
spellcheck.maxResultsForSuggest	By default, the correctlySpelled response parameter is set to false, and the suggestion is returned only if a query term is missing in both the dictionary and index. Setting this parameter to a value greater than 0 returns a suggestion if the index has results of up to the specified number. For example, a value of 10 will return a suggestion if the response has up to 9 results, and no suggestion if there are 10 or more results.

3. Query for search results with the spell-checking feature enabled.

Builds the spell-checker and then generates a spelling suggestion

```
$ curl "http://localhost:8983/solr/hellosolr/select?q=wikipadia
&spellcheck=true&spellcheck.build=true"
```

Any request for a spelling suggestion will fetch a result only when the dictionary has been built. Hence, `spellcheck.build=true` should be triggered at least once before requesting a spelling suggestion. The build operation can be costly and should be triggered infrequently.

Request suggestions for the user query

```
$ curl "http://localhost:8983/solr/hellosolr/select?q=wikipadia
&spellcheck=true&spellcheck.count=5&spellcheck.accuracy=0.6"
```

Autocomplete

Autocomplete is a crucial feature for the user search experience. It's a type ahead search, which completes the word or predicts the rest of words as soon as the user types in a few characters. The suggestions are refined for each additional character typed by the user. Most modern search engines support this feature.

Here are some of the key reasons for implementing autocomplete:

- The simplest reason for implementing autocomplete is to avoid spelling mistakes. If the suggestion provided is correct and the user selects it, the query will be free of spelling mistakes.

- If the prediction is correct, the user won't need to key in the complete query. The user can choose one of the suggestions and press Enter.

- At times users knows what they want but don't know how to express it in words. You may have experienced this when a search keyword has many common synonyms or you are seeking an answer to a question. Google autocomplete does a decent job with this, and if a suggestion pops up, you can be fairly confident that you are formulating a correct query.

- Autocomplete helps in query classification and applying filters. In e-commerce, suggestions are provided to classify products based on their primary facets. For example, the query *jeans* may give you suggestions such as *jeans (for men)* or *jeans (for women)*, and the query *apple* may give you suggestions such as *apple (in mobiles)* or *apple (in laptops)*.

- The feature is also used for generating recommendations based on a query. It's again widely used in e-commerce to suggest top-selling products to the user with respect to the query. For example, as soon as you type *Nikon*, autocomplete will suggest top-selling products such as *Nikon 3200* along with its price and probably even an image.

Autosuggestion can be of various types and can be based on various sources. The suggestion provided to the user can be a complete phrase or a specific word. Phrases can be extracted either from a Solr index or from user logs. If the search engine is being used widely and has a large user base, the phrases extracted from the log can generate more-practical suggestions. The queries from logs should go through a chain of processing, such as filtering out queries that result in no match in an index; queries with a spelling error should either be filtered out or spell-corrected; a web search engine would filter out queries on sensitive topics and objectionable content before being consumed for generating phrases. The phrases should be collapsed before suggesting so that the same or a similar phrase is not suggested multiple times.

Phrase suggestion can be combined with other approaches such as token suggestion, which can act as a fallback mechanism. When no phrase suggestion is available for the user-typed query, the system can complete the word being typed by the user.

Solr provides multiple provisions and implementations to achieve autocompletion. Each has its own benefits and limitations. The one or combination you choose depends on your requirements. Since a suggestion is provided for each key pressed by the user, whichever approach you take should not ignore performance, and suggestions should be generated fast. The implementations offered by Solr can be broadly categorized into two types of approaches:

> *Traditional approach*: This approach leverages the existing analyzers and components of Solr to get the feature in place.

> *SuggestionComponent*: A component developed specifically to support the feature of autocompletion.

Traditional Approach

The traditional approach of autosuggestion refers to the provisions introduced in Solr prior to release 3.0. In this approach, autocompletion is implemented by leveraging the features already available in Solr. All you need to do is configure it appropriately to get it to work.

In this approach, appropriate analyzers should be configured on the field depending on the type of suggestion you want to generate. For suggesting a phrase, KeywordTokenizerFactory is appropriate; and for suggesting words, StandardTokenizerFactory or WhitespaceTokenizerFactory is appropriate. You can use both, giving a higher weightage to phrase fields.

The field for generating suggestions should be analyzed to lowercase to perform a case-insensitive search. Some components (discussed in detail next) don't support query-time analysis, and in those cases, the client program might need to convert the query to lowercase. Any other processing can be handled at index-time analysis for matching the tokens appropriately.

The following are the traditional approaches for implementing autosuggestion.

TermsComponent

TermsComponent provides direct access to terms indexed in a field and returns the count of documents containing the term. This component directly accesses the Lucene term dictionary, so retrieval is fast.

Benefits

Following are the benefits of using TermsComponent for autosuggestion:

- TermsComponent directly looks up the term dictionary and so is the fastest among all traditional approaches of autosuggestion.

- It allows you to execute a prefix as well as an infix query.

Limitations

Following are the limitations of this approach:

- TermsComponent directly looks up the term dictionary, so a filter cannot be applied to restrict the result to a subset of documents. For example, you cannot retrieve only products that are in stock.

- Another limitation due to direct lookup is that it also considers the terms that are marked for deletion.

- TermsComponent doesn't analyze the query.

Usage

The following are the steps for configuring TermsComponent for autosuggestion:

1. Define the TermsComponent in solrconfig.xml.

   ```
   <searchComponent name="terms" class="solr.TermsComponent"/>
   ```

2. Register the component to the desired request handler.

   ```
   <requestHandler name="/terms" class="solr.SearchHandler" startup="lazy">
     <lst name="defaults">
       <bool name="distrib">true</bool>
     </lst>
     <arr name="components">
       <str>terms</str>
     </arr>
   </requestHandler>
   ```

Table 9-9 defines the important parameters of TermsComponent for supporting autocomplete.

Table 9-9. *TermsComponent Important Request Parameters*

Parameter	Description
terms	Specifying terms="true" enables TermsComponent. By default, the component is disabled.
terms.fl	Specifies the field name from which the terms should be retrieved.
terms.limit	Specifies the maximum number of terms to retrieve.
terms.prefix	Specifies the user-typed query in this parameter to retrieve all the tokens that start with it.
terms.regex	Specifies the regex pattern for retrieving the terms. It's useful for infix autocompletion. This operation can be costlier to execute than terms.prefix but allows an infix operation. The user query will require preprocessing to form the regex before requesting the handler.

(*continued*)

Table 9-9. (*continued*)

Parameter	Description
terms.regex.flag	Specifies terms.regex.flag=case_insensitive to execute case-insensitive regex.
terms.mincount	Terms with document frequency less than the value specified will not be returned in the response. This parameter can be useful in avoiding misspelled content, assuming them to have low frequency.
terms.maxcount	Terms with document frequency more than the value specified will not be returned in the response. This parameter can be useful to eliminate terms that can be prospective stopwords.
terms.sort	Specifying terms.sort=count sorts the terms with highest frequency first, and specifying terms.sort=index sorts in index order.

3. No specific text analysis is required on the fieldType. You may just want to convert all tokens to lowercase for case-insensitive matching. A typical fieldType is defined as follows:

```
<fieldType name="autocomplete" class="solr.TextField" positionIncrementGap="100" >
  <analyzer type="index">
    <tokenizer class="solr.KeywordTokenizerFactory"/>
    <filter class="solr.LowerCaseFilterFactory"/>
  </analyzer>
  <analyzer type="query">
    <tokenizer class="solr.KeywordTokenizerFactory"/>
    <filter class="solr.LowerCaseFilterFactory"/>
  </analyzer>
</fieldType>
```

4. Define the field for autosuggestion. The field need not be stored.

```
<field name="brand" type="autocomplete" indexed="true" stored="false" />
```

5. Send a request for each character typed by the user.

Suggest all terms beginning with specified characters

```
$ curl "http://localhost:8983/solr/hellosolr/terms?terms=true&terms.fl=brand"
```

Suggest all terms containing the specified characters

```
$ curl "http://localhost:8983/solr/hellosolr/terms?terms=true&terms.fl=brand
&terms.regex=.*eebo.*&terms.regex.flag=case_insensitive&terms.limit=5"
```

Facets

Faceting can be used to implement autosuggestion. It's beneficial for generating suggestions on fields such as category. Facets also return the count along with the term. Chapter 7 provides details on faceting.

Benefits

The following is a benefit of using FacetComponent for autosuggestion:

- It allows you to filter the suggestion to be run on a subset of documents. For example, you can retrieve only products that are in stock.

Limitations

The following are the limitations of this approach:

- Faceting is a memory-intensive process, especially if the number of unique tokens is high. Also its response time is high compared to TermsComponent.

- It doesn't support retrieving infix terms.

- It doesn't analyze the query.

Usage

The FacetComponent is by default available to the handler and doesn't require it to be registered. The following are the steps to configure autosuggestion using faceting:

1. Define the fieldType for text analysis of the faceted field.

```
<fieldType name="autocomplete" class="solr.TextField" positionIncrementGap="100" >
  <analyzer type="index">
    <tokenizer class="solr.KeywordTokenizerFactory"/>
    <filter class="solr.LowerCaseFilterFactory"/>
  </analyzer>
  <analyzer type="query">
    <tokenizer class="solr.KeywordTokenizerFactory"/>
    <filter class="solr.LowerCaseFilterFactory"/>
  </analyzer>
</fieldType>
```

2. Define the field for autosuggestion. The field need not be stored.

```
<field name="autocomplete" type="autocomplete" indexed="true" stored="false" />
```

3. Leverage the facet.prefix request parameter provided by faceting for generating a suggestion. The value supplied to this parameter is not analyzed, so as a convention always lowercase the value before supplying it to the field.

Generate a suggestion using the facet.prefix feature of FacetComponent

```
$ curl "http://localhost:8983/solr/hellosolr/select?q=*:*
&rows=0&facet=true&facet.field=brand&facet.mincount=5
&facet.limit=5&facet.prefix=ree"
```

Table 9-10 describes the important parameters of FacetComponent for supporting autosuggestion.

Table 9-10. *FacetComponent Parameters for Autosuggestion*

Parameter	Description
facet	Specifying facet=true enables the FacetComponent.
rows	Set rows=0, as you don't need to fetch search results from Solr.
facet.prefix	Specifies the user query to retrieve all the suggestions that start with it.
facet.field	Specifies the field on which faceting should be performed.
facet.mincount	This parameter can be used to avoid misspelled content, assuming that terms with a count less than a threshold might not be of interest.
facete.limit	This parameter limits the number of suggestions generated.

EdgeNGram

We discussed NGram while discussing schema design in Chapter 4. EdgeNGram breaks the token into subtokens of different sizes from one of the edges. For autocomplete, only the tokens created from the front edge would be of interest.

Benefits

Following are the benefits of using EdgeNGram for autosuggestion:

- EdgeNGram is useful for generating suggestions when you need to search the whole document instead of just the spelling suggestion. A typical example in e-commerce is suggesting popular products to the user, where you also want to return the image of the product as well as its price.

- It allows you to restrict the result to a subset of documents. For example, you can retrieve only the in-stock products.

- Documents can be boosted—for example, if you want popular matching documents to rank higher in the suggestion list.

- Query-time analysis can be performed.

Limitations

Following are the limitations of this approach:

- This approach generates many tokens, increasing the index size.

- EdgeNGram can have performance issues and slow type-ahead defies the purpose of autocompletion.

- The search query is executed on the EdgeNGram field, and the response can contain duplicate tokens. Thus multiple documents should not have the same value for the suggestion field. If you cannot remove the redundant documents, you need to use a hybrid approach of EdgeNGram with faceting. EdgeNGram can be beneficial when you have a separate index created out of a user query log for generating suggestions.

Usage

Here are the steps to configure autosuggestion using EdgeNGram:

1. Define a fieldType to use EdgeNGram.

```
<fieldType name="edgengram" class="solr.TextField" positionIncrementGap="100"
omitNorms="true" omitTermFreqAndPositions="true">
  <analyzer type="index">
    <tokenizer class="solr.KeywordTokenizerFactory"/>
    <filter class="solr.LowerCaseFilterFactory"/>
    <filter class="solr.EdgeNGramFilterFactory" minGramSize="3" maxGramSize="15" />
  </analyzer>
  <analyzer type="query">
    <tokenizer class="solr.KeywordTokenizerFactory"/>
    <filter class="solr.LowerCaseFilterFactory"/>
  </analyzer>
</fieldType>
```

Set the attribute minGramSize to specify the minimum characters from which suggestions should start coming up. Specify the attribute maxGramSize to specify the characters beyond which you don't want to provide any refinement. The EdgeNGramFilterFactory should be applied only at index time.

In the preceding fieldType text analysis, you have defined EdgeNGramFilterFactory to generate grams from a minimum size of 3 to a maximum size of 15.

2. Define the field for generating suggestions.

```
<field name="autocomplete" type="edgengram" indexed="true" stored="true" />
```

3. Execute the query to generate suggestions.

```
$ curl "http://localhost:8983/solr/hellosolr/select?q=autocomplete:lapt"
```

SuggestComponent

Solr 3.1 introduced a dedicated component to address the problems of autosuggestion. This approach uses the suggester module of Lucene and is more powerful and flexible than the previously discussed approaches.

The two important aspects of SuggestComponent are dictionary and lookup algorithm. You need to choose the implementation for both while configuring the suggester. Both aspects are described next.

Dictionary

The dictionary specifies the source for maintaining the terms. The implementations offered by Solr use the Dictionary interface. Broadly speaking, the dictionary can be of the following two types:

- *Index-based*: Uses a Lucene index as the source for generating the suggestion

- *File-based*: Uses text files from the specified location for generating the suggestion

Following are the implementations provided by Solr.

DocumentDictionaryFactory

DocumentDictionaryFactory is an index-based dictionary that uses terms, weights, and optionally payloads for generating the suggestion. The following are the additional parameters supported by this implementation.

> weightField: If you want to assign weight to the terms, specify in this parameter the fieldname that contains the weight. The default weight assigned is 0. This field should be stored.

> payloadField: If you want to assign a payload to the terms, specify in this parameter the fieldname that contains the payload. This field should be stored.

DocumentExpressionDictionaryFactory

This factory provides an implementation of DocumentValueSourceDictionary that extends the DocumentDictionary to support a weight expression instead of a numeric weight.

Following are the additional parameters supported by this implementation:

> weightExpression: You can specify an expression to compute the weight of the terms. It uses a Lucene expression module for computing the expression. The expression definition is similar to the function query expressions. For example, "((div(rating,10) + 1) + sqrt(popularity))" is a valid expression. The fields specified in the expression should be numeric. This parameter is mandatory.

> payloadField: If you want to assign a payload to the terms, specify in this parameter the fieldname that contains the payload. This field must be stored.

HighFrequencyDictionary

This is the default implementation for an index-based dictionary, which allows you to consider only the frequent terms for building the dictionary. Terms with frequency less than the threshold are discarded.

Following is the additional parameter supported by this implementation:

> `threshold`: This parameter specifies the threshold for the terms to be added to the dictionary. The value can be between 0 and 1, which signifies the fraction of documents in which the term should occur. This parameter is optional. If not specified, all terms are considered.

FileDictionaryFactory

This is the only file-based dictionary implementation supported, which allows you to read suggestions from an external file. Similar to an index-based dictionary, weights and payloads are allowed, which can be specified following the term separated by a delimiter.

Following is the additional parameter supported by this implementation:

> `fieldDelimiter`: Specifies the delimiter for separating the terms, weights, and payloads. The default value is tab.

Here is a sample file for maintaining the suggestions.

suggestions.txt

```
# File based suggestions
mobile\t1.0
mobile phone\t3.0
mobile cases\t2.0
```

Algorithm

After selecting the suitable dictionary implementation, you need to choose the `lookupImpl` that best fits your usecase. Lucene supports a set of algorithms (or data structures) and provides different implementations for them. All the implementing classes extend the `Lookup` abstract class.

The following are the broad definitions of data structures supported:

> *Finite state transducer (FST)*: The suggester builds an automaton with all the terms, which is used to cater to all the autosuggestion requests.
>
> The automaton offers fast searches and has a low memory footprint, but the process of building the automaton is slowest among all the data structures supported. Also, terms cannot be appended to automata. For adding terms, it should be built from scratch. The automata can be persisted to disk as a binary blob for fast reload on Solr restart or core reload.
>
> *Ternary search tree (TST)*: A ternary search tree is similar to a binary search tree, but can have up to three children. It offers a fast and flexible approach for term lookup. The tree can be updated dynamically.
>
> *JaSpell algorithm*: This algorithm, written by Bruno Martins, uses a ternary tree to provide highly sophisticated suggestions. It builds the data structure fast. It supports fuzzy lookup based on the Levenshtein distance and is more sophisticated than FST. Refer to the Jaspell website at http://jaspell.sourceforge.net/.
>
> The suggestions can be ordered alphabetically or on parameters such as rating, popularity, and so forth.
>
> *Index-based*: This approach uses a Lucene index for the lookup.

The following are the implementations provided by Solr for lookup. Each defines its own set of parameters to support the functionality offered.

TSTLookupFactory

This implementation provides lookup based on a ternary search tree. Its suggester doesn't support a payload and doesn't require any additional parameters to be specified.

FSTLookupFactory

This implementation provides automaton-based lookup and is very fast. It makes a good suggester unless you need a more sophisticated one. Table 9-11 specifies the parameters supported by FSTLookupFactory.

Table 9-11. FSTLookupFactory Parameters

Parameter	Description
weightBuckets	Specifies the number of buckets to create for weights. The count can be between 1 and 255. The default number of buckets is 10.
exactMatchFirst	If set to true, exact suggestions are returned first, irrespective of prefixes of other strings being available in the automaton.

WFSTLookupFactory

This implementation is based on a weighted FST algorithm. It uses the shortest path method to find top suggestions. It supports the exactMatchFirst parameter. Table 9-11 provides information on this parameter.

JaspellLookupFactory

This implementation is based on the JaSpell algorithm. It's fast at execution and is useful for a broad range of problems.

AnalyzingLookupFactory

This implementation uses weighted FST for lookup. It's called AnalyzingLookupFactory because it analyzes the text before building the FST and during lookup. The analysis prior to the lookup offers powerful and flexible autosuggestion. The analysis chain can be configured to use features such as stopwords and synonym expansion. For example, if *cell phone* and *mobile phone* are defined as synonyms, the user text *cell* can provide suggestions such as *mobile phone cases*.

The analyzers should be configured carefully, as features like stopwords can lead to no suggestion. Also, the suggestions returned are the original text and not the analyzed form of the text. Table 9-12 specifies the parameters supported by AnalyzingLookupFactory.

Table 9-12. *AnalyzingLookupFactory Parameters*

Property	Description
suggestAnalyzerFieldType	Specifies the fieldType to use for the analysis.
exactMatchFirst	If set to true, exact matches are returned as top suggestions, irrespective of other suggestions with higher weights. By default, it's set to true.
preserveSep	If set to true, a token separator is preserved (that is, cellphone and cell phone are different). By default, it's set to true.
preservePositionIncrements	If set to true, position increments are preserved. If set to false, a user query such as best 20 would generate suggestions like *best of 2015*, assuming that *of* is a stopword. By default, it's set to false'.

FuzzyLookupFactory

FuzzyLookupFactory extends the features of AnalyzingLookup, by allowing fuzzy matching on the analyzed text based on the Levenshtein distance. It supports all the parameters of AnalyzingLookupFactory, along with the additional parameters mentioned in Table 9-13.

Table 9-13. *FuzzyLookupFactory Parameters*

Property	Description
maxEdits	Specifies the maximum number of edits allowed. The default value is 1. A hard limit on the value has been specified as 2.
transpositions	If true, transposition will be computed using a primitive edit operation. If false, the Levenshtein algorithm will be used.
nonFuzzyPrefix	Specifies the length of a lookup key, the characters at a position beyond which fuzzy matching will be performed. Only matches that contain the initial prefix characters of the key should be suggested. The default value is 1.
minFuzzyLength	Specifies the length below which the edit will not be performed on the lookup key. The default value is 3.
unicodeAware	By default, this parameter is set to false, and the preceding four parameters are measured in bytes. If this parameter is set to true, they will be measured in actual characters.

AnalyzingInfixLookupFactory

AnalyzingInfixLookupFactory uses a Lucene index for its dictionary and offers flexible prefix-based suggestions on indexed terms. Similar to AnalyzingLookupFactory, it also analyzes the input text while building the dictionary and for lookup. Table 9-14 specifies the parameters supported by AnalyzingInfixLookupFactory.

Table 9-14. *AnalyzingInfixLookupFactory Parameters*

Parameter	Definition
indexPath	Specifies the directory where the index will be stored and loaded from. By default, the index is created in the data directory.
allTermsRequired	If true, applies the Boolean operator AND on a multiterm key; otherwise, it applies the operator OR. The default value is true.
minPrefixChars	Specifies the minimum number of characters from which onward the prefixQuery is used. N-grams are generated for prefixes shorter than this length, which offers faster lookup but increases the index size. The default value is 4.
highlight	If true, which is the default value, suggestions are highlighted.

BlendedInfixLookupFactory

This implementation is an extension of AnalyzingInfixLookupFactory, which allows you to apply weights on prefix matches. It allows you to assign more weight based on the position of the first matching word. It supports all the parameters of AnalyzingInfixLookupFactory, along with the additional parameters mentioned in Table 9-15.

Table 9-15. *BlendedInfixLookupFactory Parameters*

Parameter	Description
blenderType	Specifies the blender type to use for calculating the weight coefficient. Following are the supported blender types: • linear: Computes the weight using the formula weight×(1 - 0.10×position). It gives higher weight to matches in the start. This is the default blenderType. • reciprocal: Computes the weight using the formula weight/(1+position). It gives higher weight to matches in the end.
numFactors	Specifies the multiplication factor for the number of results. The default value is 10.

FreeTextLookupFactory

This suggester has been implemented with the need for fallback suggestions when other suggesters don't find a match. It builds N-grams of the text at the time of building the dictionary and at lookup considers the last *N* words from the user query. It's suitable for handling queries that have never been seen before. Table 9-16 specifies the parameters supported by FreeTextLookupFactory.

Table 9-16. *FreeTextLookupFactory Parameters*

Parameter	Description
suggestFreeTextAnalyzerFieldType	Specifies the fieldType to use for the analysis. This field is required.
ngrams	Specifies the number of last tokens to consider for building the dictionary. The default value is 2.

How It Works

The autosuggestion feature in Solr is provided by SuggestComponent, which interacts with SolrSuggester to generate suggestions. The following are the steps followed by the component:

1. The client makes a request to a SearchHandler, which has SuggestComponent registered to it.

2. The SuggestComponent, like any other SearchComponent, executes in two phases, namely prepare and process.

3. If the received request is to build or reload the dictionary, in the prepare phase the component calls the SolrSuggester to perform the task. SolrSuggester is responsible for loading the lookup and dictionary implementations specified in the configuration.

4. In the process phase, the component calls all the registered SolrSuggesters for getting the suggested results.

5. SolrSuggestor calls the appropriate implementation, which looks up a key and returns the possible completion for this key. Depending on the implementation, this may be a prefix, misspelling, or even infix.

6. The component converts the suggested results to an appropriate form and adds to the response.

Usage

Here are the steps for configuring and using SuggestComponent in Solr:

1. Define the SuggestComponent in solrconfig.xml. Table 9-17 specifies the parameters supported by the component.

```
<searchComponent name="suggest" class="solr.SuggestComponent">
<lst name="suggester">
  <str name="name">analyzedSuggestion</str>
  <str name="lookupImpl">AnalyzingLookupFactory</str>
  <str name="dictionaryImpl">DocumentDictionaryFactory</str>
  <str name="field">brand</str>
  <str name="weightField">popularity</str>
  <str name="suggestAnalyzerFieldType">string</str>
  <str name="buildOnStartup">false</str>
</lst>
</searchComponent>
```

Table 9-17. SuggestComponent Parameters

Parameter	Description
name	Specifies the name of the suggester for generating suggestions.
dictionaryImpl	Specifies the dictionary implementation to use. By default, HighFrequencyDictionaryFactory is used for index-based, and FileDictionaryFactory is used for a file-based data structure. If the sourceLocation parameter is present, the component assumes a file-based dictionary to be used.
lookupImpl	Specifies the lookup implementation to use. If this parameter is not provided, by default JaspellLookupFactory will be used.
field	For an index-based dictionary, this parameter specifies the field to be used by the lookup implementation.
sourceLocation	If using FileDictionaryFactory, this parameter specifies the dictionary file path.
storeDir	The directory to which the dictionary will be persisted.
buildOnStartup	Setting this Boolean parameter to true builds the data structure on Solr startup and core reload.
buildOnCommit	Setting this Boolean parameter to true builds the data structure on commit.
buildOnOptimize	Setting this Boolean parameter to true builds the data structure on optimize.

2. Register the component to the desired SearchHandler. Generally, if you like to have a dedicated endpoint for autosuggestion, add it to components instead of last-components. Table 9-18 specifies the parameters that can be configured in the handler or provided in the search request.

```
<requestHandler name="/suggest" class="solr.SearchHandler" startup="lazy">
  <lst name="defaults">
    <str name="suggest">true</str>
    <str name="suggest.count">10</str>
  </lst>
  <arr name="components">
    <str>suggest</str>
  </arr>
</requestHandler>
```

Table 9-18. *SuggestComponent Parameters for the Request Handler*

Parameter	Description
suggest	Setting this Boolean parameter to true enables the SuggestComponent.
suggest.q	The user query for which the suggestion should be retrieved. If this parameter is not specified, the component looks for a value in the q parameter.
suggest.dictionary	This parameter is mandatory. It specifies the name of the suggester component to use for generating suggestions.
suggest.count	Specifies the maximum number of suggestions to retrieve.
suggest.build	Setting this parameter to true builds the suggester data structure. The build operation can be costly, so trigger the process as per your need. Table 9-17 provides other options for building the suggester.
suggest.buildAll	Setting this parameter to true builds the data structure for all the suggesters registered in the component.
suggest.reload	Setting this parameter to true reloads the suggester data structure.
suggest.reloadAll	Setting this parameter to true reloads the data structure for all the suggesters registered in the component.

3. Define the fieldType for text analysis.

```
<fieldType class="solr.TextField" name="textSuggest"
positionIncrementGap="100">
  <analyzer>
    <tokenizer class="solr.StandardTokenizerFactory"/>
    <filter class="solr.StandardFilterFactory"/>
    <filter class="solr.LowerCaseFilterFactory"/>
  </analyzer>
</fieldType>
```

4. Define the field. The field must be set as stored. You might want to copy all the fields on which the suggestion should be generated to this field.

5. Query for results. If you are using a dedicated handler for suggestions, you can set suggest=true and other infrequently changing parameters in it, so that you don't need to provide those parameters with each request. The following are the sample queries for generating suggestions.

Request to build specific suggester data structures

```
$ curl "http://localhost:8983/solr/hellosolr/suggest?suggest=true&suggest.buildAll=true"
```

Request to build all the suggester data structures

```
$ curl "http://localhost:8983/solr/hellosolr/suggest?suggest=true
&suggest.build=true&suggest.dictionary=analyzedSuggestion"
```

Request for suggestions in the analyzedSuggestion dictionary

```
$ curl "http://localhost:8983/solr/hellosolr/suggest?suggest=true
&suggest.dictionary=analyzedSuggestion&wt=json&suggest.q=lapt"
```

Document Similarity

The primary purpose of developing a search engine is to retrieve documents that are most relevant to the user query. Once the user previews a retrieved document, it's highly probable that he might be interested in other similar documents. If the application is being developed for searching news, journals, and blogs, suggesting similar documents becomes even more crucial. Another area where you may be interested in finding similar documents is duplicate detection, plagiarism, and fingerprinting.

Solr provides the MoreLikeThis feature to address the problem of finding similar documents. This feature can also be used for building a content-based recommendation system, which is basically a machine-learning problem. The content-based recommendation systems use the items features or keywords to describe the items, which you already have available in Solr fields. Now, if you maintain a user profile or extract common attributes of the products from the user's purchase history and "likes," you can query MoreLikeThis with these common keywords or attributes to generate recommendation for the users.

MoreLikeThis takes the bag-of-words approach for similarity detection. It takes a document or arbitrary text as input and returns matching documents. It allows you to control the matching capabilities through configuration definition and request parameters.

Similar document detection in MoreLikeThis is a two-phase process. The following are the details of processing in the phases:

> *Detect interesting keywords*: The algorithm statistically determines the important and interesting terms in the document for which similar documents are to be retrieved. It optionally ignores the terms that are very common, very rare, very short, or very long. If boost is enabled, they are added to the terms based on TF-IDF coefficient.

> *Query for matching documents*: The terms qualified in the first phase are submitted as a search request, and the most relevant documents are retrieved.

Prerequisites

The following are the prerequisites for using the MoreLikeThis component:

- The uniqueKey field should be stored.

- Fields used in this component should store term vectors (termVectors="true"). The following is a sample field definition:

```
<field name="product" type="text_general" indexed="true" stored="true" termVectors="true" />
```

- If term vectors are disabled, the component generates terms from the stored field. Hence, at least the field should be stored (stored="true").

■ **Caution**   MoreLikeThis supports distributed search but has an open bug https://issues.apache. org/jira/browse/SOLR-4414. The shard serving the request should contain the document; otherwise, MoreLikeThis doesn't find any matches.

Implementations

MoreLikeThis has three implementations in Solr to address different user requirements. The implementations are listed here:

> MoreLikeThisComponent: This can be registered to the components list of any SearchHandler. It is useful if you want to retrieve documents similar to each document retrieved by the main query.

> MoreLikeThisHandler: This handler allows you to provide a document or content stream and retrieve documents similar to that.

> MLTQParserPlugin: This query parser forms a MoreLikeThisQuery by using the document ID and other statistical information provided.

Generic Parameters

Table 9-19 specifies the generic parameters that are applicable for all the implementations.

Table 9-19. *MoreLikeThis Generic Parameters*

Parameter	Description
mlt.fl	Specifies the fields in which interesting terms should be identified to determine the similarity. This parameter is not applicable for MLTQParserPlugin.
mlt.qf	Specifies the field to be queried for determining similar documents. These fields must also be specified in the mlt.fl parameter. The field name can be followed by a carat operator (^) and respective boost.
boost	If this parameter is set to true, the interesting terms in the query will be boosted. This parameter is not applicable for MLTQParserPlugin.
mlt.mintf	Specifies the minimum term frequency. Terms with a count less than the specified value will be ignored from the interesting terms list. The default value is 2.
mlt.mindf	Specifies the minimum document frequency. Terms that occur in fewer documents will be ignored. The default value is 5.
mlt.maxdf	Specifies the maximum document frequency. Terms that occur in documents more than the value specified will be ignored.
mlt.minwl	Specifies the minimum word length. Words of smaller length will be ignored. The default value is 0, which is programmed to have no effect.
mlt.maxwl	Specifies the maximum word length. Words that are longer than this will be ignored. The default value is 0, which is programmed to have no effect.
mlt.maxqt	Specifies the maximum number of terms to be used in the second phase for forming the query. The default value is 25.
mlt.maxntp	If the term vector is disabled, this parameter specifies the maximum number of tokens to parse for each stored field. The default value is 5000.

> ■ **Note**   Prior to Solr 5.3, MLTQParserPlugin doesn't support these generic parameters. The parameters should not be prefixed with mlt. in MLTQParserPlugin.

MoreLikeThisComponent

If you configure the MoreLikeThisComponent to any handler, it returns similar documents for each document returned by the main query. The operation would be costly to execute, and it's less likely that a user will want similar documents for all results of the main query. It can be suitable for scenarios such as fingerprinting and duplicate detection, for processing a batch of documents. Table 9-20 represents the generic parameters.

Table 9-20. *MoreLikeThisComponent Specific Parameters*

Parameter	Description
mlt	If set to true, this Boolean parameter enables the MoreLikeThis component. By default, it's set to false.
mlt.count	Specifies the number of similar documents to return for each result of the main query. The default value is 5.

How It Works

Here are the steps followed by the MoreLikeThisComponent for processing requests:

1. The client requests a SearchHandler that has MoreLikeThisComponent registered to it. The handler invokes the MoreLikeThisComponent.

2. The MoreLikeThisComponent does no processing in the prepare phase.

3. In the process phase, all the matching documents retrieved by the main query are provided to MoreLikeThisHelper for retrieving similar documents.

4. This helper class creates a new Query object by extracting the interesting terms from the documents and executes it on index to retrieving similar documents. This process is followed for each document retrieved by the main query and so is costly to execute.

5. The retrieved documents are added to response and returned to the client.

> ■ **Note**   If you are interested in the details of internal processing or are planning customization, you can refer to these steps; otherwise, Solr doesn't require you to know them.

Usage

MoreLikeThisComponent is among the default components for all SearchHandlers, so it doesn't need to be registered. Here is a sample query:

```
$ curl 'http://localhost:8983/solr/hellosolr/select?q=apple
&mlt=true&mlt.fl=product&mlt.mindf=5&mlt.mintf=3&fl=product'
```

MoreLikeThisHandler

MoreLikeThisHandler is a dedicated handler provided by Solr for finding similar documents. Unlike MoreLikeThisComponent, the handler will return documents similar to the document specified in the request. This is the preferred approach of using MoreLikeThis and can be invoked when the user previews a document. You can find similar documents by providing a query or a ContentStream. This handler supports common parameters such as fq, defType, and facets. Along with the generic MoreLikeThis parameters, Table 9-21 mentions the additional parameter supported by the MoreLikeThisHandler.

Table 9-21. *MoreLikeThisHandlerSpecific Parameters*

Parameter	Description
mlt.match.include	This Boolean parameter specifies whether the matching document should be included in the response. The default value is true. It applies only when using a query for finding similar documents.
mlt.match.offset	Specifies the offset of the document returned in response to the main query, for which similar documents should be retrieved. It applies only when using a query for finding similar documents.
mlt.interestingTerms	Specifies how the interesting terms should be returned in the response. Solr supports three styles for interesting terms: • none: Disables the feature. This is the default value. • list: Shows the terms as a list • details: Show the terms along with its boosts.

How It Works

Here are the steps followed by MoreLikeThisHandler for processing requests:

1. MoreLikeThisHandler accepts either a content stream or a query.

2. If a query is provided, the handler parses it by using a defined query parser and forms a Solr Query object. If a content stream is provided, it creates a Reader object.

3. Solr runs the query, if applicable, on the index and retrieves matching document IDs but considers only the first retrieved document for MoreLikeThis matching.

4. The document ID or the reader is provided to MoreLikeThisHelper for retrieving similar documents.

5. This helper class creates a new Query object by extracting the interesting terms from the document or content stream and executes it on index to retrieve the matching documents.

6. The retrieved documents are added to the response, as well as the interesting terms and facets if specified.

7. The generated response is returned to the client.

■ **Note**   If you are interested in the details of internal processing or are planning customization, you can refer to these steps; otherwise, Solr doesn't require you to know them.

Usage

It's easy to use the MoreLikeThis handler. Here are the steps:

1.   Define MoreLikeThisHandler in solrconfig.xml.

     ```
     <requestHandler name="/mlt" class="solr.MoreLikeThisHandler" />
     ```

2.   Query for MoreLikeThis documents.

Find documents similar to document with id APL_1001

```
$ curl "http://localhost:8983/solr/mlt?q=id:APL_1001
&mlt.fl=product&mlt.mintf=2&mlt.mindf=5"
```

MLTQParserPlugin

MLTQParserPlugin is a factory for the query parser, which allows you to retrieve documents similar to the document specified in the query. This provision allows you to enable highlighting and pagination and can be mentioned either in q, fq, or bq. The parser expects the uniqueKey of the document as a value, and the Lucene internal document ID or any arbitrary query is not supported.

Starting in Solr 5.3, this parser supports all the generic parameters except fl and boost. The parameter name should not be prefixed with mlt.

How It Works

Here are the steps followed by Solr for parsing a query using MLTQParserPlugin:

1.   The parser creates a query by using the document ID provided and retrieves the matching document. If document with the specified ID doesn't exist, Solr will report an exception.

2.   For the retrieved document, Solr extracts the vector and term frequency of all the terms in the field list.

3.   Using the terms and frequency, it filters out unnecessary terms and creates a PriorityQueue.

4.   Finally, it creates MoreLikeThisQuery from terms in PriorityQueue.

■ **Note**   If you are interested in the details of internal processing or are planning customization, you can refer to these steps; otherwise, Solr doesn't require you to know them.

Usage

MLTQParserPlugin doesn't require any definition in solrconfig.xml. The value of the UniqueKey field should be provided as a document identifier. The parser can be used as follows. Specifying at least one qf field is mandatory. The following is a sample query:

```
$ curl "http://localhost:8983/solr/hellosolr/select?
q={!mlt qf=product mintf=2 mindf=5 maxdf=100}APL_1001"
```

Summary

This chapter covered the following Solr features in detail: sponsored search, spell-checking, autocompletion, and document similarity. You learned about the approaches for getting these features in place and how to tune the configuration to customize and control the behavior of results.

In the next chapter, you will learn various approaches for scaling Solr, including the SolrCloud mode. You will see what makes Solr a highly scalable and distributed search engine and how to set it up in your environment.

■ ■ ■

CHAPTER 10

Traditional Scaling and SolrCloud

Chapter 2 covered setting up a stand-alone instance of Solr, core management, memory management, and other administrative tasks. The next chapters covered indexing, searching, and other advanced features of Solr. This single instance of Solr works well for proof of concept, development, feature testing, and simple production deployment. But when it comes to mission-critical deployment, you need to think of aspects such as performance, scalability, availability, and fault tolerance.

In this chapter, you will learn about various models supported by Solr to get your system production-ready. You can choose the one that best suits your needs. You will first explore traditional models and then focus on SolrCloud, which is the ultimate model provided by Solr to run a cluster of servers together.

This chapter covers the following topics:

- Stand-alone instance

- Sharding

- Master-slave architecture

- Hybrid of sharding and master-slave

- SolrCloud

- Frequently asked questions

Stand-Alone Mode

Stand-alone mode is the simplest Solr setup: a Solr server (also called an instance) running on a specific port to address all your search requirements. In this mode, documents are indexed to and queried upon the same instance. A stand-alone instance is the preferred mode for development activities, where you do frequent changes, reload, and restart. If high availability is not crucial and data volume is limited, you can run in this mode in production also.

Solr introduced the concept of multiple cores, so that each core can have its own index and configurations instead of you having a separate Solr setup, each running on a different port for each type of index. Multiple cores in Solr are analogous to a database having multiple tables.

Having multiple cores allows you to easily manage and administer multiple indices. A core can be easily loaded, unloaded, renamed, swapped, and optimized at runtime through the Solr admin interface. For indexing and searching, the URL should contain the core name; that's all the change required.

Previous chapters have already explored cores, their usage, and the core.properties file, so I assume that by now you understand the benefits of having multiple cores instead of multiple instances. Multicore as a feature is not limited to stand-alone mode and can be set up in any architecture.

Figure 10-1 demonstrates a stand-alone Solr instance with N cores and the same instance being requested for both indexing and searching.

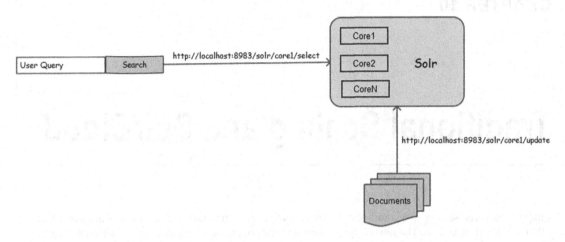

Figure 10-1. *Stand-alone Solr instance with multiple cores*

Sharding

Once you start indexing more and more documents, the index size will increase, and the search performance will be affected. If you are close to hitting the threshold for an acceptable response time for your application, it's time for sharding.

Sharding is the process of breaking a large index into smaller partitions, which are physically distributed across servers but logically make a single unit. The index is divided vertically and distributed over a network of Solr servers; each individual unit is called a *shard*.

Suppose you are indexing documents for a manufacturer with point-of-sales information for multiple countries. If the index size is small, all documents can be fit into a single Solr instance. But as business grows, the data volume will grow, and you may want to partition the index into shards. The sharding strategy will depend on your needs and the data volume. The documents can simply be sharded by using a hashing function, or the sharding can be based on custom logic. Figure 10-2 demonstrates two sharding strategies: one partitions the document based on its country such as United States (US) or United Kingdom (UK); and the other on the basis of a region such as North America, Europe, Middle East, and Africa (EMEA) and Asia-Pacific (APAC).

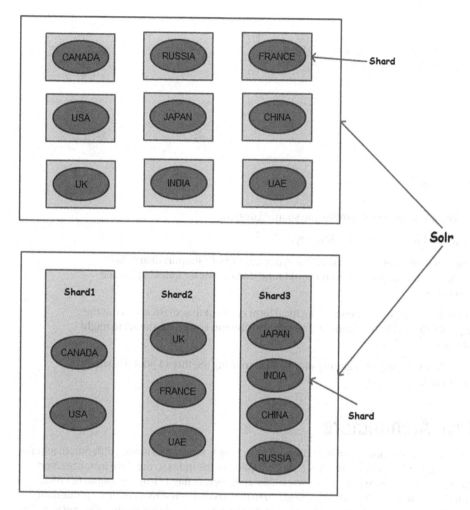

Figure 10-2. *Concept of sharding*

The search application should be aware of the shard URLs and can query all or a few on them as needed. The request should be sent to any of the instances with the additional shards parameter that specifies the list of other shards to query. The instance receiving the request distributes the query to all the shards mentioned in the shards parameter, gets their results, merges them, and responds to the client. This approach offers better query response time.

The following is an example to query Solr with multiple shards:

```
$ curl 'http://localhost:8983/solr/core1/select?q=*:*&shards=localhost:8984/solr/
core1,localhost:8985/solr/core1'
```

Figure 10-3 depicts a multisharded architecture in which all the requests are made to the Solr instance running on port 8983 that distributes the query to other shards. It's worth noting that documents are indexed to each instance separately, whereas a query can be sent to any of the shards for distribution.

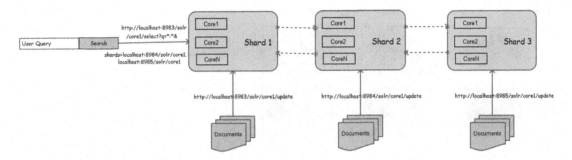

Figure 10-3. *Sharding in Solr*

Here are some key points to note regarding the sharded design:

- The schema should contain a uniqueKey.

- The approach offers only distributed querying and doesn't support distributed indexing. The indexing application should send documents for indexing to each shard separately.

- The inverse document frequency is the local term count in that shard and is not the aggregated value of all the shards. If the term distribution is skewed, the score might get affected.

- Solr distributes the requests among shards, so increasing the thread pool size should be considered.

Master-Slave Architecture

In a *master-slave architecture*, the process of indexing and searching is segregated among different machines. All the documents are indexed to the master server, which replicates the index to the slave instances, and the client sends the search requests to any of the slaves. This architecture has a clear separation of tasks: indexing is done on the master, and the search requests go to the slaves. Each slave contains a redundant copy of the master's indices, so the client can send requests to any one of the slaves. Optionally, you can introduce a load balancer that will provide a single URL to the client and redirect the search requests to one of the slaves on a round-robin basis. The load balancers are generally capable of detecting failures of instances and sending requests to live servers. This approach helps to scale Solr to handle large numbers of requests and also supports high availability and fault tolerance.

In this architecture, the indexing application is simple, and the process is the same as indexing on a stand-alone instance. For search requests, typically a load balancer sits before the client application to route the requests among slave instances.

Figure 10-4 depicts a sample master-slave architecture in which all the indexing requests are sent to the master and the search requests are sent to the slave. Also, you can see a load balancer sitting in front of the application to route the requests.

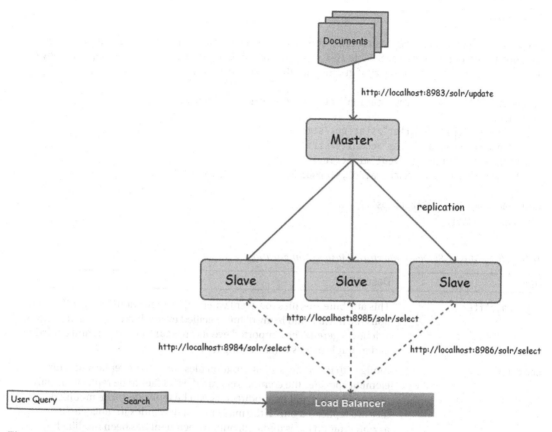

Figure 10-4. Master-slave architecture

▪ **Note**   The master instance is capable of handling search requests, but it's a norm that is followed to have dedicated slaves for searching.

To set up a master-slave architecture, Solr requires you to make a few configuration changes to support the replication of the index from master to slave. Apart from replication changes, you might want to optimize the master instance for indexing and the slave instances for searching.

The replication process is implemented by `ReplicationHandler`. To get the master-slave architecture working, this handler should be registered in `solrconfig.xml`. In the handler, you need to specify the server type (master or slave) and use the appropriate settings to get the desired behavior.

It's important to note that the master server doesn't know about the slaves. It's the slave that knows its master. The slave instances are configured with the URL of the master and they keep polling the master at specified intervals for updates.

Master

The replication handler of the master server should contain an element named `master`, and slaves should contain an element named `slave`. Table 10-1 shows the details of replication parameters supported by the master. The following is a sample configuration for the master instance.

```
<requestHandler name="/replication" class="solr.ReplicationHandler" >
<lst name="master">
  <str name="replicateAfter">startup</str>
  <str name="replicateAfter">commit</str>
  <str name="backupAfter">optimize</str>
  <str name="confFiles">schema.xml,stopwords.txt,elevate.xml</str>
</lst>
<int name="maxNumberOfBackups">2</int>
</requestHandler>
```

Table 10-1. *Master-Slave Architecture: Master Configuration*

Name	Description
replicateAfter	This attribute specifies the event when replication should trigger. The slave polls the master, and if any of the specified events has occurred, replication will be triggered. The supported events are startup, commit, and optimize, and multiple events can be configured.
confFiles	Along with the indices, configuration files can also be replicated. This element specifies the comma-separated list of files to be replicated. Only files inside conf and its subdirectory can be replicated. The modified files are replicated only if the master has a new index to replicate (if a configuration file is updated, but no document has been modified, replication will not be triggered).
backupAfter	This parameter is not related to replication, but backup. It specifies the event after which the index should be backed up. This topic is covered in detail in Chapter 2.
maxNumberOfBackups	This attribute specifies the number of backups to maintain.
commitReserveDuration	This parameter specifies the maximum allowed time to stream 5MB from master to slave.

The provision to replicate configuration files saves you from the redundant work of applying the changes in all instances. You should perform the configuration in the master instance, and replication takes care of deploying it to the slaves. But there is a challenge: with this architecture, the solrconfig.xml files of the master and slave instances are supposed to be different, and you cannot replicate the master's copy to the slave. For that, you can add a separator colon (:) after the file name and specify the name with which it should be replicated to the slave. The following is an example for replicating solrconfig_slave.xml in the master instance to the slave instance as solrconfig.xml:

```
<str name="confFiles">solrconfig_slave.xml:solrconfig.xml,schema.xml</str>
```

To replicate files from a subdirectory in conf, you can specify the relative path as follows. The files outside conf will not be replicated.

```
<str name="confFiles">schema.xml,velocity/template.html</str>
```

With this, you are set up with the master server.

Slave

The slave instance should be aware of its master and the frequency at which it should poll it. Table 10-2 shows the details of the replication parameters supported by the slave. The following is a configuration to enable replication in the slave instance:

```
<requestHandler name="/replication" class="solr.ReplicationHandler">
  <lst name="slave">
    <str name="masterUrl">http://localhost:8983/solr/core1/replication</str>
    <str name="pollInterval">00:00:30</str>
  </lst>
</requestHandler>
```

Table 10-2. *Master-Slave Architecture: Slave Configuration*

Name	Description
masterUrl	Specifies the URL of the master replication handler.
pollInterval	Specifies the interval (in HH:mm:ss) at which this slave polls its master to check for an update. A higher interval will delay changes being reflected in the slave. Replication can also be triggered through the replication API, and in that case you might want to disable polling. Polling can be disabled by removing this parameter.
httpConnTimeout	Specifies the HTTP connection time-out.
httpReadTimeout	Specifies the HTTP read time-out.
httpBasicAuthUser	If the master requires authentication, a username can be specified in this parameter.
httpBasicAuthPassword	Specifies the password corresponding to the username.

Shards with Master-Slave

Sharding allows Solr to process distributed requests, whereas the master-slave architecture helps achieve replication. If your application requires both, you can build a hybrid system in which each shard can have a master for indexing and a set of slaves for searching.

Figure 10-5 shows a design that uses sharding and the master-slave model together. The model contains two shards, and each shard has its own master and slave instances.

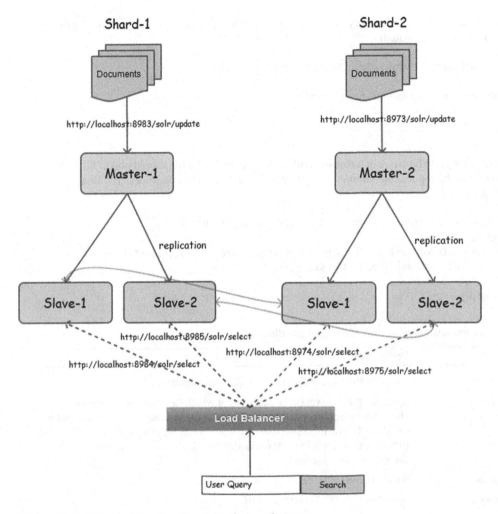

Figure 10-5. *Hybrid of shards with master-slave architecture*

This approach is the most sophisticated among all the traditional approaches, but it has a couple of limitations. This model of scaling Solr is complex and difficult to manage, monitor, and maintain.

To address the limitation of the traditional architecture, SolrCloud was introduced. If you are planning to implement a hybrid approach, I recommend you consider SolrCloud, covered in the next section.

SolrCloud

In the previous sections, you looked at the traditional approach of scaling Solr and putting it together, which has the following limitations:

- The indexing process is not distributed, and all documents should be indexed to the master instance. The master can be a single point of failure; if the master goes down, indexing has to stop.

- The client application needs to contain some of the logic, such as routing of the document and load balancing.

- It's difficult to achieve real-time updates with the replication process, because the slave instance polls the master at frequent intervals and the index is replicated to slaves.

- Inverse document frequency is not supported.

SolrCloud was introduced in release 4.0 and is a step ahead of all the models presented so far. It addresses the previous limitations and provides a true distributed architecture.

SolrCloud provides a highly available and scalable solution along with support for load-balancing, automatic routing, optimistic concurrency, failover, and robustness.

SolrCloud sets up a cluster of servers in which the data is partitioned into shards and distributed over multiple machines. It also maintains multiple copies of shards for fault tolerance and high availability, and documents can be indexed to and searched upon any shard in the cluster. The cluster automatically distributes the documents to the appropriate shard for indexing and syncs up the replicas. Similarly, the search request can be accepted by any shard in the cluster for processing. The cluster takes cares of routing, merging, and availability. If any of the failed nodes becomes available, the cluster automatically syncs it up. The client is abstracted from all the implementation details and process of distribution and coordination.

You can set up this architecture even on a farm of hundreds of machines and manage it centrally from the Solr admin interface. This model even offers lots of convenience in terms of monitoring and maintenance and even can be run on commodity machines.

Understanding the Terminology

SolrCloud introduces some new terminology, as well as terminology that may be familiar but requires understanding from a fresh perspective. Chapter 2 briefly introduced some of this terminology, and this section elaborates further. Without much ado, let's get started.

Node

A *node*, commonly referred to as a *server*, is a Java Virtual Machine instance running Solr on a specific port on a machine. Figure 10-6 depicts a SolrCloud node.

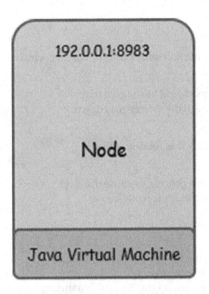

Figure 10-6. *A SolrCloud node*

Cluster

A set of two or more nodes is a *cluster*. A cluster abstracts the outside world from the implementation details and makes the nodes appear as a single unit. Nodes can be added to or removed from the cluster to dynamically expand or contract the cluster, and the client doesn't have to know anything about this change. The client simply makes a request to the cluster, and if it is acknowledged, the client doesn't need to worry about anything else. It's the job of the cluster to ensure the atomicity and further handling of the request.

Figure 10-7 represents a SolrCloud cluster, which appears as a single unit to the indexing and search application.

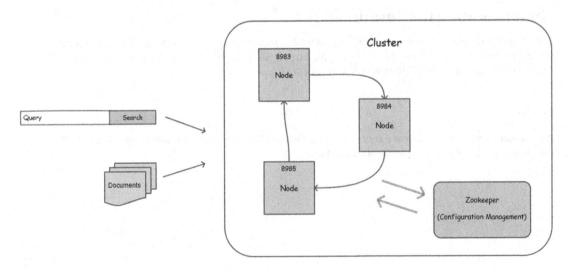

Figure 10-7. *SolrCloud cluster*

The cluster relies on ZooKeeper for coordinating and managing the configurations. ZooKeeper is discussed later in this chapter.

Core

Throughout this book, we have been referring to a core as a single index. If you want to create two types of index, you need to create two cores. But in SolrCloud, the scenario is different. An index can physically reside over multiple nodes but can logically be distributed over several machines. Each physical index in a node can be considered a *core*, and each logical index can consist of multiple cores.

■ **Note**   *Core* has multiple meanings. In a stand-alone Solr instance, a core corresponds to a logical/physical index. In SolrCloud, a collection defines a logical index, whereas a core corresponds to a physical index residing in a node, which is a portion of the logical index.

Collection

A *collection* is a complete logical index in a cluster. A cluster can have multiple collections (multiple types of indexes), a collection can have multiple shards, and a shard can have multiple replicas, which can be distributed across multiple nodes in the cluster.

Shards

The concept of sharding is not new to SolrCloud. You read about it in terms of the traditional distributed architecture also. In a stand-alone approach, all the documents are indexed in the same machine. In this approach, an index is distributed among shards, which maintains a physical copy of a portion of the logical index. The user query is distributed to all the shards for processing and is finally merged by one of the shards before responding to the user.

The traditional approach of sharding requires the client application to contain the sharding logic, but SolrCloud handles it automatically.

Figure 10-8 shows the Cloud tab in the Solr admin UI, which has a `hellocloud` collection containing two shards. The setup contains a two-node cluster running on ports 8983 and 7574. This example is running two instances on different ports, but on the same machine. In a production environment you would want to run the nodes on different machines.

Figure 10-8. Sharding in SolrCloud

Replica

A *replica* is the physical copy of a shard that runs in a node as a Solr core. Suppose that only a single physical copy of a shard exists and that if it goes down, Solr will be able to process only the partial result. To achieve high availability, redundant copies of the shard are maintained, and each of these is called a replica. Each replica corresponds to a core in the Solr admin console.

In the admin interface, replicas are represented by circles connecting the shards. If a circle is marked in green, it's live and available to accept requests. Figure 10-8 shows an example, where each shard has two replicas.

Leader

One replica of each shard is elected as the *leader*, which takes the responsibility of coordination for indexing and query requests. The leader ensures that all replicas are updated and are in sync. They are elected on a first-come, first-served basis. If a leader goes down, one of the available replicas will automatically be promoted to leader.

Figure 10-9 shows a typical SolrCloud cluster running four nodes. The cluster represents a collection of two shards, one starting with name S1 and the other starting with name S2. Each of the boxes starting with name S represents a replica. The replicas ending with L are the leaders for respective shards, and all the S1 (or S2) boxes put together make the shard.

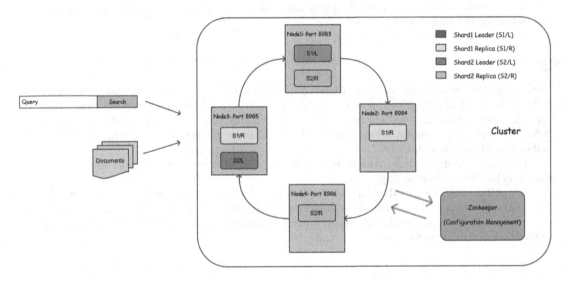

Figure 10-9. *A typical SolrCloud cluster*

Unlike the master-slave architecture, in which the master machine is configured at the time of setting up the instance, the leader is elected dynamically. Any replica, on any node in the cluster, can be appointed as the leader.

In the Solr admin console, leaders are denoted by a solid blank circle. Figure 10-8 shows replicas on the node running on port 7574 are the leaders for shard1 and shard2.

Starting SolrCloud

In Chapter 2, you learned to set up Solr in stand-alone mode, which is different from setting up SolrCloud. Here, you will first learn about starting a SolrCloud instance, which is the obvious prerequisite to perform any other operation. Once you have started the SolrCloud instance, you need to perform other setup steps. The easiest way to start and setup SolrCloud is in interactive mode. If you have no prior experience in SolrCloud, I recommend that you start Solr in this mode, play around and experiment with its features and behavior, and once you are comfortable with it, you can start SolrCloud using the standard approach.

The following are the general steps you need to perform for setting up SolrCloud cluster for indexing and searching documents.

1. Start Solr in cloud mode

2. Design the schema and create the required configurations files. Alternatively, you can use a named configset or choose to go schemaless.

3. SolrCloud doesn't reads the schema.xml and other configurations from `conf` directory but relies on ZooKeeper for it. Solr bundles a ZooKeeper and by default starts it for you. Alternatively, you can start a separate ZooKeeper ensemble. Upload the configurations to the preferred ZooKeeper.

4. Create a collection by specifying the ZooKeeper path and other required information.

Interactive Mode

The `bin/solr` script allows you to quickly launch a small cluster of nodes on your local workstation, without requiring you to perform the steps mentioned in the preceding list. The interactive process automatically instantiates a number of nodes on different ports on the local machine, and sets up the shards and its replicas and the configset for creating the cluster.

If you choose to experiment with schemaless mode, setting up Solr is as simple as downloading and starting and you are good to rock 'n' roll!

For interactive mode, run the script as follows:

```
$ bin/solr start -e cloud
```

This script will get you a SolrCloud instance running in interactive manner. The setup process is easy and self-explanatory. Even if you go ahead by pressing the Enter key for all the options, you will set up a two-node cluster of a collection named `gettingstarted`.

If you want to bypass the interactive steps and start with default settings, run the script with the `-noprompt` option:

```
$ bin/solr start -e cloud -noprompt
```

On successful start, the terminal will print the following message:

```
"SolrCloud example is running, please visit http://localhost:8983/solr"
```

Standard Mode

In this mode, you need to do all the hard work yourself. First, you start the SolrCloud instance by passing an additional parameter to the solr script as follows:

```
$ bin/solr start -c -z <zkHost>
```

> -c: This parameters instructs Solr to start the instance in Cloud mode. Alternatively, -cloud can also be provided as an option.

> -z: By default, SolrCloud starts an embedded ZooKeeper instance, whose port number is 1,000 more than the current instance port number. If, for example, you start Solr node on port 8983, the embedded ZooKeeper will be started on port 9983. To specify an external ZooKeeper ensemble, the -z parameter can be used.

After running this command, SolrCloud should start successfully. But you still need to create the collection; by following the "Creating a Collection" steps. Once that is done, you can start adding documents and searching for results in the collection.

If you have already set up the configurations and $SOLR_HOME, the solr script can be provided the -s parameter, which refers to your $SOLR_HOME directory. Here is an example for starting an instance with the path to $SOLR_HOME:

```
$ bin/solr start -c -s "/home/dev/solr-5.3.1/server/solr"
```

Suppose you are starting another node or want to refer to an existing ZooKeeper ensemble. Here is an example:

```
$ bin/solr start -c -s "/home/dev/solr-5.3.1/server/solr" -z localhost:9983 -p 8984
```

Refer to the complete manual for starting options available in the bin/solr script by providing the -help argument:

```
$ bin/solr start -help
```

Restarting a Node

The options to restart a node are similar to those for starting a node. This example restarts the node running on port 8983:

```
$ bin/solr restart -c -p 8983 -s "/home/dev/solr-5.3.1/server/solr"
```

Creating a Collection

For creating a collection, there are a few prerequisites. First, the schema and other configurations should be defined. You can even use a named configset. Second, the number of shards in the collection should be determined at the time of collection creation. It's not possible to expand or contract a shard on the fly, though you can split a shard into two. I know, it's difficult to predict the corpus size, so determining the exact shard count might not be possible. In that case, you can create an approximate number of shards and then split it when the need arises.

SolrCloud nodes read the configuration from ZooKeeper, so the configuration used by the collection must be uploaded to ZooKeeper. Solr provides a script to upload a collection directory to ZooKeeper. It is discussed in next section.

Here is a sample command for creating the collection:

```
$ bin/solr create -c hellocloud -d sample_techproducts_configs
  -n hellocloud -shards 2 -replicationFactor 2
```

- -c specifies the collection name.

- -d specifies the path of the configuration directory or the name of the existing configset that should be uploaded to ZooKeeper and used.

- -n specifies the name of the collection in ZooKeeper. If this parameter is not specified, the value of the -c argument will be considered.

- -shards specifies the number of shards to create.

- -replicationFactor specifies the number of replicas to create for the shard. If the factor is specified as 2, one leader and one replica will be created.

You can also alternatively use the create_collection option. To see all the options available for creating a collection, run the script as follows:

```
$ bin/solr create_collection -help
```

SolrCloud offers the Collections API for managing the collection. If you want to create a collection by using the API, it can done as follows:

```
$ curl 'http://localhost:8983/solr/admin/collections?
action=CREATE&name=hellocloud&collection=hellocloud&numShards=2&replicationFactor=2'
```

Using the Collections API, you cannot specify the configset or configuration directory. Instead, it should be loaded to ZooKeeper beforehand, and its name should be provided in the collection.configName parameter.

■ **Note**   Refer to the Solr official reference guide for a complete set of Collections APIs provided by Solr at https://cwiki.apache.org/confluence/display/solr/Collections+API.

Uploading to ZooKeeper

In the previous examples, you saw that Solr automatically uploads the configuration to ZooKeeper. If you want to upload the configuration to ZooKeeper manually, Solr provides the ZooKeeper command-line interface (also called zkCLI). The zkCLI script can be located in the $SOLR_DIST/server/scripts/cloud-scripts directory. The zkcli.sh should be used in *nix machines, and zkcli.bat should be used in Windows machines.

This example uses zkcli.sh to upload the configuration to ZooKeeper:

```
$ ./zkcli.sh -cmd upconfig -zkhost  localhost:9983 -confname hellocloud
-solrhome /home/dev/solr-5.3.1/server/solr
-confdir /home/dev/solr-5.3.1/server/solr/configsets/hello_configs/conf
```

■ **Note**   Refer to the Solr wiki for a complete set of command set utilities at https://cwiki.apache.org/confluence/display/solr/Command+Line+Utilities.

Deleting a Collection

A collection can be deleted from a cluster, using the `bin/solr` script as follows:

```
$ bin/solr delete -c hellocloud -deleteConfig false -p 8983
```

- `-c` specifies the name of the collection to be deleted.
- `-deleteConfig` specifies whether ZooKeeper should retain the configuration or delete it.
- `-p` specifies the port on the local instance to reference for deleting the collection.

Instead of deleting the collection by using `bin/solr` script, you can delete it by using the Collections API as follows:

```
$ curl 'http://localhost:8983/solr/admin/collections?action=DELETE&name=hellocloud'
```

Indexing a Document

SolrCloud eases the indexing process for the client application. In a traditional distributed architecture, the client program indexes all the documents to the master instance, which gets replicated to slaves for searching. Also, the client application is responsible for routing the document to the appropriate shard. SolrCloud automatically determines which shard to send the document to for indexing, without the client worrying about the master instance or routing to the appropriate shard.

The client program sends the document to any shard in the cluster for indexing. If the shard receiving the request is a replica, it sends the document to its leader for processing. The leader identifies the shard to which the documents should be indexed and sends the request to the leader of that shard. This leader appends the document to the transaction log, indexes it, and then routes it to all its replicas for indexing. If the update succeeds on the leader but fails on the replica, the client still will be responded to with a success status. When the failed replicas recover, they can reconcile by syncing up with the leader.

In a traditional master-slave architecture, all the documents are indexed in the master, and the master replicates the index segments to the slave. There is no indexing process in the slave instance. In contrast, in SolrCloud the leader indexes the document and then sends it to the replicas for indexing. The leader typically transports the documents instead of the segments, and indexing is done in both the leader and replicas.

In SolrCloud, you generally avoid triggering a commit from the client application and should rely on autocommit. If there are multiple applications indexing documents and you find it difficult to ensure that none of them trigger a commit, you can register `IgnoreCommitOptimizeUpdateProcessorFactory` to the process chain to disallow a commit from the client applications. Here is an example configuration for disabling a commit:

```
<updateRequestProcessorChain name="preprocessor">
  <processor class="solr.IgnoreCommitOptimizeUpdateProcessorFactory">
    <int name="statusCode">403</int>
    <str name="responseMessage">External commit is disabled on this collection!</str>
  </processor>
  <processor class="solr.LogUpdateProcessorFactory" />
  <processor class="solr.DistributedUpdateProcessorFactory" />
  <processor class="solr.RunUpdateProcessorFactory" />
</updateRequestProcessorChain>
```

Load Balancing

SolrCloud automatically load balances the request, and you don't need to have a load balancer in front, as in the case of traditional architecture. But it's still advised to have a load balancer or a smart client for making requests to the cluster. Suppose you make all requests to the same node, which will forward the request to its leader, and this leader in turn will determine the shard that should handle the request and then forward it to the leader of that shard. If your client application itself knows the shard to which the request should be sent, the initial routing can be avoided and will save the network from being overwhelmed. A smart client like SolrJ provides a load balancer that distributes the request on a round-robin basis.

If you send all requests to the same shard and that shard goes down, all the requests will start failing. To address such a single point of failure, SolrJ enables you to provide a reference of ZooKeeper instead of Solr node. Because ZooKeeper is always aware of the status of the cluster, it will never direct the request to a node that is unavailable. To avoid such a single point of failure, requests to SolrJ should be configured as follows:

```
import org.apache.solr.client.solrj.impl.CloudSolrServer;
import org.apache.solr.common.SolrInputDocument;

// Provide ZooKeeper address as argument
CloudSolrServer server = new CloudSolrServer("localhost:9983");
server.setDefaultCollection("hellocloud");

// Create document
SolrInputDocument document = new SolrInputDocument();
document.addField( "productId", "Mac152016");
document.addField( "name", "Apple MacBook Pro");
server.add(document);

// Let Solr autocommit
// server.commit();
```

Document Routing

By default, SolrCloud distributes the documents among shards by using the hashing function. If you want, you can fine-tune the behavior by specifying the parameter router.name=compositeId while creating the collection. This parameter also requires the numShards parameter to be specified, which defines the number of shards among which the documents should be distributed.

If the compositeId router is used, the document's uniqueKey should be prefixed with a string that Solr would use to generate a hash for identifying the shard to which the document should be indexed. The prefix should be followed by an exclamation mark (!) to differentiate it from the uniqueKey. Suppose the original uniqueKey is Mac152016 and you want to route the documents on the basis of the manufacturer. In that case, you can prefix the document with the manufacturer name, such as Apple!Mac152016.

Solr supports routing up to two levels, separated by the addition of an exclamation mark. For example, if you want to route on the basis of manufacturer and product category, the document ID should be modified to something like Apple!Laptop!Mac152016.

If documents are routed by using compositeId, then while searching, the prefix information should be provided in an additional parameter, _router_. This information will help Solr in routing the query to the right shard instead of being sent to all the shards. Here is an example of query routing:

Using the _router_ parameter, a sample query would be q=mac&_router_=Apple.

```
$ curl 'http://localhost:8983/solr/hellocloud/select?q=*:*&_router_=Apple'
```

Working with a Transaction Log

Solr uses transaction logs to mitigate the risk of data loss. Introduced in Solr 4.0, it is an append-only write-ahead log that records all the index operations on each shard. In SolrCloud, all shards, both leader and replica, have their own log file.

A transaction log is also referred to as tlog and is created in the tlog directory inside the data directory (adjacent to the index directory). Figure 10-10 shows the directory structure of tlog.

Figure 10-10. *Solr transaction log directory*

Solr appends all documents to the end of the transaction log and is rolled over on hard commit. When the request is for atomic update, tlog records the old value as well as the new value, which allows you to roll back the document. If the hard commit is performed after a long duration or the documents are indexed at high velocity, the files can grow really large and recovery can be costly.

Performing a Shard Health Check

The indexing client can send an additional parameter, min_rf, meaning minimum replication factor, to know whether the shard is in a degraded state and whether the replication factor of the documents is below the expected threshold. This information can be helpful, if you want to take any preventive action.

Querying Results

Sending a query to SolrCloud is almost as simple as always, as the cluster hides all the implementation details from the client application. The steps taken by SolrCloud for processing the search request are as follows:

1. The client application sends a request to any node in the cluster.

2. The receiving node determines the eligible shards and sends the query to any available replica of each of them.

3. Each replica returns the matching documents to the receiver shard.

4. The receiver shard merges the results and triggers another request to the replicas, for getting the stored values for the documents to be returned.

5. The receiver responds to the client with the matching documents.

■ **Note**   The query requests are not routed to the shard leader and can be processed by any of the shard replicas.

It's advised to use a smart client such as SolrJ or a load balancer to query the cluster. Solr has built-in support for load balancers, but if all queries are sent to the same node, it will have to do all the routing and may get overwhelmed with requests. In turn, a load balancer would distribute the queries among nodes and offer better performance. A smart client such as SolrJ gets the cluster state from ZooKeeper and resends the request to one of the active nodes.

The process of searching results on the complete index is the same as before, and you may not even know that you are querying a cluster. If you want to query a portion of the index (a specified set of shards), all you need to do is pass an additional parameter, shards, as in the case of traditional sharded architecture. Here is an example for each of them:

- Query the whole collection/complete index.

```
$ curl 'http://localhost:8983/solr/hellocloud/select?q=*:*'
```

- Query a specific set of shards by specifying the shards parameter with a comma-separated list of URLs.

```
$ curl 'http://localhost:8983/solr/hellocloud/select?q=*:*&shards=
localhost:8983/solr,localhost:7574/solr'
```

- Query a specific set of shards and load balance among its replicas by separating the shard URL with the pipe (|) operator.

```
$ curl 'http://localhost:8983/solr/hellosolr/select?q=*:*
&shards=localhost:8983/solr|localhost:8483/solr'
```

■ **Note**   A simple client such as curl can be used for evaluation and development, but it's advised to have a smart client like SolrJ in production.

If you want to get information about the shards that processed the query, pass the additional parameter shards.info=true to the request.

Performing a Recovery

Failures are common, especially when you are running a large cluster and that too on commodity machines. SolrCloud provides recovery from such failure by automatically syncing up with other shards when the failed node is back.

When a nonleader that was down recovers, it syncs up with the shard leader and gets active for accepting requests only after it gets up-to-date. The process of recovery can be long if the number of documents to be replayed is large.

When a leader goes down, Solr appoints another replica as the leader. When this failed node becomes available, it syncs with the current leader for the updates it would have missed.

It's important to note that when a replica recovers from a failure, it gets the documents from the leader's tlog and replays it. But if it finds that it's too far behind, the segments are replicated as in the traditional approach.

Shard Splitting

The Solr Collections API allows you to split a shard into two partitions. The documents of the existing shard are divided into two pieces, and each piece is copied to a new shard. The existing shard can be deleted later as per convenience.

Here is an example to split shard1 in the hellocloud collection into two shards:

```
$ curl 'http://localhost:8983/solr/admin/collections?action=SPLITSHARD
&collection=hellocloud&shard=shard1'
```

Adding a Replica

SolrCloud offers the elasticity to expand and contract a cluster. Suppose you want to scale the system to handle more queries or you got new hardware; in that case, you might want to add a node to the cluster and assign replicas to it.

You can add replicas to the collection by using the Solr Collections API. This example adds a node to the shard shard1 in the hellocloud collection:

```
$ curl 'http://localhost:8983/solr/admin/collections?action=ADDREPLICA
&collection=hellocloud&shard=shard1&node=192.10.8.120:7573_solr'
```

ZooKeeper

Apache ZooKeeper is a mature and fast open source server widely used in distributed systems for coordinating, synchronizing, and maintaining shared information. It's capable of handling hundreds of thousands of transactions per second and is quite popular among distributed systems including Hadoop, Spark, and HBase.

ZooKeeper maintains information in memory and builds an ensemble of servers that maintain redundant copies of these configurations to achieve fast performance and high availability. The primary server is called the leader, and has a set of followers for redundancy. Figure 10-11 depicts a ZooKeeper ensemble and how it fits in the SolrCloud architecture.

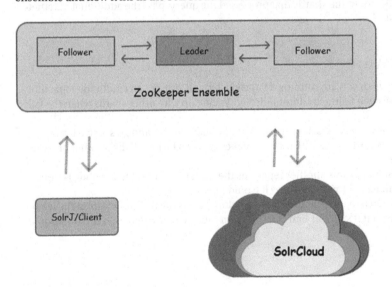

Figure 10-11. *ZooKeeper ensemble*

> ■ **Note** Refer to the official Apache ZooKeeper web site for more details: `https://zookeeper.apache.org/`.

In SolrCloud, ZooKeeper is used by the cluster for coordination among shards and maintaining the configuration. Broadly speaking, SolrCloud uses ZooKeeper for the following:

> *Configuration management*: All your configuration files in the `core/conf` directory, including `solrconfig.xml` and `schema.xml`, are centrally maintained in ZooKeeper. The nodes refer to ZooKeeper for all the configuration. Any change in the configuration should be uploaded to ZooKeeper.

> *Cluster coordination*: ZooKeeper maintains information about the cluster, its collections, live nodes, and replica states, which are watched by nodes for coordination.

> *Leader election*: Each shard should have a leader and can have multiple replicas. If the leader goes down, one of the replicas has to be elected as leader. ZooKeeper plays an important role in this process of leader election.

Solr comes bundled with ZooKeeper, which makes a good starting point for evaluation, development, and initial testing. But because the ZooKeeper ensemble expects a quorum of more than half the servers, it's advised to run an external ensemble in the production environment.

> *A quorum is a gathering of the minimal number of members of an organization to conduct business.*
>
> —`www.vocabulary.com`

> ■ **Note** Refer to Solr's official guide for setting up an external ZooKeeper ensemble at `https://cwiki.apache.org/confluence/display/solr/Setting+Up+an+External+ZooKeeper+Ensemble`.

Frequently Asked Questions

The section covers a few frequently asked questions related to SolrCloud.

Why is the size of my data/tlog directory growing drastically? How can I handle that?

This directory contains the transaction logs that are used by atomic updates and SolrCloud. All index updates are recorded in these files and are truncated at hard commit. The files grow huge if your system is indexing at high velocity but a hard commit is being performed infrequently.

You can control the size of `tlog` by performing autocommits more frequently. Here is how you can configure it in `solrconfig.xml`:

```
<autoCommit>
    <maxTime>${solr.autoCommit.maxTime:30000}</maxTime>
    <maxTime>${solr.autoCommit.maxDocs:100000}</maxTime>
    <openSearcher>false</openSearcher>
</autoCommit>
```

Can I totally disable transaction logs? What would be the impact?

You can disable `tlog` by commenting out the following section in `solrconfig.xml`:

```
<updateLog>
    <str name="dir">${solr.ulog.dir:}</str>
    <int name="numVersionBuckets">${solr.ulog.numVersionBuckets:65536}</int>
</updateLog>
```

It's strongly recommended not to disable transaction logs. The high availability of SolrCloud, along with features such as atomic updates and near real-time searches rely on `tlog`, and disabling it will impact the support of those features.

I have recently migrated from traditional architecture to SolrCloud. Is there anything that I should be careful of and not do in SolrCloud?

With SolrCloud, many things have changed in Solr and reading through this chapter gives you a fair idea about those changes. Here are some of the key things you should take care of:

- You should avoid triggering a commit from a client program and instead use Solr's `autocommit` and `softCommit` features.

- Always stop the node gracefully. If you had been doing `kill -9`, stop that.

- Avoid searching all the shards.

I am migrating to SolrCloud, but it fails to upload the configurations to ZooKeeper. What could be the reason?

ZooKeeper limits the size of the configuration to less than 1MB. If the size of your configset is larger, ZooKeeper will fail to upload it. Usually the size of the `conf` directory is large due to a huge synonym file or custom plug-in integrating taxonomies. You need to have a better datasource to address the limitation.

Summary

In this chapter, you learned about various traditional approaches offered by Solr for scalability. Based on your requirements, you can choose one of these approaches or a combination of them. You also learned about the limitation of these approaches and why SolrCloud was introduced.

This chapter also covered the prominent features of SolrCloud and its underlying concepts and how these features revolutionized distributed scaling in Solr. You also had an overview of ZooKeeper.

CHAPTER 11

■ ■ ■

Semantic Search

You have reached the last chapter of this book, and in this journey you have learned about the significant features of Solr and the nitty-gritty of using it. In previous chapters, you also learned about information retrieval concepts and relevance ranking, which are essential for understanding Solr's internals and the how and why of scoring. This knowledge is indispensable for what you will be doing most of the time: tuning the document relevance. With all of this information, you should be able to develop an effective search engine that retrieves relevant documents for the query, ranks them appropriately, and provides other features that add to the user experience.

So far, so good, but users expect more. If you look at some of the search applications on the market, they are implementing lots of innovative capabilities and plugging in diverse frameworks and components to take the search experience to the next level. As the expectations are set high, matching beyond keywords to understand the underlying semantics and user intent is needed. Google, for example, also acts like a question-answering system. It applies enormous intelligence to understand the semantics of the query and acts accordingly. If you analyze your query logs, you will find that a considerable number of queries contain the user's intent and not just the keywords, though that depends on the domain.

At this point, you should be able to develop a decent keyword-based search engine, but with a few limitations. When you put it all together, the system won't understand the semantics. If your application caters to a medical domain, for example, a user query of *heart attack* will fail to retrieve results for *cardiac arrest*, which might be more interesting to the medical practitioners.

A *semantic search* addresses the limitations of a keyword-based search by understanding the user intent and the contextual meaning of terms. The acquired knowledge can be utilized in many ways to improve the search accuracy and relevance ranking.

Semantic search is an advanced and broad topic, and presenting its techniques of text analytics would require a dedicated book. In this chapter, you will learn about some of the techniques in their simplest forms as well as references to resources that can be utilized to explore further. This chapter covers the following topics:

- Limitations of keyword-based systems

- Introduction to semantic search

- Common tools for building the semantic capabilities

- Techniques for integrating semantic capabilities to Solr

- Identifying the part-of-speech of tokens

- Extracting named entities such as person, organization, and location from the unstructured data

- Semantic enrichment

Limitations of Keyword Systems

Keyword-based document ranking fundamentally depends upon the statistical information about the query terms. Although they are beneficial for many use cases, they often do not provide users with valuable results if the user fails to formulate an appropriate query or provides an intent query. If the user is rephrasing the same query multiple times while searching, it implicitly signifies the need for extending the search engine to support advanced text processing and semantic capabilities. Computer scientist Hans Peter Luhn describes the limitations of keyword systems:

> *This rather unsophisticated argument on "significance" avoids such linguistic implications as grammar and syntax....No attention is paid to the logical and semantic relationships the author has established.*

The primary limitations of a keyword-based system can be categorized as follows:

Context and intent: Keyword-based systems are not context aware and do not consider the cognitive characteristics of the documents. A query of *white formal shirt* indicates user intent, but a keyword system might retrieve documents that are irrelevant to user expectations. Similarly, in a music search engine, a query for *top songs of this year* is a pure intent query, and a keyword-based system might end up retrieving albums or titles containing these tokens, which is irrelevant to what the user is looking for.

Significant terms: A keyword-based search engine determines the importance and significance of terms on the basis of statistical information and ignores the underlying semantics.

Synonymy: A keyword-based engine retrieves documents containing matching tokens but ignores the terms that linguistically refer to the same thing. These ignored tokens treated as irrelevant by the system can actually be more relevant, as in the previous *heart attack* example.

You may debate that `synonyms.txt` addresses the problem of synonyms, but that has two limitations. First, the file should be manually created and is limited to handcrafted synonyms. Second, it ignores the semantics and the fact that synonyms of a word can differ based on context.

Polysemy: In English, words are polysemous (a word can have different meanings). The synonyms defined in `synonyms.txt` can go terribly wrong for such words. For example, if *heart* is mapped to *emotion* in the `synonyms.txt` file, the query *heart attack* will be expanded to *emotion attack*, when instead it should have ideally expanded to *cardiac arrest*.

Unstructured data: Unstructured data is basically for human consumption, and an enormous amount of information is hidden inside it. The keyword-based system fails to fully utilize the knowledge available in this unstructured data.

Semantic Search

Semantic search refers to a set of techniques that interprets the intent, context, concept, meaning, and relationships between terms. The idea is to develop a system that follows a cognitive process to understand terms similar to the way we humans do. Technopedia.com provides this definition of semantic search:

> *Semantic search is a data searching technique in which a search query aims to not only find keywords, but to determine the intent and contextual meaning of the words a person is using for search.*

The potential of leveraging semantic capabilities in your search application is unbound. The way you utilize them depends a lot on your domain, data, and search requirements. Google, for example, uses semantic capabilities for delivering answers and not just links. Figure 11-1 shows an example of the semantic capabilities of Google, which precisely understands the user intent and answers the query.

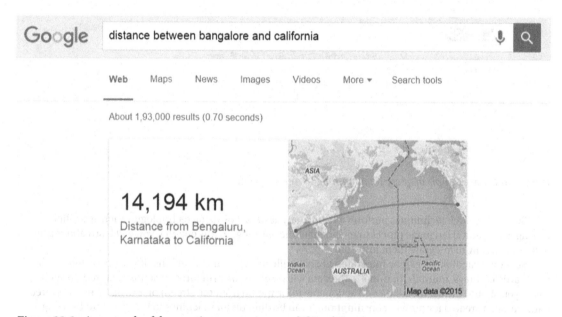

Figure 11-1. An example of the question-answering capability of Google

Historically, search engines were developed to cater to keyword-based queries, but due to their limitations, the engines also provided advanced search capabilities. This is acceptable in some verticals (for example, legal searches), but it is something that very few users find appealing. The user prefers a single box because of its ease of use and simplicity. Since the search box is open-ended (you can type whatever you want), users provide queries in natural language, using the linguistics of day-to-day life. Earlier Google had the advanced search option on its home page, but it was hidden in 2011. Google's advanced search is now available in its home page settings and requires an extra click, or you need to go to www.google.com/advanced_search. Advanced search is where you provide details about the query terms and the fields to which they apply. It is generally preferred by librarians, lawyers, and medical practitioners.

Figure 11-2 shows an example of an intelligent search, performed by Amazon.com for the user query *white formal shirt for men*. The search engine finds exactly what you want by using built-in semantic capabilities.

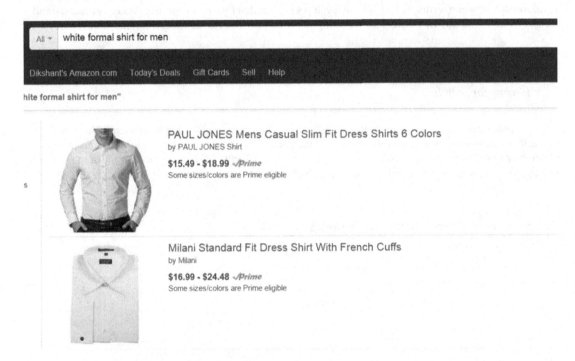

Figure 11-2. An example of query intent mining in Amazon.com

Semantic search techniques perform a deep analysis of text by using technologies such as artificial intelligence, natural language processing, and machine learning. In this chapter, you will learn about a few of them and how to integrate them into Solr.

Semantic capabilities can be integrated in Solr while indexing and searching. If you are dealing with news, articles, blogs, journals, or e-mails, the data will be either unstructured or semistructured. In such cases, you should extract metadata and actionable information from the stream of text. Since unstructured data has been created for human consumption, it can be difficult for machines to interpret, but by using text-processing capabilities such as natural language processing, useful information can be extracted.

Semantic processing broadly depends on the following:

> *Knowledge base*: The semantic knowledge source contains information regarding the entities or facts related to the terms and concepts. The knowledge can be available as an ontology, taxonomy, thesauri, other controlled vocabulary, trained models, or even a set of rules. The knowledge can be provided by a third-party vendor, crowd-sourced by a community, or developed in-house.

> *Text processing*: This refers to the processing, inference rules, and reasoning applied on the knowledge to detect the entities, establish the logical connection, or determine the context.

Tools

This section presents some of the tools and technologies that you might want to evaluate while processing text for semantic enrichment. You can extend a Solr component to plug in the tool that suits your text-processing requirements. Before proceeding further in this section, refer to the "Text Processing" section of Chapter 3 for a refresher on these concepts.

OpenNLP

The *Apache OpenNLP* project provides a set of tools for processing natural language text for performing common NLP tasks such as sentence detection, tokenization, part-of-speech tagging and named-entity extraction, among others. OpenNLP provides a separate component for each of these tasks. The components can be used individually or combined to form a text-analytics pipeline. The library uses machine-learning techniques such as maximum entropy and the perceptron to train the models and build advanced text-processing capabilities. OpenNLP distributes a set of common models that perform well for general use cases. If you want to build a custom model for your specific needs, its components provide an API for training and evaluating the models.

This project is licensed under the Apache Software License and can be downloaded at https://opennlp.apache.org/. Other NLP libraries are available, such as Stanford NLP, but they are either not open source or require a GPL-like license that might not fit into the licensing requirements of many companies.

OpenNLP's freely available models can be downloaded from http://opennlp.sourceforge.net/models-1.5/.

OpenNLP integration is not yet committed in Solr and is not available as an out-of-the-box feature. Refer to the Solr wiki at https://wiki.apache.org/solr/OpenNLP for more details. Later in this chapter, you will see examples of integrating OpenNLP with Solr.

■ **Note** Refer to JIRA https://issues.apache.org/jira/browse/LUCENE-2899 for more details on integration.

Apache UIMA

As you know, *UIMA* stands for *Unstructured Information Management Architecture*, an Apache project that allows you to develop interoperable, complex components and combine them to run together. This framework allows you to develop an analysis engine, which can be used to extract metadata and information from unstructured text.

The analysis engine allows you to develop a pipeline, which you can use to chain the annotators. Each annotator represents an independent component or feature. The annotators can consume and produce an annotation, and the output of one annotation can be input to the next in the chain. The chain can be formed by using XML configuration.

UIMA's pluggable architecture, reusable components, and configurable pipeline allow you to throw away the monolithic structure and design a multistage process in which different modules need to build on each other to get a powerful analysis chain. This also allows you to scale out and run the components asynchronously. You might find the framework a bit complex; it has a learning curve.

Annotations from different vendors are available for consumption that can be added to the pipeline. Vendors such as Open Calias and AlchemyAPI provide a variety of annotations for text processing but require licenses.

Solr integration for UIMA is available as a contrib module, and Solr enrichments can be done with just a few configuration changes. Refer to the Solr official documentation at `https://cwiki.apache.org/confluence/display/solr/UIMA+Integration` for UIMA integration.

Apache Stanbol

Apache Stanbol is an OSGi-based framework that provides a set of reusable components for reasoning and content enhancement. The additional benefit it offers is built-in CMS capabilities and provisions to persist semantic information such as entities and facts and define knowledge models.

No Solr plug-in is available, and none is required for this framework as Stanbol internally uses Solr as document repository. It also uses Apache OpenNLP for natural language processing and Apache Clerezza and Apache Jena as RDF and storage frameworks. Stanbol offers a GUI for managing the chains and offers additional features such as a web server and security features.

You might want to evaluate this framework if you are developing a system with semantic capabilities from scratch, as it offers you the complete suite.

Techniques Applied

Semantic search has been an active area of research for quite some time and is still not a solved problem, but lots of advancement has happened in the area. A typical example is IBM's Watson; this intelligent system, capable of answering questions in a natural language, won the Jeopardy challenge in 2011. Building a semantic capability can be a fairly complex task, depending on what you want to achieve. But you can employ simple techniques to improve result quality, and sometimes a little semantics can take you a long way.

Figure 11-3 provides an overview of how semantic techniques can be combined with different knowledge bases to process input text and build the intelligence. The information gained from these knowledge bases can be used for expanding terms, indicating relationships among concepts, introducing facts, and extracting metadata from the input text. Chapter 3 provides an overview of these knowledge bases. In this section, you will see how to utilize this knowledge to perform a smart search.

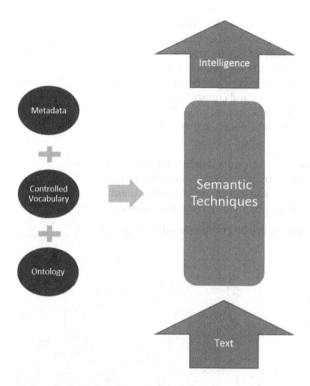

Figure 11-3. Semantic techniques

Earlier in this book, you learned that Solr ranks a document by using a model such as the vector space model. This model considers a document as a bag of words. For a user query, it retrieves documents based on factors such as term frequency and inverse document frequency, but it doesn't understand the relationships between terms. Semantic techniques such as these can be applied in Solr to retrieve more relevant results:

> *Query parsing*: Semantic techniques can be applied on the query for mining the user intent. Based on the domain, you can mine the user intent by developing a text classification system or other techniques. The feature can be plugged into Solr by writing a custom query parser. Based on the understanding of the intent, the parser can either reformulate the query or expand the query terms with synonyms and other related concepts. Reformulation can be a difficult task and should be performed with care.

> *Text analysis*: The tokens can be enriched with semantically related words while performing text analysis, similar to the way you do it using a synonym filter factory. You can plug in the enrichment by writing a custom token filter that can be applied either while indexing the fields of the documents or while querying for a result. A sample implementation for expanding the synonyms automatically is presented later in this chapter.

> *Query reranking*: Intent mining can even be applied by writing a custom reranking query, which you learned about in Chapter 7, for changing the order of retrieved documents. Query reranking will not introduce a totally new document, as in the case of a custom query parser.

Indexing documents: Structured content is more valuable than unstructured content. If you are indexing unstructured data, such as the text of a book or journal, you should structure it. You can apply several techniques to extract the entities and hidden facts from such content and automatically generate metadata. Fields containing these extracted entities can be boosted based on its significance, can be used for generating facets and controlling the manner in which results can be represented. Later in this chapter, you will learn to write a custom update request processor for automatically extracting metadata from unstructured content.

Ranking model: The ranking model used for scoring documents can be tuned to consider the semantic relationship of terms, but that would not be a trivial task. I suggest you consider other approaches that can contribute to the document ranking, by using an existing model such as by applying boosts or payloads.

Figure 11-4 depicts how semantic capabilities can be applied to Solr for improving relevancy.

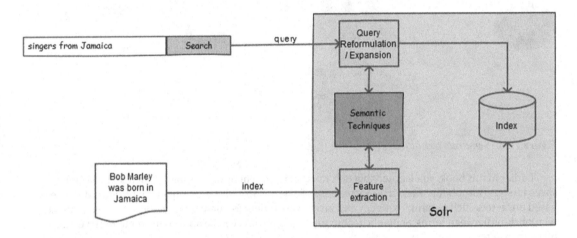

Figure 11-4. *Application of semantic techniques in Solr*

Next you will look at various natural language processing and semantic techniques that can be integrated in Solr for improving the precision of results.

Part-of-Speech Tagging

Each word in a sentence can be classified into a lexical category, also called a *part of speech*. Common parts of speech include noun, verb, and adjective. These can be further classified—for instance, a noun can be categorized as a common noun or proper noun. This categorization and subcategorization information can be used to discover the significance of terms in context and can even be used to extract lots of interesting information about the words. I suggest that you get a fair understanding of parts of speech, as it may help you decipher the importance and purpose of words. For example, nouns are used to identify people, places, and things (for example, shirt or Joe), and adjectives define the attributes of a noun (such as red or intelligent). Similarly, the subclass, such as common noun, describes a class of entities (such as country or animal), and a proper noun describes the instances (such as America or Joe). Figure 11-5 provides sample text and its parts of speech. In Figure 11-5, the tags NNP, VBD, VBN and IN refer to proper noun (singular), verb (past tense), verb (past participle) and conjunction (preposition or subordinating) respectively.

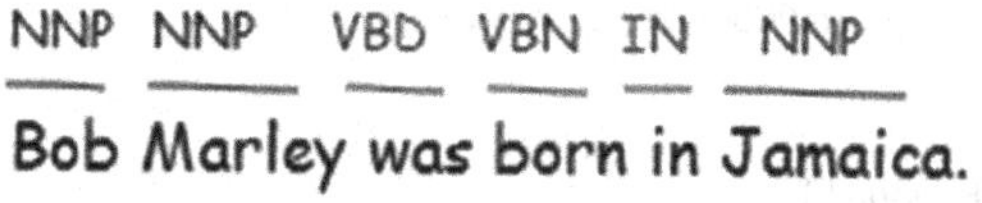

NNP NNP   VBD VBN IN   NNP
____ ____   ____ ____ __   ____

Bob Marley was born in Jamaica.

Figure 11-5. *Part-of-speech tagging*

With an understanding of parts of speech, you can clearly make out that not all words are equally important. If your system can tag parts of speech, this knowledge can be used to control the document ranking based on the significance of the tokens in the context. Currently, while indexing documents, you boost either a document or a field, but ignore the fact that each of the terms may also need a different boost. In a sentence, generally the nouns and verbs are more important; you can extract those terms and index them to separate fields. This gives you a field with a smaller and more focused set of terms, which can be assigned a higher boost while querying. Solr features such as MoreLikeThis would work better on this field with more significant tokens. You can even apply a payload to them while indexing.

The part-of-speech tagging can be a necessary feature and a prerequisite for many types of advanced analysis. The semantic enrichment example, which you will see later in this chapter, requires POS tagged words, as the meaning and definition of a word may vary based on its part of speech. A POS tagger uses tags from the Penn Treebank Project to label words in sentences with their parts of speech.

Solr Plug-in for POS Tagging

In this section, you will learn to extract important parts of speech from a document being indexed and populate the extracted terms to a separate Solr field. This process requires two primary steps:

1. Extract the part of speech from the text. In the provided sample, you'll use OpenNLP and the trained models freely available on its web site. The model can be downloaded from http://opennlp.sourceforge.net/models-1.5/.

2. Write a custom update request processor, which will create a new field and add the extracted terms to it.

The steps to be followed for adding the desired part of speech to a separate Solr field are provided next in detail.

1. Write a Java class to tag the part of speech by using OpenNLP. The steps for part of-speech tagging in OpenNLP are provided next. These steps doesn't relate to Solr but is called by the plugin for getting the POS.

    a. Read the trained model using FileInputStream and instantiate the POSModel with it. The path of model is passed to the InputStream during instantiation. OpenNLP prebundles two POS models for English and a few other languages. You can use en-pos-maxent.bin, a model which is based on maximum entropy framework. You can read more details about maximum entropy at http://maxent.sourceforge.net/about.html.

    ```
    InputStream modelIn = new FileInputStream(fileName);
    POSModel model =  new POSModel(modelIn);
    ```

b. Instantiate the POSTaggerME class by providing the POSModel instance to its constructor.

```
POSTaggerME tagger = new POSTaggerME(model);
```

c. POSTaggerME as a prerequisite requires the sentence to be tokenized, which can be done using OpenNLP tokenization. If this code had been part of an analysis chain, the sentence could be tokenized using Solr provided tokenizer. The simplest form of tokenization can even be built using Java String's split() method, also used in this example, though it's prone to creating invalid tokens.

```
String [] tokens = query.split(" ");
```

d. Pass the tokenized sentence to the POSTaggerME instance, which returns a string array containing all the tagged parts of speech.

```
String [] tags = tagger.tag(tokens);
```

e. Iterate over the array to map the tags to the corresponding tokens. You have populated the extracted tags to the PartOfSpeech bean that holds the token and its corresponding part of speech.

```
int i = 0;
List<PartOfSpeech> posList = new ArrayList<>();
for(String token : tokens) {
  PartOfSpeech pos = new PartOfSpeech();
  pos.setToken(token);
  pos.setPos(tags[i]);
  posList.add(pos);
  i++;
}
```

2. Write a custom implementation of UpdateRequestProcessor and its factory method. Follow the next steps to add the terms with specified parts of speech to a separate field. (Refer to Chapter 5 if you want to refresh your memory about writing a custom update request processor.)

a. Read the parameters from NamedList in the init() method of POSUpdateProcessorFactory, the custom factory, to populate the instance variables for controlling the tagging behavior. Also, set up the POS tagger that can be used for extraction, as mentioned in step 1.

```
private String modelFile;
private String src;
private String dest;
private float boost;
private List<String> allowedPOS;
private PartOfSpeechTagger tagger;
```

```
public void init(NamedList args) {
        super.init(args);

        SolrParams param = SolrParams.toSolrParams(args);

        modelFile = param.get("modelFile");
        src = param.get("src");
        dest = param.get("dest");
        boost = param.getFloat("boost", 1.0f);

        String posStr = param.get("pos","nnp,nn,nns");
        if (null != posStr) {
                allowedPOS = Arrays.asList(posStr.split(","));
        }

        tagger = new PartOfSpeechTagger();
        tagger.setup(modelFile);
};
```

b. In the processAdd() method of POSUpdateProcessor, a custom update
    request processor, read the field value of the document being indexed and
    provide it to the tagger object for tagging the parts of speech. Create a new
    field and add the important tag to it.

```
@Override
public void processAdd(AddUpdateCommand cmd) throws IOException {
  SolrInputDocument doc = cmd.getSolrInputDocument();

  Object obj = doc.getFieldValue(src);
  StringBuilder tokens = new StringBuilder();
  if (null != obj && obj instanceof String) {
    List<PartOfSpeech> posList = tagger.tag((String) obj);

    for(PartOfSpeech pos : posList) {
      if (allowedPOS.contains(pos.getPos().toLowerCase())) {
        tokens.append(pos.getToken()).append(" ");
      }
    }
    doc.addField(dest, tokens.toString(), boost);
  }
  // pass it up the chain
  super.processAdd(cmd);
}
```

3. Add the dependencies to the Solr core library.

```
<lib dir="dir-containing-the-jar" regex=" solr-practical-approach-\d.*\.jar" />
```

4. Define the preceding custom processor in `solrconfig.xml`. In the parameters, you need to specify the path of the model, the source field, the destination field, the parts of speech to be extracted, and the boost to be provided to the destination field.

```
<updateRequestProcessorChain name="nlp">
  <processor class="com.apress.solr.pa.chapter11.opennlp.
POSUpdateProcessorFactory">
    <str name="modelFile">path-to-en-pos-maxent.bin</str>
    <str name="src">description</str>
    <str name="dest">keywords</str>
    <str name="pos">nnp,nn,nns</str>
    <float name="boost">1.4</float>
  </processor>
  <processor class="solr.LogUpdateProcessorFactory" />
  <processor class="solr.RunUpdateProcessorFactory" />
</updateRequestProcessorChain>
```

5. Register the defined update chain to the `/update` handler.

```
<str name="update.chain">nlp</str>
```

6. Restart the instance and index documents. The terms with the specified part of speech will be automatically added to the keywords field, which is defined as a destination field in `solrconfig.xml`. The following is an example of the resultant document.

```
{
  "id": "1201",
  "description": "Bob Marley was born in Jamaica",
  "keywords": "Bob Marley Jamaica "
}
```

Named-Entity Extraction

If your search engine needs to index unstructured content such as books, journals, or blogs, a crucial task is to extract the important information hidden in the stream of text. In this section, you will learn about different approaches to extract that information and leverage it to improve the precision and overall search experience.

Unstructured content is primarily meant for human consumption, and extracting the important entities and metadata hidden inside it requires complex processing. The entities can be generic information (for example, people, location, organization, money, or temporal information) or information specific to a domain (for example, a disease or anatomy in healthcare). The task of identifying the entities such as person, organization, and location is called *named-entity recognition* (NER). For example, in the text *Bob Marley was born in Jamaica*, NER should be able to detect *Bob Marley* as the person and *Jamaica* as the location. Figure 11-6 shows the entities extracted in this example.

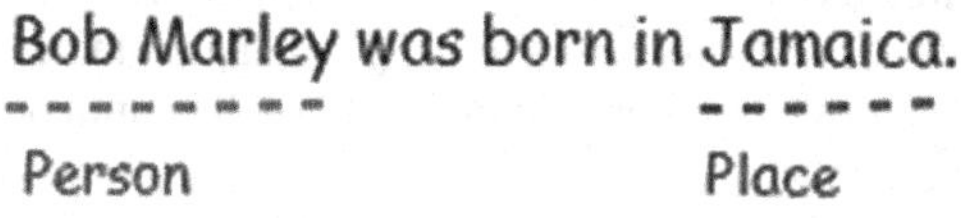

Bob Marley was born in Jamaica.

Person   Place

Figure 11-6. *Named entities extracted from content*

The extracted named entities can be used in Solr in many ways, and the actual usage depends on your requirements. Some of the common uses in Solr are as follows:

- Supporting faceted navigation using the entities

- Sorting the results on the entities

- Finding out entities such as a person's name for the autosuggestion dictionary

- Assigning different boosts to the entities, to vary their significance in the domain

- Query reformulation to search a limited set of fields based on the detected entity type.

The approaches for NER can be divided into three categories, detailed in the following subsections. The approach and its implementation depend on your requirements, use case, and the entity you are trying to extract. The first two approaches can be implemented by using the out-of-the-box features of Solr or any advanced NLP library. For the third approach, you will customize Solr to integrate OpenNLP and extract named entities. The customization or extraction can vary as per your needs.

Using Rules and Regex

Rules and regular expressions are the simplest approach for NER. You can define a set of rules and a regex pattern, which is matched against the incoming text for entity extraction. This approach works well for extraction of entities that follow a predefined pattern, as in the case of e-mail IDs, URLs, phone numbers, zip codes, and credit card numbers.

A simple regex can be integrated by using `PatternReplaceCharFilterFactory` or `PatternReplaceTokenFilterFactory` in the analysis chain. A regex for determining phone numbers can be as simple as this:

```
^[0-9+\(\)#\.\s\/ext-]+$
```

For extracting e-mail IDs, you can use `UAX29URLEmailTokenizerFactory` provided by Lucene. Refer to `http://wiki.apache.org/solr/AnalyzersTokenizersTokenFilters#solr. UAX29URLEmailTokenizerFactory` for details of the tokenizer. You may find it interesting that there is an official standard regex for e-mail, known as RFC 5322. Refer to `http://tools.ietf.org/html/ rfc5322#section-3.4` for details. It describes the syntax that valid e-mail addresses must adhere to, but it's too complicated to implement.

If you are looking for complex regex rules, you can evaluate the Apache UIMA-provided regular expression annotator, where you can define the rule set. Refer to `https://uima.apache.org/downloads/ sandbox/RegexAnnotatorUserGuide/RegexAnnotatorUserGuide.html` for details of the annotator. If you are using a rule engine such as Drools, you can integrate it into Solr by writing a custom update processor or filter factory.

If you want to use OpenNLP for regex-based NER, you can use `RegexNameFinder` and specify the pattern instead of using `NameFinderME`. Refer to the example in the section "Using a Trained Model", where you can do the substitution by using `RegexNameFinder`.

The limitation of this NER approach is that anything unrelated that follows the specified pattern or satisfies the rule will be detected as a valid entity; for example, a poorly formatted five-digit salary could be detected as a zip code. Also, this approach is limited to entity types that follow a known pattern. It cannot be used to detect entities such as name or organization.

Using a Dictionary or Gazetteer

The dictionary-based approach, also called a gazetteer-based approach, of entity extraction maintains a list of terms for the applicable category. The input text is matched upon the gazetteer for entity extraction. This approach works well for entities that are applicable to a specific domain and have a limited set of terms. Typical examples are job titles in your organization, nationality, religion, days of week, or months of year.

You can build the list by extracting information from your local datasource or external source (such as Wikipedia). The data structure for maintaining the dictionary can be anything that fits your requirements. It can be as simple as a Java collection populated from a text file. An easier implementation for a file-based approach to populate the entities in a separate field can be to use Solr's KeepWordFilterFactory. The following is a sample text analysis for it:

```
<analyzer>
  <tokenizer class="solr.StandardTokenizerFactory"/>
  <filter class="solr.LowerCaseFilterFactory"/>
  <filter class="solr.KeepWordFilterFactory" words="keepwords.txt"/>
</analyzer>
```

The list can be maintained in database tables, but a large list is likely to impair performance. A faster and performance-efficient approach is to build an automaton. You can refer to the FST data structure in the Solr suggestions module or one provided by David Smiley at https://github.com/OpenSextant/SolrTextTagger.

If you want to look up phrases along with individual terms, the incoming text can be processed by using either the OpenNLP Chunker component or ShingleFilterFactory provided by Solr. The following is the filter definition for generating shingles of different sizes. The parameter outputUnigrams="true" has been provided to match the single tokens also.

```
<filter class="solr.ShingleFilterFactory" maxShingleSize="3" outputUnigrams="true"/>
```

The benefit of this approach is that it doesn't require training but is less popular as it's difficult to maintain. It cannot be used for common entities such as name or organization, as the terms can be ambiguous and not limited to a defined set of values. This approach also ignores the context. For example, this approach cannot differentiate whether the text *Tommy Hilfiger* refers to a person or an organization.

OpenNLP offers a better approach for dictionary-based extraction by scanning for names inside the dictionary and letting you not worry about matching phrases.

Here are the steps for NER in OpenNLP using a dictionary:

1. Create an XML file containing the dictionary terms.

    ```
    <dictionary case_sensitive="false">
      <entry ref="director">
        <token>Director</token>
      </entry>
      <entry ref="producer">
        <token>Producer</token>
      </entry>
    ```

```
<entry ref="music director">
  <token>Music</token><token>Director</token>
</entry>
<entry ref="singer">
  <token>Singer</token>
</entry>
</dictionary>
```

2. Create a `FileInputStream` and instantiate the dictionary with it.

```
InputStream modelIn = new FileInputStream(file);
Dictionary dictionary = new Dictionary(modelIn);
```

Alternatively, the `Dictionary` object can be created using a no-arg constructor and tokens added to it as shown here:

```
Dictionary dictionary = new Dictionary();

dictionary.put(new StringList("Director"));
dictionary.put(new StringList("Producer"));
dictionary.put(new StringList("Music",  "Director"));
dictionary.put(new StringList("Singer"));
```

3. Create the `DictionaryNameFinder` instance by using the `Dictionary` and assigning a name to it.

```
DictionaryNameFinder dnf = new DictionaryNameFinder(dictionary, "JobTitles");
```

Refer to the implementation steps in the following "Using a Trained Model" section, as the rest of the steps remain the same.

You can use a hybrid of a rules- and gazetteer-based approach if you feel that it can improve precision.

Using a Trained Model

The approach of using trained models for NER falls under the supervised learning category of machine learning: human intervention is required to train the model, but after the model is trained, it returns a nearly accurate result.

This approach uses a statistical model for extracting entities. It is preferred for extracting entities that are not limited to a set of values, such as in case of name or organization. This approach can find entities that are not defined or tagged in the model. This model considers the semantics and context of the text and easily resolves the ambiguity between entities, as in the case of person name and organization name. These problems cannot be addressed using the earlier approach; the trained model is the only way to go. It doesn't require creating large dictionaries that are difficult to maintain.

Solr Plug-in for Entity Extraction

In this section, you will learn to extract the named entities from documents being indexed and populate the extracted terms to a separate Solr field. This process requires two primary steps:

1. Extract the named entities from the text. In the provided sample, you'll use OpenNLP and the trained models freely available on its web site. The model can be downloaded from http://opennlp.sourceforge.net/models-1.5/.

2. Write a custom update request processor, that will create a new field and add the extracted entities to it.

Here are the detailed steps to be followed for adding the extracted named entities to a separate field:

1. Write a Java class to extract the named entities by using OpenNLP. Here are the steps for extraction:

    a. Read the trained model by using FileInputStream and instantiate the TokenNameFinderModel with it. OpenNLP requires a separate model for each entity type. To support multiple entities, a separate model should be loaded for each entity.

    ```
    InputStream modelIn = new FileInputStream(fileName);
    TokenNameFinderModel model = new TokenNameFinderModel(modelIn);
    ```

    b. Instantiate the NameFinderME class by providing the model to its constructor. A separate instance of NameFinderME should be created for each entity type.

    ```
    NameFinderME  nameFinder = new NameFinderME(model);
    ```

    c. NameFinderME as a prerequisite requires the sentence to be tokenized, which can be done using the OpenNLP tokenization component. If this code is part of the analysis chain, the sentence can be tokenized by using the Solr-provided tokenizer. The simplest form of tokenization can even be using Java String's split() method, also used in this example, though it's prone to creating invalid tokens.

    ```
    String [] sentence = query.split(" ");
    ```

    d. Pass the tokenized sentence to the NameFinderMe instance, which returns the extracted named entity.

    ```
    Span[] spans = nameFinder.find(sentence);
    ```

    e. Iterate the Span array to extract the named entities. We have populated the extracted entities to the NamedEntity bean that holds the entity and its corresponding entity type.

    ```
    List<NamedEntity> neList = new ArrayList<>();
    for (Span span : spans) {
      NamedEntity entity = new NamedEntity();
      StringBuilder match = new StringBuilder();
      for (int i = span.getStart(); i < span.getEnd(); i++) {
    ```

```
      match.append(sentence[i]).append(" ");
    }
    entity.setToken(match.toString().trim.());
    entity.setEntity(entityName);
    neList.add(entity);
  }
```

f. After processing the sentences of a document, call clearAdaptiveData() to
    clear the cache, which is maintained by OpenNLP to track previous entity
    extraction of a word.

```
    nameFinder.clearAdaptiveData();
```

2. Write a custom implementation of UpdateRequestProcessor and its factory
    method. The following are the steps to be followed for adding the extracted
    entities to a separate field. (Refer to Chapter 5, if you want to refresh your
    memory about writing a custom update request processor.)

    a. Read the parameters from NamedList in the init() method of
        NERUpdateProcessorFactory, the custom factory, to populate the
        instance variables for controlling the extraction behavior. Also, set up the
        NamedEntityTagger that can be used for extraction as mentioned in step 1.

```
    private String modelFile;
    private String src;
    private String dest;
    private String entity;
    private float boost;

    private NamedEntityTagger tagger;

    public void init(NamedList args) {
      super.init(args);

      SolrParams param = SolrParams.toSolrParams(args);

      modelFile = param.get("modelFile");
      src = param.get("src");
      dest = param.get("dest");
      entity = param.get("entity","person");
      boost = param.getFloat("boost", 1.0f);

      tagger = new NamedEntityTagger();
      tagger.setup(modelFile, entity);
    };
```

b. In the processAdd() method of NERUpdateProcessor, a custom update request processor, read the field value of the document being indexed and provide it to the NER object for extracting the entities. Create a new field and add the extracted entities to it.

```
@Override
public void processAdd(AddUpdateCommand cmd) throws IOException {
  SolrInputDocument doc = cmd.getSolrInputDocument();

  Object obj = doc.getFieldValue(src);
  if (null != obj && obj instanceof String) {
    List<NamedEntity> neList = tagger.tag((String) obj);

    for(NamedEntity ne : neList) {
      doc.addField(dest, ne.getToken(), boost);
    }
  }
  super.processAdd(cmd);
}
```

3. Add the dependencies to the Solr core library.

```
<lib dir="dir-containing-the-jar" regex=" solr-practical-approach-\d.*\.jar" />
```

4. Define this custom processor in solrconfig.xml. In the parameters, you need to specify the path of the model, the source field, the destination field, the entity to be extracted, and the boost to be provided to the destination field. The destination field should be multivalued, as multiple entities can be extracted from the text.

```
<updateRequestProcessorChain name="nlp">
  <processor class="com.apress.solr.pa.chapter11.opennlp.
NERUpdateProcessorFactory">
    <str name="modelFile">path-to-en-ner-person.bin</str>
    <str name="src">description</str>
    <str name="dest">ext_person</str>
    <str name="entity">person</str>
    <float name="boost">1.8</float>
  </processor>
  <processor class="solr.LogUpdateProcessorFactory" />
  <processor class="solr.RunUpdateProcessorFactory" />
</updateRequestProcessorChain>
```

5. Register the defined update chain to the /update handler.

```
<str name="update.chain">nlp</str>
```

6. Restart the instance and index documents. The extracted entities will be automatically added to the destination field. The following is an example of a resultant document.

```
{
"id": "1201",
"description": "Bob Marley and Ricky were born in Jamaica",
"ext_person": [
  "Bob Marley ",
  "Ricky "
]
}
```

This source code extracts only one type of entity. In real-life scenarios, you may want to extract multiple entities and populate them to different fields. You can extend this update request processor to accommodate the required capabilities by loading multiple models and adding the extracted terms to separate fields.

OpenNLP uses a separate model for each entity type. In contrast, Stanford NLP, another NLP package, uses the same model for all entities.

This approach of entity extraction is supposed to return accurate results, but the output also depends on tagging quality and the data on which the model is trained (remember, garbage in, garbage out). Also, the model-based approach can be costly in terms of memory requirements and processing speed.

Semantic Enrichment

In Chapter 4, you learned to use SynonymFilterFactory to generate synonyms for expanding the tokens. The primary limitation of this approach is that it doesn't consider semantics. A word can be polysemous (have multiple meanings), and synonyms can vary based on their part of speech or the context. For example, a typical generic synonym.txt file can have the word *large* specified as a synonym for *big*, and this would expand the query *big brother* as *large brother*, which is semantically incorrect.

Instead of using a text file that defines the list of terms and its synonyms, more sophisticated approaches can be applied using controlled vocabularies such as WordNet or Medical Subject Headings (MeSH), which require no manual definition or handcrafting. Synonym expansion is just one part of it. The vocabularies and thesauri also contain other useful information such as hypernyms, hyponyms, and meronyms, which you will learn about further. This information can be used for understanding the semantic relationship and expanding the query further.

These thesauri are generally maintained by a community or an enterprise that keeps updating the corpus with the latest words. The vocabulary can be generic or it can be specific to a particular domain. WordNet is an example of a generic thesaurus that can be incorporated into any search engine and for any domain. MeSH is a vocabulary applicable to a medical domain.

You can also perform semantic enrichment by building taxonomies and ontologies containing the concept tree applicable to your domain. The query terms can be matched against a taxonomy for extracting broader, narrower, or related concepts (such as altLabel or prefLabel) and perform the required enrichment. You can get some of these taxonomies over the Web, or you can have a taxonomist define one for you. You can also consume resource such as DBpedia that provide structured information extracted from Wikipedia as RDF triples. Wikidata is another linked database which contains structured data from Wikimedia projects including Wikipedia.

These knowledge bases can be integrated into Solr in various ways. Here are the ways to plug the desired enrichment into Solr:

Text analysis: Write a custom token filter that expands the tokens with the synonyms or other relationships extracted from the controlled vocabulary. The implementation can be similar to the Solr-provided SynonymFilterFactory that uses a controlled vocabulary file instead of the synonyms.txt file. SynonymFilterFactory has a support for WordNet in its simplest form. You will see a custom implementation for synonym expansion later in this chapter.

Query parser: Write a query parser for expanding the user query with its related or narrower term. For example, in an e-commerce web site for clothing, the user query *men accessories* can be expanded to search for belts or watches. This additional knowledge can be extracted from a taxonomy that contains accessories as a broader term, and belts and watches as its narrower terms. Figure 11-7 specifies the relationship between the broader and narrower concepts. Instead of just expanding the query, you can extend the system to reformulate the query to build a new query.

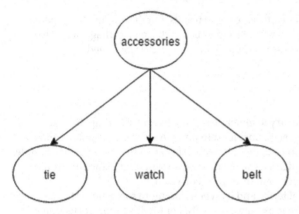

Figure 11-7. *Concept tree*

Synonym Expansion

In this section, you will learn how to automatically expand terms to include their synonyms. This process requires implementing the following two tasks:

1. Knowledge extraction: The first step is to extract the synonyms from the controlled vocabulary. The extraction process depends on the vocabulary and supported format. In the following example, you will extract knowledge from WordNet by using one of the available Java libraries.

2. Solr plug-in: The feature can be plugged into any appropriate extendable Solr component. In this section, you will expand the synonym by using a custom token filter.

Before performing these tasks, you'll learn about the basics of WordNet and the information it offers, and then get hands-on with synonymy expansion.

WordNet

WordNet is a large lexical database of English. It groups nouns, verbs, adjectives, and adverbs into sets of cognitive synonyms called *synsets*, each expressing a distinct concept. Synsets are interlinked by means of conceptual, semantic, and lexical relationships. Its structure makes it a useful tool for computational linguistics and natural language processing. It contains 155,287 words, organized in 117,659 synsets, for a total of 206,941 word-sense pairs.

WordNet is released under a BSD-style license and is freely available for download from its web site, https://wordnet.princeton.edu/. You can also evaluate the online version of the thesaurus at http://wordnetweb.princeton.edu/perl/webwn.

The main relationships among words in WordNet is synonymy, as its synset groups words that denote the same concept and are interchangeable in many contexts. Apart from synonyms, the thesaurus also contains the following primary information (among others):

> *Hypernymy/hyponymy*: This refers to an IS-A relation between words. It links a generic synset such as *accessory* to a more specific one, like *belt*. For example, *accessory* is a hypernym of *belt*, and *belt* is a hyponym of *accessory*. These relationships maintain the hierarchy and are transitive.

> *Meronymy*: This is a whole-part relationship between words. For example, *button* is a meronym of *shirt*.

> *Troponymy*: This refers to verbs that express increasingly specific manners characterizing an event. For example, *whisper* is a troponym of *talk*.

> *Gloss:* This is a brief definition of a word. In most cases, it also contains one or more short sentences illustrating the use of the synset members.

WordNet requires the part of speech along with the words as a prerequisite.

A handful of Java libraries are available for accessing WordNet, each with its own pros and cons. You can refer to http://projects.csail.mit.edu/jwi/download.php?f=finlayson.2014.procgwc.7.x.pdf for a paper that compares the features and performance of the primary libraries.

Solr Plug-in for Synonym Expansion

This section provides steps for developing a mechanism for a simple expansion of terms. Below are the two steps needed to implement the feature

1. Write a client to extract synonmys from wordnet.

2. Write a Solr plugin to integrate the extracted synonyms for desired expansion. In this section, the enrichment is integrated to Solr using a custom token filter.

Synonym Expansion Using WordNet

To extract synonyms from WordNet, you have two prerequisites:

1. Download the database from WordNet's download page at https://wordnet. princeton.edu/wordnet/download/current-version/ and extract the dictionary from tar/zip to a folder.

2. You will need a Java library to access the dictionary. The example uses the Java WordNet Library (JWNL). You can use any other library that suits your requirements.

This steps provided are in their simplest form; you may need optimizations to make the code production ready. Also, the program extracts only synonyms. You can extend it to extract other related information discussed previously. Another thing to note while extracting related terms from a generic thesaurus such as WordNet is that you may want to perform disambiguation to identify the appropriate synset for the term being expanded; words such as *bank*, for example, are polysemous and can mean *river bank* or *banking institution*, depending on the context. If you are using a domain-specific vocabulary, the disambiguation will not be that important. (Covering disambiguation is beyond the scope of this book.)

Here are the steps for synonym expansion using WordNet:

1. The JWNL requires an XML-based properties file to be defined. The following is a sample properties file. The path of the extracted WordNet dictionary should be defined in the `dictionary_path` parameter in this file.

```xml
<?xml version="1.0" encoding="UTF-8"?>
<jwnl_properties language="en">
  <version publisher="Princeton" number="3.0" language="en"/>
  <dictionary class="net.didion.jwnl.dictionary.FileBackedDictionary">
    <param name="dictionary_element_factory"        value="net.didion.jwnl.
    princeton.data.PrincetonWN17FileDictionaryElementFactory"/>
    <param name="file_manager"
        value="net.didion.jwnl.dictionary.file_manager.FileManagerImpl">
      <param name="file_type"
          value="net.didion.jwnl.princeton.file.
          PrincetonRandomAccessDictionaryFile"/>
      <param name="dictionary_path" value="/path/to/WordNet/dictionary"/>
    </param>
  </dictionary>
  <resource class="PrincetonResource"/>
</jwnl_properties>
```

2. Create a new `FileInputStream` specifying the path of the JWNL properties file and initialize the JWNL by providing the `FileInputStream`. Create an instance of `Dictionary`.

```java
JWNL.initialize(new FileInputStream(propFile));
Dictionary dictionary = Dictionary.getInstance();
```

3. WordNet requires the part of speech to be specified for the tokens, and that value should be converted to a POS enum that is accepted by the dictionary. The part of speech can be tagged by using the OpenNLP part-of-speech tagger, as discussed in the previous example, or any other package you are familiar with.

```java
POS pos = null;
switch (posStr) {
case "VB":
case "VBD":
case "VBG":
case "VBN":
case "VBP":
case "VBZ":
  pos = POS.VERB;
  break;
```

```
case "RB":
case "RBR":
case "RBS":
  pos = POS.ADVERB;
  break;
case "JJS":
case "JJR":
case "JJ":
  pos = POS.ADJECTIVE;
  break;
// case "NN":
// case "NNS":
// case "NNP":
// case "NNPS":
//   pos = POS.NOUN;
//   break;
}
```

This code snippet has a section commented out to ignore the synonym expansion for nouns as nouns will introduce more ambiguity. You can uncomment it, if you introduce a disambiguation mechanism.

4. Invoke the getIndexWord() method of the Dictionary instance by providing the word and its POS. The returned value is IndexWord.

```
IndexWord word = dictionary.getIndexWord(pos, term);
```

5. The getSenses() method of IndexWord returns an array of Synset, which can be traversed to get all the synonyms. The synset returned varies on the basis of the POS provided. The following block of code populates the synonyms Java set with all the extracted synonyms.

```
Set<String> synonyms = new HashSet<>();
Synset[] synsets = word.getSenses();
  for (Synset synset : synsets) {
    Word[] words = synset.getWords();
    for (Word w : words) {
        String synonym = w.getLemma().toString()
                        .replace("_", " ");
        synonyms.add(synonym);
  }
}
```

Custom Token Filter for Synonym Expansion

In the previous section, you learned to extract synonyms from WordNet. Now the extracted synonyms have to be added to the terms being indexed. In this section, you will learn to write a custom token filter that can be added to a field's text-analysis chain to enrich the tokens with its synonyms.

Lucene defines classes for a token filter in the package `org.apache.lucene.analysis.*`. For writing your custom token filter, you will need to extend the following two Lucene classes:

TokenFilterFactory: The factory creating the `TokenFilter` instance should extend this abstract class.

TokenFilter: In Chapter 4, you learned that a token filter is a token stream whose input is another token stream. `TokenFilter` is an abstract class that provides access to all the tokens, either from a field of a document or from the query text. The custom implementation should subclass this `TokenFilter` abstract class and override the `incrementToken()` method.

The following are the steps to be followed for writing a custom token filter and plugging it into a field's text-analysis chain:

1. Write a custom implementation of `TokenFilterFactory` that creates the `TokenFilter`. Here are the steps:

   a. Extend the `TokenFilterFactory` abstract class. The `ResourceLoaderAware` interface is implemented by classes that optionally need to initialize or load a resource or file.

   ```
   public class CVSynonymFilterFactory extends TokenFilterFactory implements
   ResourceLoaderAware {
   }
   ```

   b. Override the `create()` abstract method and return an instance of the custom `TokenStream` implementation, which you will create in the next step. You can optionally pass additional parameters to the implementing class. Here you pass the instantiated resources:

   ```
   @Override
   public TokenStream create(TokenStream input) {
     return new CVSynonymFilter(input, dictionary, tagger, maxExpansion);
   }
   ```

   c. If you want to read parameters from the factory definition in `schema.xml`, you can read it from the map that is available as an input to the constructor. You have read the path of the JWNL properties file, the OpenNLP POS model, and the maximum number of desired expansions.

   ```
   public CVSynonymFilterFactory(Map<String, String> args) {
     super(args);
     maxExpansion = getInt(args, "maxExpansion", 3);
     propFile = require(args, "wordnetFile");
     modelFile = require(args, "posModel");
   }
   ```

d. Initialize the required resources by overriding the `inform()` method provided by the ResourceLoaderAware interface.

```
@Override
public void inform(ResourceLoader loader) throws IOException {

    // initialize for wordnet
    try {
        JWNL.initialize(new FileInputStream(propFile));
        dictionary = Dictionary.getInstance();
    } catch (JWNLException ex) {
        logger.error(ex.getMessage());
        ex.printStackTrace();
        throw new IOException(ex.getMessage());
    }

    // initialize for part of speech tagging
    tagger = new PartOfSpeechTagger();
    tagger.setup(modelFile);
}
```

2. Create a custom class by extending the `TokenFilter` abstract class that performs the following tasks.

a. Initialize the required attributes of the tokens. You have initialized the CharTermAttribute, PositionIncrementAttribute, PositionLengthAttribute, TypeAttribute, and OffsetAttribute that contain the term text, position increment information, information about the number of positions the token spans, the token type, and the start/end token information, respectively.

```
private final CharTermAttribute termAttr = addAttribute(CharTermAttribute.class);
private final PositionIncrementAttribute posIncrAttr
    = addAttribute(PositionIncrementAttribute.class);
private final PositionLengthAttribute posLenAttr
    = addAttribute(PositionLengthAttribute.class);
private final TypeAttribute typeAttr = addAttribute(TypeAttribute.class);
private final OffsetAttribute offsetAttr = addAttribute(OffsetAttribute.class);
```

b. Define the constructor and do the required initialization.

```
public CVSynonymFilter(TokenStream input,
        Dictionary dictionary, PartOfSpeechTagger tagger, int maxExpansion) {
    super(input);
    this.maxExpansion = maxExpansion;
    this.tagger = tagger;
    this.vocabulary = new WordnetVocabulary(dictionary);

    if (null == tagger || null == vocabulary) {
        throw new IllegalArgumentException("fst must be non-null");
    }
```

```
      pendingOutput = new ArrayList<String>();
      finished = false;
      startOffset = 0;
      endOffset = 0;
      posIncr = 1;
    }
```

c. Override the incrementToken() method of TokenFilter. The method
   should play back any buffered output before running parsing and then
   do the required processing for each token in the token stream. The
   addOutputSynonyms() method extracts the synonym for each term
   provided. When the parsing is completed, the method should mandatorily
   return the Boolean value false.

```
@Override
public boolean incrementToken() throws IOException {
  while (!finished) {
    // play back any pending tokens synonyms
    while (pendingTokens.size() > 0) {
      String nextToken = pendingTokens.remove(0);
      termAttr.copyBuffer(nextToken.toCharArray(), 0, nextToken.length());
      offsetAttr.setOffset(startOffset, endOffset);
      posIncAttr.setPositionIncrement(posIncr);

      posIncr = 0;
      return true;
    }

    // extract synonyms for each token
    if (input.incrementToken()) {
      String token = termAttr.toString();
      startOffset = offsetAttr.startOffset();
      endOffset = offsetAttr.endOffset();

      addOutputSynonyms(token);
    } else {
      finished = true;
    }
  }

  // should always return false
  return false;
}

private void addOutputSynonyms(String token) throws IOException {
  pendingTokens.add(token);

  List<PartOfSpeech> posList = tagger.tag(token);

  if (null == posList || posList.size() < 1) {
    return;
  }
```

```
    Set<String> synonyms = vocabulary.getSynonyms(token, posList.get(0)
      .getPos(), maxExpansion);

    if (null == synonyms) {
      return;
    }
    for (String syn : synonyms) {
      pendingTokens.add(syn);
    }
  }

  @Override
  public void reset() throws IOException {
    super.reset();
    finished = false;
    pendingTokens.clear();
    startOffset = 0;
    endOffset = 0;
    posIncr = 1;
  }
```

The processing provided here tags the part of speech for each token instead of the full sentence, for simplicity. Also, the implementation is suitable for tokens and synonyms of a single word. If you are thinking of getting this feature to production, I suggest you refer to SynonymFilter.java in the org.apache.lucene.analysis. synonym package and extend it using the approach provided there.

3. Build the program and add the Java binary JAR to the Solr classpath. Alternatively, place the JAR in the $SOLR_HOME/core/lib directory.

```
<lib dir="./lib" />
```

4. Define the custom filter factory to the analysis chain of the desired fieldType in schema.xml.

```
<fieldType name="text_semantic" class="solr.TextField"
positionIncrementGap="100">
  <analyzer type="index">
    <tokenizer class="solr.StandardTokenizerFactory"/>
    <filter class="solr.StopFilterFactory" ignoreCase="true" words="stopwords.txt" />
    <filter class="solr.LowerCaseFilterFactory"/>
  </analyzer>
  <analyzer type="query">
    <tokenizer class="solr.StandardTokenizerFactory"/>
    <filter class="solr.StopFilterFactory" ignoreCase="true" words="stopwords.txt" />
    <filter class="com.apress.solr.pa.chapter11.enrichment.CVSynonymFilterFactory"
maxExpansion="3" wordnetFile="path-of-jwnl-properties.xml" posModel="path-to-en-
pos-maxent.bin" />
    <filter class="solr.LowerCaseFilterFactory"/>
  </analyzer>
</fieldType>
```

5. Restart the instance, and you are good to query for semantic synonyms. If the token filter has been added to index-time analysis, the content should be reindexed. Verify the expansion in the Analysis tab in the Solr admin UI.

Summary

In this chapter, you learned about the semantic aspects of search engines. You saw the limitations of the keyword-based engines and learned ways in which semantic search enhances the user experience and findability of documents. Semantic search is an advanced and broad topic. Given the limited scope of this book, we focused on simple natural language processing techniques for identifying important words in a sentence and approaches for extracting metadata from unstructured text. You also learned about a basic semantic enrichment technique for discovering documents that were totally ignored earlier but could be of great interest to the user. To put it all together, this chapter provided sample source code for integrating these features in Solr.

Here you've come to the end of this book. I sincerely hope that its content is useful in your endeavor of developing a practical search engine and that it contribute to your knowledge of Apache Solr.

Index

■ G

■ H

■ I

Get the eBook for only $5!

Why limit yourself?

Now you can take the weightless companion with you wherever you go and access your content on your PC, phone, tablet, or reader.

Since you've purchased this print book, we're happy to offer you the eBook in all 3 formats for just $5.

Convenient and fully searchable, the PDF version enables you to easily find and copy code—or perform examples by quickly toggling between instructions and applications. The MOBI format is ideal for your Kindle, while the ePUB can be utilized on a variety of mobile devices.

To learn more, go to www.apress.com/companion or contact support@apress.com.

Printed in the United States
By Bookmasters